THE EFFECTIVENESS OF SOCIAL CASEWORK

CONTRIBUTORS

William C. Berleman
Jerome Cohen
Harvey L. Gochros
Walter W. Hudson
Edward J. Mullen
Bernice W. Polemis
William J. Reid
Herbert S. Strean
Eugene Talsma
Francis J. Turner
Harold D. Werner

In concentrating on the careful examination of issues regarding casework effectiveness and accountability, this book provides the tools necessary for the analysis of research; reviews and analyzes the findings of research on effectiveness; and discusses the implications of the findings for future research and practice. The book also provides a platform for the discussion of several viewpoints on these topics, thus exploring the range of both practical and scholarly issues in social work research.

The issues raised in this book are central to the ongoing mission of casework, and pose serious questions about future directions of the field. Because of the role of casework within the profession as a whole, these findings are crucial to the entire spectrum of social work. Students, undergraduate as well as graduate, can utilize this book in social work courses dealing with either research or practice. Professional practitioners and administrators will also find this volume valuable for its presentation of new directions in practice, including the planning of social work intervention programs. The vital significance of this volume to the core of social work is destined to make it a classic in the field.

Ubi explorari vera
non possunt, falsa
per metum augentur.

Quintus Curtius Rufus
De Rebus Gestis
Aleandri Magni

THE EFFECTIVENESS OF
SOCIAL CASEWORK

By

JOEL FISCHER, D.S.W.

Professor
School of Social Work
University of Hawaii
Honolulu, Hawaii

With a Foreword by

H. J. Eysenck, Ph.D., D.Sc.

Professor
Institute of Psychiatry
University of London
London, England

CHARLES C THOMAS · PUBLISHER
Springfield · Illinois · U.S.A.

Published and Distributed Throughout the World by

CHARLES C THOMAS • PUBLISHER

Bannerstone House

301-327 East Lawrence Avenue, Springfield, Illinois, U.S.A.

*With THOMAS BOOKS careful attention is given to all details of
manufacturing and design. It is the Publisher's desire to present books that are
satisfactory as to their physical qualities and artistic possibilities and
appropriate for their particular use. THOMAS BOOKS will be true to those
laws of quality that assure a good name and good will.*

Printed in the United States of America

C-1

Library of Congress Cataloging in Publication Data

Fischer, Joel.
    The effectiveness of social casework.

    Bibliography: p.
    1. Social case work—Research. I. Title.
HV43.F52   361.3   75-20325
ISBN 0-398-03491-5

This book is dedicated to the authors whose work is presented in Part II and to other social workers like them who recognize that a profession will be viable only as long as its members continue to question.

FOREWORD

D URING THE LAST fifty years or so, there has been a tremendous
flowering of applied social science. New ideas have grown
up in psychiatry, penology, social work, education, vocational
guidance, occupational selection—everywhere students are being
trained in the new methods which have grown from these ideas,
and great claims are being made for the help that social science
can give to people engaged in the evergrowing "social help" in-
dustry. The picture now is of a number of extremely active, pur-
poseful, well-trained individuals pursuing important, worthwhile
occupations which make a significant contribution to social well-
being. A technology has come into being which promises to trans-
form our old-fashioned, unsuccessful methods of dealing with
social problems; this tendency claims to be an applied science,
and believes itself entitled to all the honour due to disciplines recognized as "scientific." In the world-wide chorus of mutual con-
gratulation on these is hardly a dissonant note; we get busier and
busier training more and more people to use the methods worked
out and taught in these fields, and we less and less take the trouble to look at the one crucial problem which confronts us—the
outcome problem.

The fable of the *Emperor's New Clothes* comes to mind.
There was unanimity about the wonderful new raiments worn
by the king—until the little boy piped up and pointed out that
the Emperor was in fact naked! One can well imagine the outcry
that this innocent remark provoked; yet the little boy was simply
telling the truth, unaffected by the warp of social approval and
the woof of mutual back slapping that constitutes the web of
our professional interactions. In all the fields mentioned above,
there has appeared such a little boy, innocently (or not so innocently) asking for proof that these wonderful new methods
actually produced what they were alleged to produce—better

vii

methods of psychological treatment, better methods of dealing with offenders, and rehabilitating them, better methods of education, resulting in greater knowledge, social competence, or whatever was judged to be the aim of education. And in all cases the answer has been the same—not the desired proof, but rather an exhortation to the little boy to keep silent, not to disturb his elders and betters with absurd requests, and finally the threat of expulsion from the group if he persisted with his infernal questioning.

This book extends the list of intrepid questioning to the field of social work; another little boy has joined the small band of people more concerned with the facts of the situation than with preserving professional decorum, and more concerned with the samples of suffering humanity whom we seek to help than with the status and the power of those seeking to provide this help. We hold out certain implied promises to those who suffer; it does not seem too much to ask that we should have some proof to demonstrate that what we are promising, we can actually perform. Yet such proof has never been forthcoming in any of the fields we are discussing; rehabilitation of prisoners remains as much a chimera as ever, psychotherapy may perform many incidental wonders, but it does not cure patients, and social casework does not seem to have any of the effects claimed for it. These are important truths, and while those who put them before the public are not likely to be popular among their colleagues, they nevertheless deserve the gratitude of the great mass of the people for their courage in pointing out the god who failed. For no improvement in a desperate situation is likely until we recognize that the situation *is* desperate; as long as we are all scurrying around, busily filling our quotas and doing what we have been taught to do, not looking right or left to see if we are actually doing anything useful, so long will we delay carrying out the research that alone will give us methods that actually accomplish what we seek to accomplish. Debunking is not fashionable, but it is necessary before the rebuilding that is so urgently required can take place.

It is surely odd, and something of an enigma, that in social science the null hypothesis is so extraordinarily difficult to disprove. Whatever we do seems to have much the same effect. Put the young wrongdoer on probation, send him to prison, let him off with a caution, give him parole or not—when you follow up groups of prisoners treated in these varied ways you will find it very difficult indeed to discover any differences in their future behaviour! The same can be said about your neurotic patient—psychoanalyze him or give him placebo pills, leucotomize him or let him talk to his priest, there is little probability that any significant differences will emerge when you study his future conduct and well-being. Social work now joins the rest of the social disciplines which have had to learn this sad truth; it is easy to make claims, and to do busy work that seems to get somewhere, but it is very difficult to come up with any proof that might convince the sceptic that what you are doing is anything but just that —busy work. The fact that you may enjoy what you are doing, that you are making sacrifices in doing it, and that your motives are of the best, can do nothing to disguise the fact that you might just as well not do anything at all; there is simply no proof that your actions have any positive (or even negative) effect on the people you are trying to help. This is sad, even tragic, but it must be recognized if we are ever to achieve the aims social science sets for itself so proudly: *Pro bono publico!*

We all ought to be grateful to Dr. Fischer for having done such a scholarly job in presenting us with the available evidence, discussing the results of these studies in depth, and getting a number of experts together to discuss the outcome. If personal experience is any guide, I am afraid that gratitude is the least likely result to crown his efforts; few people enjoy having the rug pulled from under their feet, and it would be idle to imagine that groups of social workers, or psychiatrists, or penologists would give thanks to the person who proved, however impeccably, that the time spent on their professional training was in fact spent uselessly, in acquiring a nonexistent expertise. There is an irresistible temptation to sweep the dirt under the mat, and to go on as if nothing had happened, with just a few barbed words uttered in the direction of the person who disturbed the peaceful scene. The whole process is often accompanied by semi-scholarly criticisms of methods of investigation used, of statistical devices used, and of the rigor of the deductions made; what is seldom or never done is to point to even one single example of a properly designed and executed study that contained a proper control group, and that showed clearly, without any quibbling, that the methods under investigation actually worked! Until such proof is forthcoming, the depressing and indeed damning conclusions of this book will have to be accepted.

Protagonists of existing methods are unlikely to be convinced, or to change their ways; it is the coming generation of students that are most likely to benefit, and to question the doctrines they are being taught. This is true even in physics and other hard sciences. As Max Planck, the Nobel Laureate and inventor of quantum theory, once put it: "A new scientific truth does not win its way by convincing its opponents, and gaining their adherence; it becomes established because its opponents gradually die, and the growing generation is taught from the beginning to accept it." Very slowly the outlook has been changing with respect to psychotherapy, where the new development of behaviour therapy is beginning to eclipse and will soon completely outstrip the older, unproven, and probably ineffective methods. In social work, this book constitutes the first, essential step towards the development of genuine, effective, scientifically meaningful methods; the second step will be even harder—the actual use of psychological and sociological principles in order to create such new methods and prove them to be effective. Let us drink to the successful accomplishment of the first step and to the prospective accomplishment of the second!

H. J. EYSENCK. PH.D., D.SC.

PREFACE

MANY SOCIAL WORKERS behave as though the whole field of knowledge about the effectiveness of methods for practice is wide open and there are no facts yet established. Conversely, many others act as though the final word is in regarding which approaches to use. I disagree as strongly with those who say "nothing is known" as I do with those who say "everything is known." Both perspectives are destructive to our profession.

The "know-nothings" are destructive because they are dead wrong. We know a good deal about some new approaches that are effective and a good deal about some old approaches that are not. The "know nothing" philosophy basically amounts to "anything goes; do your own thing"—a perspective that appears unencumbered by the facts: the findings of a considerable body of research. If it is assumed that nothing is known (or the logical extension of that, that nothing can be known), the professional will be deluding himself into using a philosophic and semantic shroud to deny reality.

The other extreme, the "everything is known" school is one to which many caseworkers belong, particularly those who continue to use methods of practice in the face of evidence they are not effective. This perspective is destructive to our profession because it leads to a lock-step rigidity for professional education and practice. Since everything (or everything "important") is known, there is no need to continuously search for new approaches for practice that might prove effective in helping people. Adhering to this perspective precludes any real progress.

I take a middle position on this issue which I hope this book reflects. I believe that while a good deal is indeed known about casework practice, it is crucial to the viability of our profession to go much further and continue to engage in the search for something better. Obviously, the arena for discussion of these issues in this book involves the effectiveness of casework practice, particularly *research* on the effectiveness of practice. It is the achievement of effectiveness which is central to our profession's—indeed, to any profession's—mission, and this book has as its goal the exploration of what is known about the effectiveness of social work practitioners.

To accomplish this exploration, the book is organized into three major parts:

Part I consists of a review and analysis of all the available controlled research on the effectiveness of the largest segment of the social work profession—social casework. The results of this research, to say the least, appear rather disquieting for our profession. So, in the last chapter of Part I, Chapter 6, I have presented a brief overview of some additional material that also is "known." This material illustrates a variety of both practice and research technologies that appear to have great potential for moving social casework in new and more effective directions. Based on evidence that already is available, I believe these new directions will substantially improve the effectiveness of the vast majority of social workers in providing services to clients.

But the issues regarding the results of research on effectiveness are not necessarily always clearcut. There usually is room for reasonable disagreement among reasonable people. Obviously, issues such as professional effectiveness, because they are central to the existence of a profession, need an airing. Therefore, to contribute toward that airing, I invited a group of noted social work educators, theorists, administrators, practitioners, and researchers (including some who conducted the original studies reviewed in this book) to review Part I and write their own comments, critiques, and points of view on the material contained therein.

Part II consists of the discussion of these scholars. While not all of the individuals I invited were able to participate, I think that those who did were articulate and frank in presenting their points of view, positions which they knew would lead to disagreement and controversy.

The material in Part II, presented in alphabetical order of the authors, provides an excellent, open discussion of many of the theoretical and research issues raised in Part I. While some of the discussants agreed with, or perhaps accepted, the conclusions reached in Part I, a number of them clearly did not. But either way, they presented a variety of important ideas whether they were in challenge to my material, or in the development of innovative notions about future directions for research and practice in social casework.

I am deeply indebted to these scholars; the obvious time and energy they put into their work is greatly appreciated. It is their willingness to discuss differences of opinion, and their openness about it, that I think provides an excellent model for all of us to emulate. It is to the authors whose work is presented in Part II that this book is respectfully dedicated.

In Part III, I have attempted to briefly summarize some of the major issues raised by the discussants in Part II. The purpose of Part III is to open up and, to the extent possible, clarify those issues. Although there were several areas of disagreement between some of the discussants and me and between the discussants themselves, I think that all of us agree that a good deal of work is necessary for social work in the years ahead—in the areas of research, theory and practice. If anything, I hope the message of this book is: let's get to it!

Finally, I would like to express my appreciation to H. J. Eysenck for writing the foreword for this book. Although not a social worker, through his work in his own field, one which is closely related to ours, Dr. Eysenck established both the necessity and precedent for critical evaluations of research regarding the effectiveness of professional practice. Beyond this, he has set and maintained consistently high standards for conducting such evaluations. Whether we agree or disagree with some of the conclusions he has reached, I believe all of us in the helping professions are in his debt for encouraging us to constantly re-evaluate the empirical basis for the services we provide. His goal (if I can presume to speak for him) and the goal of this book are one and the same: to stimulate a continuing examination of professional competence and effectiveness, with the aim of ultimately insuring that helping professionals really do help.

JOEL FISCHER
Honolulu, Hawaii

CONTENTS

Page

Foreword

  H. J. Eysenck vii

Preface xi

Part I

RESEARCH ON CASEWORK EFFECTIVENESS

Chapter

1. INTRODUCTION 5
2. STUDIES WITH UNTREATED CONTROLS 22
3. STUDIES WITH OTHER-TREATED CONTROLS 72
4. DETERIORATION EFFECTS IN CASEWORK 98
5. SUMMARY ANALYSIS OF STUDIES 110
6. IMPLICATIONS 140

Part II

DISCUSSION

7. A CAUTIONARY CHEER: SOME RESERVATIONS REGARDING THE INTERPRETATION OF FINDINGS
    William C. Berleman 169
8. A BRIEF COMMENT: EVALUATING THE EFFECTIVENESS OF AN UNSPECIFIED "CASEWORK" TREATMENT IN PRODUCING CHANGE.
    Jerome Cohen 176
9. THE EFFECTIVENESS OF EFFECTIVENESS RESEARCH
    Harvey L. Gochros 190
10. SPECIAL PROBLEMS IN THE ASSESSMENT OF GROWTH AND DE-TERIORATION
    Walter W. Hudson 197
11. SPECIFYING CASEWORK EFFECTS
    Edward J. Mullen 225
12. IS THE CASE CLOSED?
    Bernice W. Polemis 232

Chapter	Page

13. NEEDED: A NEW SCIENCE FOR CLINICAL SOCIAL WORK
    William J. Reid 262
14. IS THE PSYCHOANALYTIC MODEL OBSOLETE?
    Herbert S. Strean 273
15. SOME BRIEF COMMENTS ON THE MATTER OF CASEWORK EVALUATION
    Eugene Talsma 279
16. THE EFFECTIVENESS OF SOCIAL CASEWORK: SOME COMMENTS
    Francis J. Turner 287
17. CASEWORK CAN BE EFFECTIVE
    Harold D. Werner 300

Part III

SUMMARY AND CONCLUSION

18. THE END OF SOCIAL CASEWORK OR A BEGINNING? 311

THE EFFECTIVENESS OF
SOCIAL CASEWORK

PART I RESEARCH ON CASEWORK EFFECTIVENESS

The entire thrust of science is a movement toward freedom from misconception.

—LEONARD P. ULLMANN AND LEONARD KRASNER
A Psychological Approach to Abnormal Behavior

CHAPTER 1 INTRODUCTION

R ESEARCH ON THE effectiveness of social casework can provide a bridge between two of the basic values of the social work profession: (1) a commitment to competence and (2) a commitment to the scientific method. The first value, commitment to competence, refers to a concern about effectiveness: Doing everything possible to be certain that professional services are being translated into demonstrable benefits for clients. The second value, commitment to the scientific method, refers to the belief that a process of rational, systematic and orderly inquiry is the best way yet devised by man to organize, understand and accumulate knowledge. An important area of convergence between these two values lies in the use of research—application of scientific procedures to answer questions—to determine whether caseworkers' commitment to effective services can in fact be demonstrated in practice.

This is not a frivolous question. Caseworkers, both in terms of educational and practice specialties, comprise by far the largest part of the social work profession (Stamm, 1968; Loavenbruck, 1973). Literally thousands of agencies across the United States, employing tens of thousands of people, expending millions of dollars, are engaged in countless man-hours of effort to bring casework services to those who need and desire them. But beyond this tremendous investment of time, energy and money by a huge educational and practice establishment, there is an even more basic assumption. That assumption holds that when professional services are provided, both clients and the communities that support those services, have the right to expect that they will be effective.

The point of this is not to say that guaranteed performance —absolute and complete effectiveness irrespective of the situation—can be expected. No profession in the human services—

5

law, medicine, nursing, social work, or any other—can promise that. But it *is* to say that once a field like social casework has defined a claim and shown it to be within acceptable bounds of realization, that field has created an expectation that it must fulfill by performance (Tropp, 1974). In other words, the burden of proof is on social caseworkers to demonstrate the effectiveness of the services they offer.

When caseworkers do offer services, they are making an implicit if not explicit claim that the client has a right to expect some degree of help from those services. *Post hoc* apologies stating that in any given instance casework oversold itself or bit off more than it could chew (e.g. Perlman, 1972) provide little comfort to clients who have received the services, and cannot overcome the more basic fact that once services are offered, that represents the claim that the services have a reasonable chance of being successful. That is the essence of professional responsibility. Indeed, the mere fact that any services whatsoever are being provided, particularly on such a widespread basis and under the auspices and sanction of a profession, can create the impression that, *ipso facto,* they *must* be effective. Or else, how could they be offered?

Unfortunately, it is generally far easier to accept as true what everyone else accepts than to question prevailing attitudes and beliefs. The history of mankind is replete with examples of beliefs and myths that had great currency for periods ranging from several years to centuries, but which were eventually proven false through one or another method of scientific investigation. These myths include such beliefs as, "the world is flat," "man will never fly," "the sun circles the earth," and belief in the efficacy of countless medical treatments, ranging from the use of leeches for bloodletting to Hippocrates' recommendation that marriage is the best remedy for female hysteria.

There is a discomforting analogy here to the practice of social casework. For well over seventy years, caseworkers have practiced as though what they were doing was effective. There actually was little reason to think otherwise, since there was basic agreement about the effectiveness of social casework at all levels of the casework establishment—academicians, practitioners and theoreticians. But this allegiance to prevailing methods of practice had never been validated in research; there was scant empirical evidence justifying caseworkers' faith in their effectiveness. Caseworkers, in essence, had created a professional myth: "A collective belief that is built up in response to the wishes of the group instead of an analysis of what it pertains to" (*American College Dictionary*, 1957, p. 805).

This is not to say that there has been no research on the effectiveness of casework services. Rather, caseworkers seem to have developed a rather widespread lack of appreciation for scientific study and research. For example, when research, particularly with negative findings, appeared, it was considered as "premature and potentially harmful" (Roberts and Nee, 1970, p. xiii); it was disregarded or ignored; it was explained away; and any number of defensive maneuvers were devised in an effort to discount results (Fischer, 1973b). A nonsocial work university administrator noted the responses of social workers to only one study showing lack of effectiveness as including, ". . . tremendous antagonism against the thrust of the study, so that social workers appeared, . . . closed minded in terms of criticism" (Lindsay, 1973, pp. 18, 19).

There was a general flurry of notoriety around the question of casework effectiveness following the publication of such well-known studies as *Girls at Vocational High* (Meyer, Borgatta and Jones, 1965), and the Chemung County Study (Brown, 1968). But the commotion almost always dissipated rapidly and before any of the issues raised at those times could be settled, or even properly discussed. In fact, one noted casework theorist, commenting on the consistency of the research reports with negative or null results, suggested that, ". . . we leave off with both breast beating and evaluative research for a time and work on new adaptations of our problem solving process" (Perlman, 1968, p. 442). There appeared to be widespread agreement to this proposal, since, for some years afterwards, almost as if by some tacit arrangement, the issue of the effectiveness of social casework largely was ignored.

The major thesis of this book, however, is that the issue of the effectiveness of practice must always be of paramount concern to the profession. It is through the use of evaluative research that the profession can assess the appropriateness of its services, the need or desirability for developing new services or for improving or discarding old. Whether research provides negative results, suggesting the necessity for new practice methodologies, or positive results, suggesting the desirability of maintaining current practices, it is largely through evaluative research that such conclusions can be obtained. The emphasis on objectively assessing the effects of practice is at the core of professional accountability.

It was precisely for the above reasons—the desirability of assessing the state of knowledge regarding the effectiveness of social casework—that an earlier review was published by the author (Fischer, 1973a). The conclusion of that review of eleven controlled studies was that professional casework had failed to demonstrate its effectiveness, and that lack of effectiveness appeared to be the rule rather than the exception. The reactions to that review largely approximated earlier reactions to negative results of research, ranging from the opinion that casework is too elusive a process to study or that research methodology is unsophisticated or invariably defective, to the argument that caseworkers should not study their effectiveness because other professions do not study theirs (e.g. "Letters to the Editor," *Social Work,* March, 1973; May, 1973; July, 1973). Not only did history recapitulate itself within social work, but there was an incredible similarity between these responses, and the types of reactions to Eysenck's (1952, 1966) critical reviews of the effectiveness of psychotherapy.

The purpose of this book is to update the earlier review by examining the literature further to see if any other studies are available to shed more light on the question of casework effectiveness. In fact, several additional studies pertinent to this discussion have been located. A second purpose of this book is to provide a basis for the kind of rational and logical discourse that this emotionally-laden topic desperately needs. To that end, as detailed in the Preface, several noted casework theorists, researchers and practitioners have been asked to respond to the analysis of research that will be presented in Part I of this book, and to express their own ideas on the topic. This is intended to insure both a balanced perspective, and the opportunity for several points of view to be discussed.

DEFINING CASEWORK

In order to draw conclusions about how *effective* casework is, it is first necessary to define just *what* casework is, or at least, what kinds of casework, or caseworkers, will be examined. Casework traditionally has been a rather vaguely defined endeavor. After reviewing a number of definitions of social casework reflecting the major streams of casework thought since its earliest days, Hartman (1971, p. 419) concluded: "Because people who define themselves as caseworkers define the practice so differently and because no one has been elected to determine the definition, I assume that we can all carve out our area and practice it, teach it, and write articles about it as long as the community, clients, universities, and editors will support us."

Such vagueness—wherein the answer to the question, what is social casework, seems to depend on who is asked—can be potentially dysfunctional for the casework enterprise. It tends to prevent caseworkers from defining or describing themselves in a uniform way. Thus, not only may there develop a poor or diffuse sense of professional identity, but caseworkers find themselves at a loss when asked to clarify the nature of casework practice to both their clients and the communities to which the profession is accountable. Further, definitional vagueness often precludes caseworkers—and, correspondingly, casework researchers—from specifying the methods and techniques of practice, and hence, expectable outcomes and goals. This inability to come to some common agreement about the precise nature of casework suggests a view of social casework, to paraphrase Raimy's (1950) classic definition of psychotherapy, as, ". . . a set of undefined techniques, applied to unspecified problems, with unpredictable outcome. For this approach, rigorous training is recommended."

On the other hand, the lack of an all-encompassing, unifying definition of social casework is also potentially advantageous. It allows significant differences in practice to emerge and be examined. It can be a motivating factor for innovation, since new modalities of practice cannot be arbitrarily excluded from consideration by practitioners due to wide-spread professional acceptance of a narrow and constricting definition of what practice ought to be like. And finally, and perhaps, above all, lack of a single definition of social casework is *realistic*. There is growing recognition that casework is not a unitary phenomenon, that caseworkers do a multitude of things in a multidude of ways, and that all of this legitimately is called casework (e.g. Roberts & Nee, 1970; Turner, 1974).

Social casework then appears to be more of a *professional* designation than one which describes either a specific theory or method, or specific techniques of practice. At the heart of this professional designation is the notion that social casework is that branch of the profession that provides individualized—and individualizing—services on a case-by-case basis. Although some caseworkers still confuse particular approaches to casework, e.g. the "problem-solving approach," the "psychosocial approach"; the "functional approach" with casework, *per se,* it is becoming increasingly clear that caseworkers can and do use many methods and many techniques. But social casework, as a combination of professional services running the gamut from intensive psychotherapy to broker and advocacy activities, depending on the needs of the case, can be and is independent of any specific theoretical orientation. This was recently acknowledged by both Hartman (1971b) and by a leading casework theorist and educator, Florence Hollis (1971), both of whom have concluded that casework, "is a broad discipline embracing a number of different models."

Assuming the appropriateness of this view of social casework as the branch of the social work profession that provides individualized services, what criteria that will be operationally specific and clear can be used to aid in the identification of studies of casework effectiveness? The first criterion that will be suggested here is that either the social workers or the researchers in a given study identify a major thrust of the services in their study as being comprised of social casework services, or there is clear reason for believing this to be the case (for example, the services were provided in clinics or agencies traditionally staffed by case-workers, or at a time when casework was almost exclusively the orientation of most social workers both in education and in practice). That is, there should be some designation within each study that it is focused on an evaluation or some form of social casework.

The second criterion for identifying studies for review is an educational one: The services provided for at least one of the groups of clients in the study must be provided by professional social workers, defined as social workers with master's degrees (M.S.W.'s) from accredited schools of social work. This criterion was selected because specification of the details of case-work services traditionally appears to have been either less important or less clearly defined than agreement within the profession that those services should be provided by persons whose educational qualifications have met the standards of the profession. This directly implies that educational criteria relate to a presumed basic minimum competence in the practice of casework for all those who have been professionally educated as casework-ers. This is recognized by the Council on Social Work Education, which, in its most recent statement of the Curriculum Policy for the Master's Degree Program in Graduate Schools of Social Work, states: "The development of competence in the practice of social work is a primary curriculum objective . . ."

Specifically for the purpose of identifying and reviewing evaluative studies, then, social casework is defined in this book as *the services provided by professional caseworkers.* This definition provides a clear basis for including any and all studies involving professional caseworkers (assuming research criteria, to be discussed below, are also met), and excluding studies that are main-ly focused on nonprofessional casework. That this is indeed a problem can be seen in other reviews of the effects of "social work" intervention (e.g. Geismar *et al.,* 1972; Mullen & Dumpson,

1972) which have combined studies evaluating the effectiveness of professional workers with those evaluating nonprofessional workers, with correspondingly jumbled conclusions of minimal value to the profession.

The definition of casework as the services of professional caseworkers is an attempt to reflect the realities of social casework practice. It assumes that casework is not a unitary or homogeneous phenomenon; it includes under its scope whatever services the professionals involved in a given project or study deemed appropriate, and hence, recognizes the necessity of individualizing services; and it provides the broadest possible base for drawing conclusions about the effectiveness of professional casework, no matter what techniques or methods are used in providing casework services.

DEFINING EFFECTIVENESS

Almost as difficult as defining social casework is the problem of specifying just what is meant by "effectiveness" (or "success" or "improvement"). This is complicated by the belief among some caseworkers that the effects of casework are too subtle, intangible or elusive to be measured. If this were so, it would seem then than there would be little reason for caseworkers to be offering services. Not only would no one, including the client, be aware of when such changes came about, but they would likely be so insignificant to the clients' personal and social functioning—his attitudes, feelings and/or behavior—as to be literally inconsequential. Intangible or elusive changes can hardly be either worthwhile goals or a basis for continuing professional practice.

It is true, however, that the effects of intervention can show up in a number of different ways, from rather subtle psychological changes to objective observable changes in such areas as school grades, delinquency rates and other performance dimensions. Thus, there are a number of ways of reporting such changes (Bergin, 1971): standardized assessment interviews, psychological tests such as the Minnesota Multiphasic Personality Inventory (M.M.P.I.), behavioral assessment, self-concept measures such as

Q-sorts, thematic stories, e.g. the Thematic Apperception Test (TAT), worker ratings and evaluations, client checklists and self-ratings, factor-analytic batteries, mood scales, peer ratings, and, of course, objective data obtained from such sources as school and police records.

One of the fascinating findings to be derived from extensive research on changes in clients in casework and related fields such as counseling and psychotherapy is that change processes tend to be divergent and multifactorial. Changes in clients in any given study may show up on one measure and not at all on other measures (Bergin, 1971). Thus, for purposes of this review, significant changes on *any* measure will be taken as evidence of effectiveness even if other measures do not reflect this change. The only exceptions to this guideline will be when the changes are likely only artifacts of multiple analyses and therefore due to chance (see Wilkinson, 1951), or when flaws in research design clearly cast doubt on the validity of the findings.

When drawing general conclusions about the effectiveness of social casework, it is clear that a greater degree of confidence can be derived when positive changes can be demonstrated across varying types of criterion measures across several studies. Also, given the scope of potential changes resulting from casework intervention, it would appear that researchers have a better chance of demonstrating significant changes in clients by using a range of measures, e.g. objective and subjective, behavioral ratings or self-administered questionnaires. On the other hand, there might also be validity in drawing conclusions about the effectiveness of social casework, certainly in a given study and even across many studies, from changes in only a few measures of outcome. This is because those few measures, e.g. an instrument designed specifically to study the effectiveness of casework, might really be the only appropriate indicators of the kinds of changes that casework services are capable of producing.

Within each individual study, it is the task of the participants —researchers, caseworkers, agency administrators—to select the appropriate outcome indicators (Herzogg, 1959). As noted above, any number of measures are available for use in casework research. Effectiveness is then defined in the individual study as a determination that scores changed significantly in a positive direction over the course of treatment on the measures selected, and that the differences significantly favored one group over another. This would denote achievement of a goal which has been specified in advance by those involved in the study (Herzogg, 1959). Obviously, this review is constrained by the fact that results only can be reported in relation to the measures that were included in the primary investigations, even though other unknown effects of potential importance may have occurred.

SELECTION OF STUDIES

The basic purpose of a study of casework effectiveness is to examine whether or not the casework services were successful in helping clients. A minimum requirement for establishing that whatever changes came about could reasonably be considered a product of the services provided is the use of a control procedure. Evidence of some change in clients, *per se,* is not necessarily evidence that the changes came about *because* of the casework services, and evidence of no change cannot be taken as a demonstration that the services had no effect, e.g. the intervention might have prevented deterioration. In either situation, the researcher cannot draw definite conclusions unless some form of controls have been introduced to minimize alternative explanations. (A detailed discussion of the need for control groups is presented in Fischer, 1975.) Therefore, the basic minimum methodological requirement (and this is indeed a minimum standard of rigor) for selection of studies for this review was that some form of control group of clients was utilized in the study.

Beginning with recent reviews (Briar, 1966, 1970; Geismar, 1971; Geismar *et al.,* 1972; Brown, 1968; Mullen & Dumpson, 1972), major social work journals, dissertation abstracts and unpublished agency reports were surveyed from the 1930's to the present. Over eighty studies were located that purported to examine the effectiveness of casework services. However, although these studies contained a great deal of valuable information, most neglected to include a control group in their design. Because of the difficulty in drawing a valid conclusion regarding cause and effect without a control group for comparison purposes, the great bulk of these studies had to be excluded from this review.

Two major types of control group were utilized in the studies eventually selected. The first kind used "untreated" controls where the effects of services upon the experimental group are compared with a group which purportedly received no treatment at all. The second kind used a specific form of "other-treated control," where the experimental group received the services of professional caseworkers (with a minimum educational requirement of a master's degree in social work), and the control or contrast group received services from non-professionals, e.g. public assistance or probation workers without a master's degree in social work.

Despite obvious differences in the two categories of studies, certain assumptions basic to professional education and practice tend to minimize the importance of these differences. Essentially, these assumptions are that, given client groups with similar problems appropriate for social work intervention: (1) caseworkers with professional degrees should achieve more successful results than nonprofessional workers; and (2) a program of professional intervention should achieve more successful outcome with clients than either no treatment at all or nonspecific or haphazardly arrived at treatment. Considerable research points to the fact that there may be very few "pure" control groups (Bergin, 1971). Even when nominally in a control group, people often seek out help wherever they can find it, including such sources as family, friends or the clergy. In such cases, it is assumed for the reasons stated above that a program of professional intervention, on the whole, still should achieve more efficacious results.

Thus, in line with the definition of casework as the services provided by professional caseworkers, this review will attempt to ascertain whether such services have been found to be more effective than no treatment whatsoever or other nonspecific or nonprofessional services with which they have been compared.

In addition to exclusion of studies that did not utilize control groups, several other categories of studies were excluded to minimize potential biasing and confounding effects which could have been introduced if they had been included. This hopefully would allow for greater precision in drawing conclusions. Studies examining casework services outside of the United States proper were not included, e.g. Wattie, 1973; Goldberg, 1970; Martin, 1969; Kuhl, 1969. Since the effectiveness of caseworkers with the professional degree (M.S.W.) is the object of attention, a range of well-known studies examining only the services of non-M.S.W.'s also were not included, e.g. Schwartz & Sample, 1967; Behling, 1961; Wilson, 1967; Rudoff & Piliavin, 1969; Geismar, 1971; Geismar *et al.,* 1972. Those studies that examined only variations in types of professional services, without utilizing an untreated or nonprofessionally treated control group were excluded as well, e.g. Reid and Shyne, 1969; Langsley *et al.,* 1968; Blenkner, Jahn & Wasser, 1964. And finally, those studies in which it appeared that social workers were only a minority of the treatment team providing services to clients in the experimental group also were omitted, e.g. Witmer & Keller, 1942; Barron & Leary, 1955. Thus, only those studies where it was clear that at least a majority of the services were provided by professional social workers were included. This was done because including studies where it was possible that non-social work professionals contributed the largest part of the services could significantly detract from both the specificity and the generality of conclusions about the effectiveness of professional casework.

Seventeen studies have been conducted that meet the minimum criteria for inclusion in this review: (1) services identified in the study involved some form of social casework; (2) services were provided mainly by professional (M.S.W.) caseworkers for at least one group of clients; and (3) use of an "untreated" or nonprofessionally treated control group. Further, since the purpose of this book is to draw general conclusions about the effectiveness of social casework, one major condition that must be met before attempting any sweeping conclusion is that success or failure must be the *rule* rather than the exception in the studies evaluated, cutting across a variety of clients, casework approaches and situations.

Now it might be argued that it is meaningless to consider a variety of projects, one next to the other, each one possibly using a different casework approach, with different categories of clients and even using different measures of success. However, the purpose of this review is to examine the results of the efforts of the largest branch of the profession of social work, regardless of the techniques or methods used by its practitioners. While specification of these practice details is of course important, the prior question, and certainly the more relevant one, must be: Is there any evidence that, either across the board or in a given situation, professional caseworkers are effective in helping their clients? It would seem fruitless, for example, to begin the investigation of such a question by attempting to identify specific components of practice, i.e. the details of the input, if research shows that no matter what the techniques used or the type of clients or outcome measures, caseworkers are not able to demonstrably help their clients. Thus, once the question of effectiveness is examined on the broadest level possible, the *next* step might be to identify specific components of practice, and to measure their contribution to either success or failure.

CRITERIA FOR RESEARCH ANALYSIS

Each of the studies reviewed in this book was evaluated using analytic criteria of demonstrated value and validity. These criteria are summarized in the framework in Table 1-I. This framework was developed by abstracting and synthesizing criteria for analysis from a number of sources, both from within and without the field of social work, e.g. Tripodi *et al.*, 1969; Paul, 1969; Campbell & Stanley, 1969; Meltzoff & Kornreich, 1970; Herzogg, 1959; Weiss, 1972; Suchman, 1967. Since the entire framework, in which each criterion is specifically explained has been pub-

TABLE 1-I.

SUMMARY OF FRAMEWORK FOR ANALYZING RESEARCH

A. Problem Formulation

	A	B	C	D
1. Clarity of purpose				
2. Clarity of auspices				
3. Clarity of orientation of researcher				
4. Adequate use of literature				
5. Clear formulation of research questions				
6. Clear definition of concepts				
7. Adequate operational definitions				
8. Clear statement of testable hypotheses				
9. Clear specification of independent variables				
10. Clear specification of dependent variables				
11. Reasonableness of assumption of relationship between 9 & 10				
12. Clarity about confounding variables				
13. Method for controlling confounding variables				
14. Reasonableness of assumptions				
15. Tests more than one independent variable				
B. Research Design and Data Collection				
16. Clear statement of research design				
17. Adequacy of design (re: purpose)				
18. Clear specification of kinds of changes desired				
19. Clarity as to signs of changes				
20. Use of appropriate (to purpose) criterion measures				
21. Validity of criterion measures				
22. Reliability of criterion measures				
23. Use of variety of criterion measures, e.g. subjective and objective				

STUDIES

	STUDIES			
	A	B	C	D
24. Clarity about how data is collected				
25. Clarity about who collects data				
26. Avoids contamination in process of data collection				
27. Clarity and adequacy of time between pre- & post-test				
28. Appropriate use of control group(s)				
29. Appropriate use of randomization procedures				
30. Appropriate use of matching procedures				
31. Experimental and control groups equivalent (at pre test)				
32. Controls for effects of history				
33. Controls for effects of maturation				
34. Controls for effects of testing				
35. Controls for effects of instrumentation				
36. Controls for statistical regression				
37. Controls for differential selection of subjects				
38. Controls for differential mortality				
39. Controls for "therapist bias"				
40. Controls for temporal bias				
41. Controls for selection-maturation interaction				
42. Overall degree of success in maximizing internal validity				
43. Sample size adequate				
44. Adequacy of representativeness of client sample				
45. Adequacy of representativeness of helper sample				
46. Controls for reactive effects of testing (interaction with independent variable)				
47. Controls for special effects of experimental arrangements, e.g. "Hawthorne effect" or "placebo effect"				
48. Controls for multiple-treatment interference				
49. Controls for interaction between selection and experimental variable				
50. Overall degree of success in maximizing external validity (representativeness)				

C. Data Analysis and Conclusions	STUDIES			
	A	B	C	D
51. Adequate manipulation of independent variable				
52. Appropriate use of a follow-up				
53. Data adequate to provide evidence for testing of hypotheses				
54. Appropriate use of statistical controls				
55. Appropriateness of statistical procedures				
56. Use of between-group statistical procedures				
57. Extent to which data support hypotheses				
58. Degree of uniformity between tables & text				
59. Extent to which researcher's conclusions are consistent with data				
60. Avoids investigator bias				
61. Clarity as to cause of changes				
62. Degree to which alternative explanations avoided in design				
63. Degree to which potential alternative explanations are dealt with in report				
64. Controls confounding effects of helpers				
65. Controls confounding effects of clients				
66. Controls confounding effects of non-specific treatment				
67. Plausibility of researcher's inferences				
68. Clarity as to meaning of changes				
69. Adequate relating of findings to literature				
70. Adequacy of conclusions in not generalizing beyond or without data				
71. Extent to which research accomplished purpose of study				
72. Appropriately handles unexpected consequences				
D. Utilization of the Research				
73. Relevance to social work practice				
74. Overall soundness of study				

	STUDIES			
	A	B	C	D
75. Generalizability of study findings				
76. Extent to which variables are accessible to control by practitioners				
77. Extent of difference in practice if variables are utilized				
78. Economic feasibility of manipulation of variables				
79. Ethical suitability of manipulation of variables				
80. Extent to which "primary question" is addressed (what methods, based on what "theory", with what helpers, working with what clients, with what kinds of problems, in what situations, are most successful?)				

lished elsewhere (Fischer, 1975), there is no need to reprint it here. Further, in-depth elaboration of the criteria summarized in Table 1-I, is also available in the original references cited above.

Use of objective, identifiable criteria such as presented in Table 1-I, on which each study can be evaluated and then compared according to the same dimension, is intended to enhance the validity and reliability of the conclusions reached. These criteria are available to the reader to be used to carefully examine the analyses of research in this book, and also to be used in the examination of other types of research important to social work.

CHAPTER 2 REVIEW OF STUDIES WITH UNTREATED CONTROLS

S INCE MANY SOCIAL workers are unfamiliar with the studies with which this book is concerned, this and the following chapter contain summaries of those studies, including basic details regarding the nature of the clients, problems, research design, casework services and findings. Knowledge about the content of these studies is obviously necessary as a basis for conclusions regarding the state of casework practice, and can also allow the reader to make his own analyses of these studies. Hopefully, this will act to bring more perspective to the elusive goal of enhancing the relationship between theory, research and practice. As mentioned previously, each study has been evaluated on the basis of the criteria presented in Chapter 1.

For clarity of exposition, the studies are examined in chronological order within two categories: (1) studies utilizing untreated control groups, to be reviewed in this chapter; and (2) studies utilizing "other-treated" control groups which received services from change agents who were not professionally trained caseworkers, which will be reviewed in Chapter 3.

As noted in Chapter 1, subjects in untreated control groups ostensibly are not receiving services. However, the reality of this situation is that such subjects may or may not have been receiving help with their problems. When help was provided, it generally was from friends, relatives, acquaintances or clergy, and rarely from professionals equivalent to those providing services in the experimental group (Bergin, 1971). Of course, such resources are available also to experimental group members, and there is no clear evidence to date that, in a given study, other help was not received in similar proportions by members of both groups. Be that as it may, however, such help often is unplanned, haphazardly selected, and offered on an informal or "unofficial" basis by people in the natural environment. Even if subjects in the control group were to receive higher proportions of such help than clients in the experimental group, the basic assumptions of professional services are that professional services still should be more efficacious. Thus, the question this chapter seeks to answer is: Are services provided by professional caseworkers more effective or in any way superior to no treatment whatsoever, or to services haphazardly or informally obtained in the natural environment?

SUCCESS AND FAILURE OF TREATMENT OF CHILDREN
(Lehrman, L. J. *et al.*, 1949)

This study was a follow-up evaluation of results achieved in the clinics of the Child Guidance Institute of the Jewish Board of Guardians, New York City. All of the cases closed in the child guidance clinics between April, 1941 and March, 1942 were included in the study. Out of a total of 403 cases, however, thirty-seven could not be located for the one-year follow-up; of the remaining 366, 196 had received treatment only at one of the Jewish Board of Guardians clinics, 110 had not received any treatment whatsoever, and sixty were rejected mainly because they had received treatment elsewhere. Thus, the total sample for the follow-up study was 306, including 196 in the treated group and 110 in the controls.

All new cases at the child guidance clinics of the Board of Guardians were seen for an observation/diagnostic period of up to six weeks prior to treatment. This six weeks was spent in evaluating the child and his family, and in determining whether the problems of the child were "within the function" of the agency. The treated group in this study was composed of those cases that completed this six-week period of observation and began treatment at a child guidance clinic. The control group was composed of cases who also completed the observation period and were found to be "within function," but who, for one reason or another (these reasons were not spelled out), had not been treated in one of the child guidance clinics of the Board of Guardians or elsewhere. Thus, this is a "terminator" or "defector" control rather than a true untreated control group. Using such cases as controls may produce important biasing factors, especially when the reasons for early termination are unknown.

In fact, although the two groups were comparable in terms of age (ranging from under 10 years to 16 years and over) and sex (mainly boys in both groups), they apparently were not comparable both in terms of diagnosis and ratings made during the observation period of the "adequacy" of the children's parents. The control group contained a higher proportion of children diagnosed as "primary behavior disorders" and a lower proportion of children diagnosed as "psychoneurotic." The researchers believed this produced a bias in favor of better prognoses for the control cases since, "the agency was specializing in primary behavior disorder cases at the time and was more successful with them than with psychoneurosis cases" (p. 61). The control group also was considered to be favored by the fact that a higher proportion of control children were evaluated as having "two adequate parents." Although the reliability of such diagnostic impressions may be open to question, the fact that they were applied to all children prior to any designation of treatment or control groups likely would tend to randomize any problems across both groups regarding unreliable or inaccurate judgments. Thus, on balance, it would appear that the groups are not completely comparable in that the control group may have been predisposed toward more favorable outcome.

Treatment was carried out by psychiatric social workers operating from a psychoanalytic framework. The bulk of treatment involved intensive individual "therapeutic sessions" with the child, although some of the children also received group therapy and other special agency services such as psychiatrically-oriented summer camps (the quantity or nature of these forms of intervention were not detailed). Length of treatment varied from one to thirty-six months (the median range was 12 to 23 months), with none of the children having fewer than five interviews and 75 percent receiving over thirty client interviews. Data on treatment of parents were not presented.

Two types of clinical ratings were used to operationalize the dependent variable of "adjustment." The first involved evaluating changes in the "objective" area of the child's functioning, including behavior at home, in school and in interpersonal relationships. Each area was rated separately and the ratings aggregated. The second evaluation was in the "subjective" area, such as anxiety, depression, guilt, and so on. Degree of improvement on these subjective dimensions was rated on a four-point sliding scale from "considerable improvement" to "worse." These two types of ratings were then translated into an overall clinical rating of "improved" ("success"), "partially improved" ("partial success") or "unimproved" ("failure").*

Two psychiatric social workers made the one-year follow-up visits in which both children and parents were interviewed. School and other collateral visits also were undertaken. The materials gathered by these research interviewers were presented to a separate evaluation committee who applied the criteria evaluating changes between intake and follow-up without knowing whether the child was in the treatment or control group.

There were two contradictory findings in this study. The first was that 50.5 percent of the children in the treated group were evaluated as "improved" ("successfully adjusted") compared with 31.8 percent of the control group. The difference was statistically significant and led the researchers to conclude that, "the positive effect of the treatment . . . was established beyond doubt" (p. 80). The second finding, which the researchers never discussed but which is evident from the tables, was that when the categories of "success" and "partial success" are combined, there were no real differences between the groups, with 74 percent of the treated group and 70 percent of the control group being considered successful.

There is probably a greater degree of reliability in this latter method, i.e. separating all cases with any degree of improvement from those with no improvement or a worsened condition, in distinguishing most clearly between effectiveness and noneffectiveness. Many studies of casework effectiveness follow this principle

---

* (Sociological criteria such as delinquency rates were also used but not reported in the study.)

(e.g. Beck & Jones, 1973); in fact, none could be located that do not consider any sign of improvement as evidence of effectiveness. This fact also is noted by most reviewers of similar research (e.g. Eysenck, 1966; Levitt, 1957; Segal, 1972). Thus, while the researchers in the Lehrman *et al.* (1949) study may have been properly enthusiastic over the results of their study, the overall findings make it unclear as to just what was the impact of the treatment for the children in the treated group. Perhaps the fairest conclusion is that the overall effectiveness of the treatment is not clear, since the results in this study point in the direction of effectiveness when the findings are viewed in one way (using only one of three outcome categories, thereby ignoring well over half of the data), and point to a conclusion of noneffectiveness (no difference between the treated and control groups) when all of the categories of outcome are employed and all the data are used.

The major flaws in this study relate to the nature of the control group. The use of "defectors" or "early terminators" simply is not the same as an untreated control group. The defectors may vary in any number of dimensions from the treatment group, including those dimensions such as "motivation for treatment" and a variety of external factors which may be difficult to measure and therefore cannot be properly ascertained. Indeed, the researchers presented no information on the reasons for defection, thus obscuring potential differences between the groups even more. A greater degree of confidence might be placed in the use of a "defector" control group when it is clear that, on any measurable dimensions, they are comparable to the treatment group. But in this study, that condition did not pertain and the controls were significantly different from the treated group in terms of diagnosis and ratings of family adequacy. This presents a serious problem in interpreting any greater change in one group in comparison to the other since their presumed noncomparability opens up the door for explanations other than the treatment factor in interpreting the reasons for those changes. (Apparently, however, the diagnostic differences between the groups in this study had little impact on the results of treatment.

Rates of change for the treatment group were virtually identical for "primary behavior disorders," with 75 percent improved or partially improved, and "psychoneuroses," with 73 percent "improved" or "partially improved." Thus, the assumption that the higher percentage of behavior disorders in the control group would bias that group in a more favorable direction seems, at best, not proven in terms of the results of this study.)

Further, since the control group did have some contact with the agency, ranging from one to five sessions during the diagnostic period, it is difficult to partial out the effects of those contacts, if any, from the overall results of the study. While such brief contacts may have had no impact whatsoever on control group children and their families, the fact that this remains one more unknown factor about the control group once again diminishes its value when comparisons are made. This is because the purpose of studies such as this is to attempt to isolate the effects of treatment—which is defined in this report only as "following the guiding principles of psychoanalytic psychotherapy" (p. 7)—a difficult process at best when both groups are exposed to the treatment.

In all, because of the above problems and the fact that outcome was reported in a way that leads to two clearly divergent conclusions depending on which data are used, this study does not clearly support or refute the effectiveness of the casework used with the clients in the treatment group. Perhaps the most appropriate conclusion that can be drawn is that no definitive conclusion can be derived about success or failure in this study.

CAMBRIDGE-SOMERVILLE YOUTH STUDY
(Powers & Witmer, 1951)

This is one of the best-known and most-quoted studies of casework intervention. The purpose of this study, conducted from 1937 to 1945 in Cambridge, Massachusetts, simply stated, was to prevent juvenile delinquency. This purpose was modified during the course of the study to include "fostering growth" and social adjustment in "predelinquent" boys. Names of boys from six to ten years old who were judged likely to become delinquent were submitted by settlement workers, teachers and police officers to this independently designed and financed project. A total of 650 boys were matched in pairs (called "twins") on variables such as I.Q., grade in school, delinquency prognoses (predictive judgments by the selection committee), and a host of socio-economic variables. The boys were then randomly assigned to either the treatment or control groups. This excellent design included large enough numbers and sufficient comparability between groups to make any results convincing, and, in most of its provisions, can serve as a model for conducting research on the effectiveness of casework intervention.

The 325 control boys were to be "left alone," i.e. they would receive whatever services they happened upon in the community during the course of their development. Each of the 325 boys in the experimental group was immediately assigned to one of the caseworkers in the project and treatment begun. The details of treatment varied from worker to worker, but the major focus with all workers was on the establishment of friendly, warm relationships with the boys through the use of individual face-to-face contacts. Supervision "with a psychiatric slant" was available, and the caseworkers attempted to individualize plans, meet specific needs and cooperate with other agencies. Most of the workers operated from a psychodynamic framework, with at least one preferring a "Rogerian nondirective technique whenever possible" (p. 130). Interviews were held in and outside of the office, in the boys' homes, and wherever conditions seemed conducive to establishing relationships. The mean length of contact per boy was four years and ten months, with an average of 27.3 contacts per boy per year. The range of contacts varied widely, though, since some of the boys presented few problems, and others presented many problems.

Since the purpose of the project was to prevent delinquency, a variety of official records were used as outcome indicators: (1) police statistics from the Cambridge Crime Prevention Bureau; (2) frequency of court appearances; (3) seriousness of offenses; and (4) commitment to correctional institutions. The results of the analyses of these data showed some measures favoring the treatment group and some favoring the control group, but none of the differences were reported as statistically significant. There were no overall trends supporting the primary hypotheses of the study. "The special work of the counselors was no more effective than the usual forces in the community in preventing boys from committing delinquent acts" (p. 337). Further, these results were maintained at a long-term follow-up. Eight years after completion of the study, McCord and McCord (1959) located 253 matched pairs of "twins" (N = 506) and found no significant differences between the groups on any measures. Clearly, both in the short- and long-run, the services offered these boys had little or no impact.

Since the project hoped not only to prevent delinquency but to "develop character of experimental boys superior to that of control group boys" (p. 385), terminal adjustment ratings were made. These terminal ratings occurred at various points for different individuals and referred to the latest point at which information about a boy would be secured. Eventually, 148 control boys were located and compared with their matched treatment "twins." Information was obtained largely from interviews with the boys and their parents, although ancillary data from schools and other official records were used when available. Ratings were based largely on judgments about the social functioning of the boys and were made on the basis of a four-point scale (which included several subcategories): "good adjustment," "fairly good adjustment," "rather poor adjustment" and "poor adjustment." When ratings for the treated boys were compared with those for control boys, they were found to be virtually identical. This was maintained when age was held constant. It was clear that both in terms of delinquency records and social functioning, control boys ". . . turned out just about as well as the boys who had the benefit of the study's services" (p. 417).

One of the most fascinating pieces of information from this study involves the ratings of the caseworkers. Throughout the program, counselors were asked on several occasions to list all of the treatment group boys they thought had "substantially benefitted" from the services offered by the project. Roughly two thirds of the boys were so listed. Further, at the end of treatment over half of the boys volunteered that they had been helped by their caseworkers. Similarly, in a follow-up of treatment group boys which included 254 boys where data could be found, global adjustment ratings suggested that two-thirds were adjusting satisfactorily, a figure that easily could have been attributed to the effects of the project. However, when data on the control group were added to the picture, it changed dramatically, showing no differences between the groups on any indicators of delinquency or social functioning. It is not necessarily that treatment group boys were not doing well. It is more that their "doing well" could not be attributed to the caseworkers' efforts since control group boys were doing equally as well.

As Teuber and Powers (1953) note: "These findings illustrate the importance of the control group, and the peculiar difficulty one has in interpreting the counselor's (or the counselee's) 'own story' unless objective behavioral indices for treatment success are available. Quantitative indices of behavior, of course, are not infallible . . . yet quantitative indices, where available, are better than professions of faith bolstered by the therapist's prestige and the skillful use of the illustrative case" (p. 140).

The Cambridge-Somerville study is not without certain flaws. The independent variable—the treatment—was poorly defined and highly variable, both in terms of methods and in terms of contacts with boys. The control group boys did receive whatever social services were available in the community, although it is improbable that with such large samples, one group of 325 boys received substantially more help than another group of 325 randomly selected boys. Further, the assumption that the kind of individual attention described in the study should be able to prevent delinquency, although perhaps widely subscribed to, seems to be a tenuous one. Additionally, since only one judge (Witmer) apparently made all ratings of social adjustment, it is not clear to what extent they were free from bias. Finally, not all of the boys in the treatment group were carried the full length of the project. Sixty-five boys were "retired" as functioning well and not in need of services with a mean period of treatment of two years and six months; 113 boys were "dropped," with a mean length of treatment of four years and two months, largely because they had moved away from the target area; seventy-two boys were terminated for various reasons including having reached age seventeen, with a mean length of treatment of five years and eleven months; and seventy-five boys were carried to the end of the project with a mean length of treatment of six years and nine months. On the whole, however, the mean length of treatment of four years and ten months, seems to provide a reasonable period of time for the evaluation of any effects of that treatment that might have appeared.

Despite these flaws, the major provisions of this study are particularly sound and well executed. It is hard to ignore or refute the conclusions from this long-term, controlled, well-designed study, that whatever the caseworkers were doing in this project, their efforts appear to have had little or no impact on the overall progress of boys in the experimental group. None of the outcome indicators employed revealed any significant degree of success in comparison to the control group.

FOLLOW-UP-EVALUATION AT A CHILD GUIDANCE CLINIC
(Levitt, Beiser & Robertson, 1959)

The purpose of this study was to evaluate the effectiveness of clinical practice at the Institute for Juvenile Research in Chicago. "Treatment" was arbitrarily defined as at least five one-hour sessions for at least one family member with a clinician at the Institute. A random sample of 1,006 cases seen at I.J.R. over a period of ten years (1944 to 1954) was drawn. Of these, 579 were in the treated group and 427 were controls. The control group was of the "defector" type—cases which had been accepted for treatment at the Institute but which had voluntarily terminated contact with the clinic without receiving any treatment interviews. Several studies were carried out to determine the appropriateness of this group serving as a control. No differences were found between defector and treatment groups on sixty-one diagnostic and background variables, or on severity of symptoms or motivation for treatment based on estimates of case materials by expert judges. Of the 1,006 cases, eventually only 330 were located who had not had subsequent treatment and who were willing to participate in the study, including 237 treated cases and ninety-three controls. Sixty-nine percent of these were male, and the average age of all cases was 15.9 years.

Treatment consisted of whatever services had been received at the clinic (variously called "psychotherapy," "child guidance" and "treatment") and was not more specifically defined than that (beyond the minimum of 5 sessions per case). The child alone was the focus of treatment in only 10 percent of the cases, the parent alone in 44 percent of the cases, and in 46 percent, both parent and child were treated. The average number of therapy interviews for the family member receiving the most interviews was eighteen; the average length of time per case was not defined, although 90 percent of the individuals were seen once per week. The bulk of the treatment—76.5 percent—was conducted by caseworkers, with nearly 87 percent of all parents treated by caseworkers. The remainder of the treatment was conducted by psychiatrists and psychologists. Since the Institute was a training agency, roughly 35 percent of the treatment was conducted by students.

The major dependent variable was defined as "adjustment" and operationalized as twenty-five specific outcome indicators, including the following: (1) objective psychological tests—a short form of the M.M.P.I., the Barron Ego-Strength Scale, the Taylor Anxiety Scale and the Bendig-Pittsburg short form of the latter. These were administered to all subjects who were at least fourteen years of age at follow-up, including 103 experimental cases and forty-nine controls; (2) objective data, such as marriage, institutionalization, completion of schooling; (3) parents' opinions and evaluations of the child and his symptoms; (4) statements about himself and his feelings by the child; and (5) clinical judgments of the child by the research interviewers. Data were collected by interviews with parent and child in roughly three quarters of the cases, parents alone were seen in 229 of the cases, and the child alone in 5 percent. An average of 5.4 years intervened between the time of the close of the case at the clinic and the follow-up interview.

Of the twenty-five variables, only two showed a significant difference between the groups; the control group had a lower score on the Taylor Anxiety Scale ($p = .02$) and the experimental group reported a greater liking for school ($p = .05$). However, the probability of finding two p-values of .05 out of twenty-five by chance alone was found to be greater than .35, resulting in the conclusion that the two significant p's were the result of chance, and could not be interpreted as a reflection of real differences between the groups brought about by the treatment. There were no differences between the sexes on the psychological inventories. However, of the twenty-five variables, the direction of the difference favored the control group on sixteen, and favored the experimental group on only nine, although this difference was not statistically significant.

A second analysis was conducted on the assumption that five interviews may not be sufficient to be called "treatment," even though the mean number of interviews was eighteen. Treatment was redefined as at least ten interviews, leaving a total of 192 cases in the experimental group, with a mean number of treatment interviews of twenty-six. Age and sex ratios changed only slightly from the original analysis. Seven of the outcome variables were also dropped because of insufficient data. There were no significant differences between the groups with this reanalysis. Of the eighteen variables, ten favored the control group, six favored the treated group and two were the same for both groups. The authors concluded that "the data of this study indicate that there is no difference at follow-up between the adjustments made by treated and untreated child patients" (p. 345).

Of course, the "treatment" methods employed in this study are not defined at all, although the period of time during which the treatment occurred (1945 to 1954) makes it likely that they were largely psychodynamically-oriented. Most of the treatment was conducted by caseworkers, although since psychiatrists and psychologists also participated, the onus of failure in this study cannot be placed solely on the caseworkers. Similarly, since roughly one third of the treatment was conducted by students, albeit under intensive supervision, the results cannot be attributed solely to the lack of impact of professional practitioners. On the other hand, as a discussion of the study pointed out (Forstenzer, 1959), clinics such as the I.J.R. are "ranked at the top" in accreditation reviews, and the intensive supervision of students, plus absence of formal data on the subject, make the real differences between both the way the students and professionals handled their cases, and even more importantly, any differences in effectiveness, unclear.

Perhaps the most serious question about this study has to do with the use of the "defector" group as controls. Although the researchers point to abundant data showing no differences between the defector and treated groups, it simply is not clear what real differences between the groups actually do exist, perhaps on untested dimensions, so that any conclusions drawn on the basis of use of a defector control group must be tentatively held.

The use of a six-year follow-up adds an important dimension to the analysis of programs of clinical effectiveness. The authors appeared to bend over backwards to examine their data for potential positive effects of intervention, especially in the reanalysis phase when all cases with less than ten interviews were dropped. The broad range of outcome indicators used—involving feelings, behaviors and social functioning, attitudes, and data from psychological tests—also add extra dimensions to this study. On the whole, it appears as though the intervention in this study—mainly provided by caseworkers—had minimal positive impact on the treated group, although such a conclusion must be advanced with caution because of the potential problems with use of the defectors as a control group. Certainly, however, unless the defectors were significantly different from the treated group in a more positive direction at the outset of the study—a fact contradicted by the pretest data comparing the two groups—the results of this study give little reason for affirming any degree of confidence in the value of the services provided.

DELINQUENTS, THEIR FAMILIES AND THE COMMUNITY
(Tait & Hodges, 1962)

The purpose of this project was to "prevent delinquency," which included forestalling or precluding any acts considered delinquent. The focus of the project was on "officially known delinquency," defined as "a youngster within the age limits prescribed in the involved community who has come to the attention of the juvenile court, police, or other duly constituted authority for an act (s) considered a 'delinquency' by the laws of that community" (p. 26). The project concentrated on an area in Washington, D.C. during the mid-50's which had the highest crime rate in the city, overcrowded housing (slums) and one of the lowest median incomes in the city.

The project, called the Maximum Benefits Program, was sponsored by the city's Youth Council and the schools, although it was eventually funded by private grants. The project centered on children from two elementary schools from the "deprived" area described above. One hundred and seventy-nine children were referred to the project from the two schools, mainly because of behavioral problems in the school. Boys outnumbered girls by approximately three to one and blacks outnumbered whites by roughly the same proportion. Children were evaluated by intensive case studies, and then predictions about their potential for future delinquency were made using the Glueck Social Prediction Table (a method for predicting delinquency). Based upon these predictions, children were assigned to treatment and control group. It is not clear whether this was random assignment, although the researchers note that they attempted to match the groups on age, sex, race, and on the likelihood of delinquency as indicated by Glueck scores (p. 34). These efforts were largely successful except for significant differences between the groups in terms of age (the untreated group averaged one-and-a-half years older) and grade (controls slightly less than one grade ahead). These differences are unfortunate because of the potential relationship between age and delinquent behaviors. The groups were also alike in terms of I.Q.

The heart of the treatment program was social casework, from a psychodynamic perspective (p. 61). The details of the treatment were not spelled out, although referrals apparently were extensively used. Treatment mainly was composed of direct interviews in the home and in the office with parents and their children and lasted an average of eleven months per case, with a mean of 4.5 interviews with each child and 10.9 with parents. These figures appeared to vary depending on the year a family was in the project, since thirty-seven families involved in the first year of the project averaged nineteen months of contact with a mean of 12.1 interviews per child.

Since the goal of the project was to prevent juvenile delinquency, the outcome indicators consisted of any records of police or court contacts. The researchers recognized the weaknesses in these measures, but justified the focus on officially known delinquency in terms of costs of crime to the community plus costs of community services. They recognized that other delinquent acts may go unreported and apparently assumed that these probably would be randomly distributed in the treated and control groups. Project treatment was begun in 1954 and all treatment terminated by 1957. In 1958, a follow-up study was conducted. Records on 108 children were located from the treated group and fifty-seven from the untreated group. There were no differences that favored the treated group. Children in the control group had fewer appearances before both the courts and the police, with 39 percent of the treated group identified as delinquent and only 25 percent of the control group so identified. This led the researchers to state: "We find it necessary to conclude that the treatment program has failed" (p. 74).

Apart from the typical problems in defining the nature of the casework treatment, certain problems are apparent in this design. The use of officially-known delinquency records was already mentioned. In addition, there was some confusion in the way the data were presented. The researchers focused mainly on cases treated during the first year of the project, apparently because data analysis for these cases was completed. Thus, much of the information about the course of treatment and the matching refers only to those cases. Outcome data on the entire treated group appeared to be added as an afterthought. Thus, it is not known if such characteristics as the matching problems regarding age are maintained for the entire sample. If they are, it is not clear what effects this would have on the outcome data, although on the surface, because the untreated control was somewhat older, the bias probably favored the treated group. The researchers did attempt a *post hoc* analysis of differences between the two groups, concluding that four out of six favored the treated group, but the true effects of these differences are not known.

Despite these problems, the real effects of which are unknown, the overall results did not support the hypothesis in this study that professional casework services can have any impact on preventing the performance of delinquent acts.

THE MIDCITY DELINQUENCY CONTROL PROJECT
(Miller, 1962)

The Midcity Project consisted of a large-scale, "total community" effort to inhibit or reduce the amount of delinquency in a "lower-class" district of Boston in the mid-1950's. The Project actually had three focal points: (1) a community program; (2) work with families in the area; and (3) work with gangs in the area, which was both the major effort of the Project, and the major target of evaluation.

The seven gangs totaling 205 members comprised the experimental group (details of their selection were not clarified). Four of these gangs were composed of white males, one was white females, one was black males and one was black females. The mean age range for the gangs during the period of worker contact was sixteen to twenty.

The control group was composed of 172 members from eleven other gangs who were not being worked with by the Project. The two groups were matched for age, sex, ethnic status and social status. However, the report was not clear how these control gangs were located, selected or matched, especially since there were more gangs but fewer subjects in the control group. Thus, the true comparability of the two groups is open to serious question.

The treatment in the Project was provided by seven workers also of mixed ethnic status, all of whom had professional degrees in casework, group work or both. The workers employed a wide variety of methods and techniques, but their approach was grounded in "psychodynamic psychiatry" and "group dynamics."

The three major phases of their work with gangs were conceptualized as: (1) contact and relationship establishment; (2) behavior modification via mutual activity involvement; and (3) termination. (Some of the details of each of these phases are presented in the original report.) Work was directed at both individuals in the gangs and gangs as a whole. The workers' activities ranged from personal counseling to recreational endeavors to broker and advocacy functions, and all but one of the workers devoted primary attention to a single gang. The "methods" which were reported as most extensively employed or successfully executed were: (1) locating and contacting gangs; (2) establishing relationships with gang members; (3) effecting formal organization and involvement in organized recreational activity; (4) provision of access to adult institutions; and (5) provision of adult role-models. The total duration of contact with the gangs ranged from ten to thirty-four months, with an average number of contacts of 3.5 per week.

The Midcity project was originally instituted in response to community concern over uncontrolled gang violence. Thus, the key dependent variable of the study was the inhibition and control of criminal behavior. Three separate measures of changes in patterns of "violative" behavior were used: (1) judgments by the workers about changes in disapproved forms of customary behavior; (2) trends in illegal acts (using both official and unofficial statistics); and (3) trends in court appearances. However, data on the former two categories were only available for the treated group, so that the only between-group comparisons were for the third category, trends in court appearances. These data were collected before, during and for four years after the project.

Not only was there not a significant decrease in overall trends in court appearances for the experimental group when measured before, during and after contact periods, but when compared with the control group, the trends were virtually identical for both groups. On all indicators—total court appearances per year, number of individuals appearing in court per year, the number of appearances per individual, the proportion of individuals who had appeared in court by age twenty-three, and the proportion who had reappeared—the figures for the two groups were almost exactly the same. In fact, where percentages are reported, the greatest difference between the groups was 1.6 percent. (In addition, the researcher reported that for the experimental group only there were no major reductions in trends in disapproved behavior or trends in illegal acts.) In reviewing the overall impact of the Project, the researcher asked rhetorically, " 'Was there a significant measurable inhibition of law-violating or morally-disapproved behavior as a consequence of Project efforts?' The answer, with little necessary qualification, is 'No' " (p. 187).

While the data appear to justify the researcher's conclusion that, on the measures used, the Project had minimal impact, there are sufficient design flaws to warrant only tentative acceptance of this conclusion. The true comparability of the experimental and treatment groups is unknown. Criteria for selection and matching of groups were unclear, and it is possible some systematic bias is present in the composition of the groups. Further, the outcome data for some unexplained reason are not presented for all members of the experimental and control groups (pp. 185-187). This leaves some question as to the results of the study with the remaining subjects. The outcome measures used, e.g. court appearances, are subject to considerable bias since court appearances really cannot be taken as an accurate indicator of the presence of delinquency. However, it is likely that this bias is present in equal proportions for both treatment and control groups.

Further, there is possibly some degree of confounding between the intensive efforts of the Project gang worker with the effects of the rest of the Project. While the researcher reported that family and community programs tended to be poorly executed, they were implemented to some degree. In fact, not only would these efforts confound the effects of the major treatment variable—which apparently was a combination of casework and group work efforts—but subjects in the control group also may have received some of the community and family services. If so (and these data were not presented), their value as a control group diminishes even more.

On balance, while on the measures used there clearly were no differences between the experimental and control groups, any conclusions about the reasons for those lack of differences must be applied cautiously because of the several problems inherent in this design.

MEASURING MARITAL SATISFACTION
(Most, 1964)

This study was concerned with assessing the effectiveness of professional casework services to clients seeking help at a family planning center. The study took place at the Margaret Sanger Research Bureau in New York City. Beginning in April, 1957, every applicant to the clinic's Marriage Consultation Service requesting help with marital problems was placed in the experimental group until a total of twenty clients was reached. Women admitted as patients to the Fertility Service of the Clinic during the same period of time were used as controls. The researcher described the two groups as "fairly similar" on most characteristics: they were, "predominantly of the white-collar class, relatively youthful (the greater number were under twenty-eight and married less than five years), and mainly white (there were two [blacks] and one mixed couple in the control group only). In each group, more than half had been educated beyond high school, and about half were of the Jewish faith" (p. 66). The one dimension where the two groups were clearly noncomparable was the most critical one: Experimental clients had requested marriage counseling and control clients had come to the clinic requesting only medical advice.

The casework was performed by the researcher, and was not defined in any way. Apparently, most or all interviews took place in the worker's office with a minimum of five contacts and an average length of contact of three months.

The main concern of this study was to measure changes in "marital satisfaction" on an instrument devised by the researcher. The questionnaire covered six areas of the marital relationship: (1) personality; (2) companionship; (3) sex relationship; (4) job/household/finances; (5) family/children/in-laws; and

(6) activities/interests/friends. In all, sixty-eight areas plus an overall rating of degree of happiness were rated on a four-point scale from "Very Satisfied" to "Very Dissatisfied." This instrument was administered at pre- and posttest to experimental and control subjects (a follow-up administration excluded control clients so is not reported here). Clients in the experimental group were demonstrated to change on this instrument in the direction of greater marital satisfaction over the course of the study to a greater degree than clients in the control group. This led the researcher to conclude that the changes occurred because of the counseling and that the program could therefore be evaluated as effective.

Unfortunately, several design flaws were present in this study, of such a serious nature that this study probably should not even be classified here as using an experimental design. Treatment was only provided by one worker whose characteristics were completely unknown. No generalizations would be possible on this basis. Further, the case worker was also the researcher, and this could introduce an important source of bias in the study; she clearly had something special to gain by demonstrating positive changes in clients.

The data on which this study were based were limited to subjective impressions by the clients, a notoriously unreliable measure. Such data are most susceptible to the "Hello-Goodbye Effect," the well-documented fact that clients often exaggerate the seriousness of complaints on entering treatment and give socially desirable, exaggerated reports of improvement on leaving treatment. Other more objective measures might have bolstered confidence in any conclusions drawn from such data. (In fact, two additional measures were used, apparently for the experimental group only, the Hunt Movement Scale and a scale reported by the Philadelphia Marriage Council. Judgments on both of these scales were not correlated to a statistically significant degree with the self-ratings of the clients.) An undetermined number of clients who did not complete five interviews were excluded from the data analysis. This could have biased the final results in either direction, although it is likely that the cases that were retained biased the findings in the direction of more favorable results. This is because clients least likely to improve are those most likely to drop out early, leaving remaining clients to spuriously inflate improvement rates. At best, the effects of this sampling bias are undetermined, although it might be argued that it perhaps is legitimate for researchers to limit their data analysis and conclusions to cases where treatment is completed to evaluate its true effects.

But the above design flaws are minimal compared to the following. As mentioned previously, the clients in the experimental group, on the most important dimension, are not comparable with the controls. Clients in the experimental group actually sought help for marital problems, while those in the control group came to the center for medical services and not marital counseling. Comparing these two groups to assess the effectiveness of marital counseling is similar to comparing clients with a headache with those without a headache to determine the effects of aspirin. Obviously, any possible changes that come about could be explainable as the result of an interaction between selection and maturation factors, where the selection of clients for treatment and control groups results in two groups with different potential for rates of change. In addition, since what essentially was being compared in this study was one group with extremely negative pretest scores (the experimental group had a median score on the scale of 114.5) with another group with high pretest scores (the control group median was 156.5 out of a possible 168), the effects are also likely a result of statistical regression, the tendency of a group selected for study *because* of extremely negative scores to show positive changes in their scores at a later date whether or not they have had any treatment. Indeed, the scores of the treatment group at posttest—with a median of 139 —were still substantially below the pretest scores of the controls.

Finally, even if none of the above problems were present, the statistics used provide an unclear basis for comparing the groups as to what changes really occurred. The researcher apparently compared changes *within* the experimental group (which were statistically significant, although barely) with changes within the control group (which were not significant, although they hardly could be expected to change dramatically from pretest). Actually, the key index for evaluating overall program effects lies in comparing differences *between* the groups. Thus, unless the appropriate statistics are used to make these between-group comparisons, it is impossible to ascertain whether differences between the treated and control groups would reach statistical significance. (Indeed, the researcher reported that the differences in Z-scores between the experimental group, 1.68, and the control group, 1.08, were rather minimal.) Of course, it should be clear that a finding of statistically significant movement within the treatment group has nothing to do at all with what caused the change. As this study clearly demonstrates, without an adequate control group, any number of explanations other than the treatment itself are possible.

In all, this study does not provide evidence of whether or not there was a significant effect of casework intervention. In terms of design characteristics, however, it probably should not even be included in this review, although the fact that the researcher considered herself to have provided a control group necessitated its analysis.

WHAT HAPPENS AFTER TREATMENT?

(Craig & Furst, 1965)

This study was part of an attempt to validate predictions of delinquency using the Glueck Social Prediction Table. The test was applied to all first-grade boys in two New York City elementary schools. The total group of boys numbered 224; they were between the ages of five and one-half and six and one-half, with the majority being black and the remainder white and Puerto Rican. The Prediction Table was focused on evaluating five areas of family and interpersonal relationships, after which a weighted score was assigned; the higher the score, the greater the presumed likelihood of delinquency.

The research design called for clinical treatment in a Board of Education child guidance clinic for all boys with a weighted score of 250 or over (which indicated a minimum of 63.5

chances per hundred of becoming delinquent). From these, twenty-two boys were assigned to the treatment group and were matched with twenty-two other boys (on the basis of Glueck scores, neighborhood, I.Q., age and ethnic group), who then comprised the control group. Seven additional boys, referred by teachers to the clinic for various reasons, were added to the treatment group, and were matched on the same characteristics as described above with seven additional boys for the control group. Thus, the total N of fifty-eight included twenty-nine boys in each group.

Treatment consisted of intensive child guidance therapy by psychiatric social workers and other clinic professionals, all of whom had at least three years of postgraduate experience. In addition to the intensive therapy, the treatment personnel engaged in several reaching-out activities including home visits, concrete services, "and other activities demonstrating interest, concern and accessibility" (p. 168). The treatment was indeed intensive, with the median length of uninterrupted contact with the clinic being fifty months; over half of the treatment boys and their families were in treatment more than four years. Further, over a fifteen-year period, each group was found to have approximately the same number of registrations with the Social Service Exchange, suggesting comparability in terms of other professional help.

Two kinds of outcome measures were used. Since the prevention of delinquency was of primary concern, delinquency records (presumably police and court records) were the major measure. These records were examined at a five-year follow-up (ten years after the initiation of the total project.) The second outcome measure consisted of annual behavior records established for nineteen boys in each group who had not become delinquent. These behavior records were based largely on teacher reports, and behavior was rated by "the research department" on a five-point scale in which "good behavior" received a rating of 1.

Analysis of all measures revealed no differences between the groups. Exactly the same number of children (10) in each group had "acquired delinquent status" at the five-year follow-up. Further, analysis of the behavior records both after the first year and when the ten-year behavior unit scores were totaled revealed no significant differences between the groups (there were slight tendencies in favor of the control boys). The researchers concluded that child guidance therapy offered in this project produced neither measurable improvement in behavior at the delinquency level nor "... measurable improvement in behavior at the lesser level of merely troublesome behavior" (p. 171).

As with many of the other studies reviewed in this book, the independent variable of "treatment" is poorly defined, although it is perhaps assumed that most readers in the 1960's understood what "intensive therapy" was. Further, the small size of the sample prevents any major generalizations from this study. Finally, the addition of seven nondelinquent boys to each group produced some minor changes in the original focus of the study, which was primarily concerned with delinquency. However, use of the annual behavior records to measure possible effects of treatment on the nondelinquent boys did tend to compensate for that problem.

Despite these rather minor flaws, this study provides clear evidence that, for this sample, intensive and long-term psychiatric and reaching-out casework (p. 170) had no impact whatsoever on either delinquency rates, or the social functioning of the children in their schools.

GIRLS AT VOCATIONAL HIGH
(Meyer, Borgatta & Jones, 1965)

This is perhaps the best known of all studies evaluating the effectiveness of social work services. The study involved a massive effort to evaluate, "... the extent to which social casework is effective in prevention" (p. 3) when applied to high school girls identified as "potentially problematic." The service project was a product of collaboration between the New York City Board of Education, a vocational high school (from which subjects were obtained), and Youth Consultation Service (Y.C.S.), the agency which provided services.

Y.C.S. was a nonsectarian, voluntary social agency in New York City that specialized for over fifty years in services to adolescent girls through a highly trained professional staff of social workers. The research was based on a concern of the agency about how to most effectively serve adolescent girls with types of problems that got them into difficulties at school and elsewhere. To that end, cooperation of a single large high school—called "Vocational High"—was enlisted. The records of all girls entering the school in the fall semester for a period of four years were reviewed by agency workers who made judgments about girls' "potential for problems" and "need for treatment." Roughly one fourth of each of the four cohorts (or entering groups of girls) were identified as potential problem girls. Over the course of four years, an eventual total of 189 girls were randomly assigned to the treatment group and 192 to the control group. Comparisons of the groups on numerous personal and demographic variables revealed them to be basically comparable. In sum, the girls were of mixed ethnic composition (white, Puerto Rican and black) from predominately lower income families.

The treatment program was provided by professional caseworkers, including the regular staff of the agency, plus additional workers employed by the agency on a part-time basis. The researchers note that, ". . . in keeping with the ideology of casework practice in which the social workers were trained . . . objectives of treatment are described in such terms as: to increase self-understanding, to develop more adequate psychological and social functioning, to facilitate maturation, to supplement emotional resources inadequate for the ordinary and extraordinary stresses of adolescence" (p. 181). It was assumed that such a treatment orientation would lead to accomplishment of such objectives as reduction of truancy, improvement of school grades and conduct, prevention of out-of-wedlock pregnancy—all goals of the project—plus numerous other more subtle changes "at the psychosocial level" (p. 181). The theoretical orientation of the workers was "diagnostic casework," grounded in principles of ego-psychology. The preventive emphasis of the project was formulated as trying ". . . to help adolescent girls who face crises to add significantly to their repertoire of reality-based problem-solving techniques and thus improve their crisis-coping capacity for the future" (p. 147).

The original plan for the study involved concentration on individual treatment for the girls. This phase was begun with the first cohort of girls (50 out of 53 referrals from the school to Y.C.S. were completed). However, after one year's experience, the staff of the agency concluded that a more proper focus would be group treatment, with individual treatment being used as an adjunct. This decision was made, according to the researchers, because "the experimental attitude pervading the activities at Y.C.S. enabled the agency . . . to profit from its day-to-day experiences" (p. 90). Thus, the bulk of the girls in the project (139 completed referrals for group treatment out of 147) received primarily group services, provided by caseworkers "with extensive experience in group therapy" (p. 100). The groups were specifically formed around the presumed needs of the girls, and ranged from activity groups to interview treatment groups. The period of time of all treatment contacts ranged from one contact to three years. Half of all girls had seventeen or more treatment contacts with social workers; 16 percent of the girls had fewer than five contacts while 44 percent had more than twenty contacts.

This study used perhaps a greater variety of outcome measures than any other study of social work effectiveness. In line with the treatment philosophy described above, both objective and subjective criteria of success were used. Following is a summary of those outcome indicators: completion of school (school status at end of project, highest grade completed); academic performance (grades, advancement with class, honors and awards); school-related behavior (attendance, truancy, conduct marks, teacher ratings); out-of-school behavior (entries on health record, attention of authorities and agencies, out-of-wedlock pregnancy); personality tests (Junior Personality Quiz, Make a Sentence Test); questionnaire responses (e.g. general feelings); and sociometric data (friendship choices). Not all of the girls were included in the analysis of the effects of the program, however, since the period of time alloted for the study elapsed before the final cohort completed high school. The first three cohorts were in the program for the full three years, while the fourth cohort (60 girls in each group) was in the program only two years.

Thus, where lapse of time was particularly relevant to outcome, e.g. graduation from high school, only the first three cohorts were included in the data analysis. All four cohorts were included on measures where time was less relevant, e.g. school grades or behavior ratings. This differential inclusion of cohorts possibly added some degree of bias to the analysis of data.

Despite the vast amount of information generated from this project, it is possible to summarize the effects of treatment rather succinctly. On almost every measure, there were no significant differences between the groups. The direction of several measures tended to favor the experimental group, but a slightly less, though still substantial, number favored the control group. Therefore, no definitive trend could be established even in terms of directionality. The few areas where the researchers reported some degree of statistical significance favoring the experimental group were grades earned for vocational and academic subjects and on one of twelve measures of the Junior Personality Quiz (experimental girls changed significantly on the factor designated as Will Control vs. Relaxed Casualness, suggesting changes toward greater self-control). However, even these reported changes are suspect. In the first place, it appears as though between-group statistical measures were not used. The researchers noted when statistically significant changes within the treated group occurred, and if significant changes did not occur within the control group, concluded that the changes were "significant." However, such within-group analysis does not provide a proper basis for making a conclusion about overall effects. This can only be done properly when the differences *between* the groups are analyzed. Indeed, particularly in the areas of grades, since precisely the same trend was demonstrated within the control group (although not to a significant degree), it is possible that use of an appropriate statistical procedure might have revealed no significant differences between the groups.

However, even more importantly than this, the second reason for doubting the validity of the observed changes (even assuming the appropriate statistics had been used) is that, given the vast number of comparisons made, the probability of finding only three as statistically significant is itself, not significant (Wilkinson, 1951). Thus, these observed changes cannot be taken as reflecting true differences between the groups, nor can they be attributed to the treatment. Instead, it is most likely that they are merely artifacts of multiple statistical comparison. This is true even isolating the Junior Personality Quiz, on which one of twelve measures showed significant changes. The probability of finding one of twelve comparisons statistically significant at the .05 level is .46, again showing that this difference likely is not a true difference between the groups brought about by the treatment.

Even the highly subjective responses of the clients in the project showed no major differences between the groups. For example, in the final testing period, in response to the question "generally speaking, how do you feel," 43 percent of the experimental group replied "excellent or very well" compared to 44 percent of the control group who answered similarly (p. 183). Thus, for this study at least, this refutes the commonly held assumption that the effects of casework, while they may not be reflected in objective indicators, tend to show up in more positive feelings of clients.

In evaluating the overall impact of service, the researchers state, ". . . the conclusion must be stated in the negative when it is asked whether social work intervention with potential problem high school girls was in this instance effective" (p. 180).

This was a particularly well-designed, and almost equally well-executed, study. However, there were some problems in design and implementation that bear discussion. Although it is neither a fault nor a criticism of the study, *per se,* the nature of the treatment provided by the caseworkers was generally vague, as were the goals for the girls to which the caseworkers subscribed. Further, major changes in the basic treatment methods during the course of the study indicates the failure of the predetermined treatment plan. In changing the treatment, however, the researchers argued that, "a measure of innovation and experimentation was not only justified but might yield significant new results" (p. 103). Changing in the direction of presumably more effective methods of treatment, then, can hardly be seen as potentially harmful to the expected results for the treatment group. Presumably, such changes are at the heart of the social work principle of finding the best available services and tailoring them to the needs of the client. Thus, if anything, these changes likely introduced a bias *favoring* more positive findings for the experimental group.

A more serious problem, perhaps, is that in the group treatment, at least, several different types of group therapy were utilized, and it is impossible from the way the data were presented to partial out potential differential effects. Further, the differences between the caseworkers, as with almost every other study reviewed in this book, were neither spelled out nor analyzed for possible differential effects. Finally, when the girls were referred for treatment from the school, the reasons were not made clear; many of the girls either did not display or were unaware of problems. Thus, although treatment was voluntary and most of the girls eventually were engaged, this perhaps does not provide the most optimal conditions.

The reliability and validity, as well as the discriminability, of some of the outcome measures is also questionable. For example, little attention is paid to reliability and validity data on the Junior Personality Quiz or the Make a Sentence Test. As a further example, the questionnaire used to determine the girls' "psychological insight" and reactions to help did not discriminate between a group of "problem" girls in the control group and girls not in the study, called "residuals," who were not considered potential problems. Hence, use of such a questionnaire to discriminate between treatment and control girls is questionable.

There also may be some question about the use of specific outcome indicators (such as out-of-wedlock pregnancies) when treatment was conceptualized more broadly. This, in essence, is a question about the reasonableness of expecting some relationship between the independent variable and changes in the dependent variable. However, the use of so many different classes and kinds of outcome indicators tends to minimize the importance of this problem. Whether the outcome criteria were objective or subjective, general or specific, the general lack of significant effects pertained. Further, all the workers were aware of the preventive purpose of the project, and it seems reasonable to include a range of measures that the workers and researchers could agree on as indicators of the presence of problems.

Finally, there were several problems with regard to data collection. Differential use of the last cohort of girls, plus measurement of effects prior to completion of treatment for a minority of them, provides a certain lack of clarity in interpreting results. However, when comparisons were made over time, e.g. year of cohort entry, first year of cohort entry and second year of cohort entry, no substantial differences appeared. It therefore appears unlikely that the loss of the final cohort on selected measures, or the incompleted treatment (which did last for a potential of two years for the final cohort) for a minority of girls in that cohort would have affected overall results. Finally, the researchers do not indicate what data if any were obtained on girls who transferred to different schools; since data were often reported as "unavailable" for substantial numbers of girls (sometimes including over 50% of the girls in the study), analyses of the different outcome measures were made with varying numbers of girls. The extent of the bias introduced into the data by these changes and differences is unclear.

However, even taking all of these flaws into consideration, the basic findings of the study remain. That is because the problems discussed above in no way prevent comparisons between the groups using the subjects and the data that were available. Indeed, the most that can be said is that the potential effects of those problems are unknown, so that any conclusions drawn from the findings must be made with caution. But the findings themselves stand. The services provided in this program, on the wide variety of outcome measures used, with all of the girls that were included in the data analyses, clearly had little or no measurable beneficial effect on the personal and social functioning of the girls in the treatment group.

A DELINQUENCY PREVENTION PROGRAM
(Berleman & Steinburn, 1967)

This study reports the results of one phase of a five-year project conducted by the Seattle Atlantic Street Center, a small settlement house, to evaluate its services to "acting-out boys." The samples for this study consisted of "high risk" boys drawn from a population of 167 black youths in the seventh grade of Seattle's two central area junior high schools. "Risk," that is potential for future delinquent behavior, was determined by two methods. The first involved a search of official records—school, police and court—to determine if any acting-out, antisocial behavior, or delinquent behavior had occurred in the boys' pasts. The second consisted of analysis of other factors—school grades and attendance, home composition, health records, and so on—that previous research had shown were correlated with actual delinquent behavior at later ages. From these data, predictions about delinquency were made. On the basis, then, of the two sources—data on actual and predicted acting-out—a continuum ranging from low to high risk was established.

From the high-risk group, where both prediction and actual acting-out indicated likelihood of future delinquency, four high-risk categories, ranging from most to least severe, were established. It was decided in advance to assign a higher proportion of the most serious types to the experimental than to the control group as a hedge against attrition. Then, the required number of specific cases were randomly assigned to each group. Twenty-eight boys were assigned to the experimental group and thirty-three boys to the control group. Attrition over the course of the study accounted for seven boys from the experimental group and seven from the controls. Thus, even though matching and randomization procedures were followed, assignment of disproportionate numbers of severe cases to the experimental group, plus the attrition factors, introduce some degree of potential bias into these groups (even though the attrition cases were known in terms of their high-risk category and equal numbers were lost from each group). The final samples included 19 percent of the control and

38 percent of the experimental group as coming from the two most severe high risk categories.

Treatment was provided by three male workers. Three groups were formed at the center composed of seven boys each. Boys and their parents were also seen in their homes and in the schools, so that a broad pattern of intensive services was established. Details of the services were not presented, although workers kept records of their activities. The service period lasted five months, with the least amount of time any boy was in contact with his worker being forty-five and one-half hours. The median amount of service time a boy and his significant others received was over seventy-five hours; as the researchers note, although the span of time was brief, the service was indeed intense (p. 418).

The dependent variable was defined as "acting-out behavior," operationalized in terms of evidence secured from school disciplinary files and police records. The school records were weighted from "1" for minor infractions to "30" for major infractions. From these data, four indices were developed: (1) an average offense score, considered the most important index because it was indicative of total performance of the group; (2) the percentage of boys in each group that actually generated the total offense scores; (3) average severity of offenses; and (4) average severity scores for boys in each group who compiled records. Data were collected in four time periods: (1) preservice; (2) during the service period; (3) the first postservice period (the six months following termination); and (4) the second postservice, or follow-up, period, up to one year after termination.

In-depth analysis with all pertinent statistical procedures unfortunately was not presented. However, after examining trends in the data, the researchers concluded that, ". . . the experimental group initially was performing in school at a somewhat poorer level than the control group, that with service, the experimental group performed at a better level; and with termination of service, the [experimental] group reverted back toward the same relative performance it had prior to service" (p. 423). On the most important index—average school disciplinary score—boys in the experimental group went from twenty-four at pretest to thirty-one at follow-up, while boys in the control group went from nineteen to twenty-five, almost an identical change. A footnote (p. 423) explains that statistical comparisons between experimental and control group were not significant, and that police records, though scanty, showed similar trends as the school data. Overall, then, there appeared to be little if any positive impact of these intensive services on the prevention of acting-out behavior.

Again, as with so many of the other studies reviewed in this book, this conclusion must be somewhat tentative. The possibility of selection and attrition biases were already mentioned in the summary of the study. However, there is also the possibility that the attrition helped to make the groups more comparable since two of the attrition cases from the experimental group (which contained more of these boys at the outset) were in the most severe high risk category while none of the attrition cases from the control group were from this category. Be that as it may, a rigorous pattern of random assignment to groups was not achieved, introducing unknown potential biases into the results. In addition, the researchers note (p. 418) that school data for seven of the boys were not available, but it is not stated which groups the boys were from, thus adding another unknown, but potentially important, source of bias.

Further, the size of the sample was particularly small, thereby limiting generalizations from this study. The operationalization of the dependent variables is not particularly clear, i.e. how judgments about the seriousness of offenses were made, nor are the characteristics of the workers or the methods they used specifically defined. Finally, it is not clear whether any other services of the settlement house, e.g. recreational activities, were also available to the boys (in either of the groups). If so, they could have confounded the effects of the independent variable, the intensive services.

Given these design problems, interpretations of the data must be made cautiously. However, at least on the measures used, follow-up data, both within the experimental group and in comparison with the controls, suggest that the services provided in this study had negligible positive impact on the behavior of the boys in the treatment group.

THE PURSUIT OF PROMISE
(McCabe, 1967)

As an expression of concern with the vast needs of deprived urban areas, the Community Service Society of New York established the East Harlem Demonstration Center to develop and test experimental social work programs to attempt to meet those needs. This Project, one of several conducted by the Center, was stimulated by concern about the failure of promising young people to develop their potentialities for achievement and leadership. The purpose of this Project—termed "The Intellectually Superior Child in a Socially Deprived Area"—was to study the characteristics of such children and their families and to test the effectiveness of a service program in sustaining or improving their functioning (p. vi).

The sample for this study was obtained from several elementary schools designated by the Board of Education as being representative of East Harlem. Children in the second to fourth grades of those schools, who had scored highly on one of two school-administered achievement tests, were administered two tests by project researchers—the Wechsler Intelligence Scale for Children (W.I.S.C.) and, to reduce the influence of verbal facility on performance, the Lorge-Thorndike Group intelligence test. Selection of the sample, for a variety of reasons, took three years. Of 273 originally given the W.I.S.C., 119 who scored highly (the operational definition of "intellectually superior") met the criteria for inclusion in this study. From this group, sixty-seven children were finally included in the sample (the remaining forty-two could not be included for reasons such as moving out of the area, refusal to participate, and so on). After being matched on the variables of sex and ethnicity, forty-two of the children were randomly assigned to the experimental group and twenty-five to the control. The larger number were assigned to the experimental group due to fear of attrition. All of the children had at least one English-speaking adult in their families, and none of the families were currently active with other services as determined by registrations with the Social Service Exchange. Two thirds of the children were male, and all but seven black (N = 37) or Puerto Rican (N = 23). By the time the program started, most of the children were nine or ten years old and in the fifth or sixth grade.

The intervention program was grounded in principles of ego-psychology. The basic assumptions of the project were as follows: "The academic and social functioning of promising children living in deprived areas is influenced by the adequacy of the child's ego functions and the nature of his family life," both of which are in turn detrimentally affected by a "pathological environment" (pp. 24 & 25). Based on these assumptions, the Project workers hypothesized that an intervention program using measures for strengthening the ego can avoid some of those negative effects and possibly improve the child's functioning.

The major thrust of the experimental program was group services provided by agency workers to both the children and their parents. "The intervention was intended to support ego strengths and to enhance constructive attitudes in the . . . children," and, for the parents, to encourage their consideration of "their crucial role in the continuing motivation of the children and to collaborate with the schools in the children's behalf" (p. 192). Five groups for the children were formed—three for boys and two for girls. The groups were combinations of discussions and activities and were conducted on similar bases, although they varied with the styles of the leaders. The intervention program lasted for three years and two months, with an average of 90.5 meetings per group. The median percent of meetings attended for the children was 71 to 80 percent of the meetings. Interestingly, all but one of the experimental families cooperated with the Project.

Two parent groups were formed, one for parents of boys and one for parents of girls. These were largely task-oriented discussion groups. Parents, one or both, from thirty of the families attended these meetings, plus open houses held for each children's group. Over half of the families (25) also were seen in casework interviews in which "ego-supportive techniques" geared toward limited goals were used. However, the Project wished to minimize the impact of such contacts in an effort to avoid contamination of the effects of the major experimental variable—the group program.

A wide range of criterion measures were employed to evaluate the effects of the program. These were employed before and after services were offered, with the time lapse between pre- and posttest being three years. The fifty-eight criterion measures that were used included twenty-eight concerned with the intellectual, academic or ego functioning of the child, twenty-two concerned with functioning of the parents, and eight dealing with selected areas of family functioning as a whole.

The measures for the children included three measures of academic achievement (Stanford Achievement Test Reading Level, Stanford Achievement Test Arithmetic Level and School Grade Average); three measures of intellectual ability (Full, Verbal and Performance W.I.S.C. I.Q.'s); two ratings of school behavior; and twenty ratings of ego functioning. These latter ratings were made on a scale to measure ego functioning especially designed for the study. Caseworkers were hired especially to rate ego functioning on the basis of interview data secured from the child, his parents and teachers. These workers were given intensive training in use of the scales and achieved satisfactory interjudge reliability (76 to 80% agreement was the median).

Data on parental and family functioning were collected by research interviewers, none of whom knew the experimental or control group status of the case. The format for parent interviews was largely a structured, question-and-answer one. Data from these interviews were rated on special schedules by trained raters with a median reliability of 91 to 95 percent agreement. Ratings of parents were on scales evaluating such dimensions as "overall parental functioning," "overall psychological functioning," and "provision of emotional nurturing," while data on total family functioning included such dimensions as "marital situation," "sharing of values," and "family solidarity."

Finally, an overall index of outcome was developed, utilizing data from all fifty-eight criterion measures. Posttest data were collected six months after termination of the intervention program. Analyses between experimental and control groups were conducted on all measures of outcome and also were carried out separately for differences between blacks and Puerto Ricans.

Of the fifty-nine outcome measures (including the overall index), only one showed a statistically significant difference between the groups favoring the experimental group. The one significant difference was on reading level. However, finding one significant difference out of fifty-nine has a probability well beyond .80 (Wilkinson, 1951) and could be expected to occur by chance alone many more times than once in fifty-nine analyses. Thus, this one significant difference cannot be assumed to be brought about by the intervention and is likely merely an artifact of multiple comparisons.

The overall index of outcome provided a succinct summary of results—66 percent of the experimental group showed an increase in functioning as compared to 72 percent of the controls, while 34 percent of the experimental group showed a decrease in functioning compared to only 28 percent of the control group. However, when independent analyses were carried out for blacks and Puerto Ricans, a differential pattern appeared, favoring Puerto Rican experimental families and apparently detrimental to black families in the experimental group. The researcher refrained from reporting any overall between-group analyses and instead concentrated on experimental and control differences for blacks and Puerto Ricans.

These results can be summarized as follows: For Puerto Ricans, the experimental group had higher means on 58 percent of the measures, while 30 percent of control group means increased. The researcher reported this to be statistically significant. For blacks, the pattern was reversed, with 76 percent of experimental group means increased, but 93 percent of control group means increased, a statistically significant difference favoring the controls. However, on all measures for both groups (in addition to the reading scores), apparently only two were statistically significant within ethnic/racial groups, and both of those (soundness of children's judgment and degree of family organization) showed differences favoring black control families over black families in the experimental group.

In sum, the almost complete lack of any statistically significant differences either within or between groups, even when divided on an ethnic/racial basis, indicates a program of negligible impact. The researcher, however, concludes, "there is substantial evidence that the service program was effective in achieving many of its goals for Puerto Ricans" (p. 261), presumably on the basis of the minor trend favoring Puerto Rican experimental families, even though not a single difference between Puerto Rican experimental and control cases reached statistical significance. The researcher's enthusiasm seems hardly warranted in view of the extensive effort, time and money invested in the program. Further, the researcher also emphasizes the achievement of the program in the area of reading performance, a result which the reanalysis above showed to be likely an artifact of multiple analyses and one which cannot be considered to be a result of the experimental program. Interestingly, while the researcher concludes that the advantages for the Puerto Rican families were due to the experimental program, she avoids the obvious corollary that the lower functioning of the black experimental group compared to the black control group then would also be due to the effects of the program (the researcher chooses to assume that there must have been some nonrandom influencing factors operating, a possibly unwarranted assumption).

In addition to this problem of interpretation of results in the original report—overemphasis of small positive findings and deemphasis of negative findings—other problems also are apparent. The size of the sample is particularly small, thereby limiting any potential for generalization. In fact, the sample itself may not have been reflective of "the intellectually superior child," since only 12 percent of the total qualified by both verbal and performance I.Q. scores, and only 22 percent by performance I.Q. alone (the remaining 66% qualified by verbal I.Q. only). Even though experimental and control groups were matched and randomly assigned, there may have been numerous pretest differences between the groups (randomization probably would have equated the groups had the sample size been larger), a fact that can be inferred from data on family background (Chapters 7 and 10). The potential for initial differences between the groups is increased also by the fact that unequal numbers of cases were assigned to the groups (42 to the experimental, 25 to the control). However, the researcher reported that analysis of covariance with pretest scores as the covariate—the appropriate statistical procedure—was used to analyze outcome data, so that any initial differences affecting overall results could likely be ruled out.

There also was evidence (p. 98) that the sample for the study was not representative of the urban district from which it was selected. In addition, several pretest differences favored the black over the Puerto Rican families, but again analysis of covariance would tend to eliminate the effects of differences in initial level of functioning. Indeed, the family background of the children in the study, plus their relatively high levels of intellectual functioning, lead to some question about the key assumptions of the study—that these children are bound to be affected by a "pathological environment." In fact, this study suggests that the concept of a "pathological environment" may be inadequate, since the data reveal that apparently "deprived" areas do not necessarily foster either emotional deprivation or other deleterious effects on children.

Finally, since there were five groups for the children conducted by five different leaders, there was a potential for differential effects based on the performance of individual group leaders. However, data were not presented in such a way as to justify that conclusion.

In all, given the long-term, intensive nature of this intervention program, and the flimsy or completely neutral (or, in many instances, negative results), the only conclusion that does seem justified is that the services provided by the workers to these children and their parents on the whole cannot be demonstrated to have any substantially positive impact whatsoever.

CASEWORK WITH WIVES OF ALCOHOLICS
(Cohen & Krause, 1971)

This study reports the results of a research and demonstration project conducted by the Family Service Agency of Cincinnati. The purpose of the project was ". . . to explore, develop and define treatment regimes which would be effective in: (1) holding in treatment the wives of male alcoholics, (2) promoting treatment of the alcoholic husband, and (3) retarding or reversing disintegration of the family" (p. 4). Four criteria were established to select cases for the project: (1) the husband's drinking was a key problem; (2) an intact marriage; (3) neither husband nor wife known to be psychotic; (4) and service not being given to the family by another agency. During the period of the project, 298 cases were referred and were assigned to one of three groups: "E," the experimental group using innovative methods; "C," "overt control," cases assigned to workers who apparently knew about the project, but were expected to handle cases in the same manner such cases typically had been handled in the agency in the past; and "D," "ostensible overflow," cases designated as overflow and assigned at random to agency workers who were unaware of their participation in the project. Cases were randomly assigned to the project in the following way: one to the E group, one to the C group, one to the E group and one to the overflow group. The number of cases in the experimental group (146), therefore, was equal to the number of cases in the two other groups.

These three groups, however, do not include an untreated control. To compensate for that problem, once quotas of cases for the three groups were filled, a fourth group, "P," consisting of the next twenty-three cases who applied to the agency and met criteria for the project, were used as untreated controls and assessed prior to their treatment (P = pretreatment) as a basis for comparison with the other three groups. While random assignment of the first three groups was appropriate, the randomization pattern was disrupted for the P group (untreated control) producing possible biasing effects. Also, since P group members were chosen after all other subjects and on a consecutive basis, they were selected at a substantially different period of time, so that the effects of the period of time may be an additional unknown factor.

Of all clients in the project, 18 percent were black and 82 percent white; 80 percent Protestant and 20 percent Catholic; 68 percent were between the ages of twenty-five and forty-five; 50 percent had incomes under $6,000 per year; 58 percent of the marriages were between five and twenty-five years in duration. The researchers generalized the findings on the nature of the client population as: "relatively more motivated, oriented toward self-help with professional assistance, and willing to reveal the family situation" (p. 128). It was not clear that these variables also described the untreated control group (P), the members of which were only seen for evaluative purposes at intake. If they did not, this constitutes a potential bias favoring outcome for project clients.

There were basically three different groups of caseworkers involved in the study. The first group, providing the E services, was comprised of five workers and a supervisor, all of whom had several months of special training and preparation for the project. They were housed in special quarters apart from the agency, and had reduced caseloads of only project clients. The C group of workers consisted of four caseworkers from the agency staff "matched as nearly as possible in skill and experience with the experimental workers" (p. 9); they carried an "undifferentiated and unprotected caseload." The overflow cases were handled by the rest of the regular staff who knew nothing about the project; they were included as a check on the Hawthorne Effect, the possibility that special effects of being in the experiment itself may have contaminated outcome in the E and C groups.

A substantial part of the report of this study consists of descriptions of the theoretical framework and innovative treatment approach and techniques of the E workers. Briefly, the major components of the casework process employed by the experimental staff were: (1) the worker's assertion and demonstration of his competence to help the client deal with the problem of alcoholism; (2) the use of reading material; (3) the detailed exploration of the man's drinking and its connection with other family problems; (4) the worker's accessibility to the client; (5) the worker's assistance to the family in adapting to change; and (6) the use of community resources (p. 48). The E staff viewed alcoholism as a chronic, progressive disease, as opposed to the remainder of the staff (who were characterized as using "traditional methods"), who viewed alcoholism as a "symptom." However, both views appear to be rooted in a more or less psychodynamic framework, and without clear operational indicators of what was different about what E workers actually did (beyond engaging in far more intensive study of the subject of alcoholism), it is difficult to note specific procedural differences between E and C workers.

The focus of the E workers was on the wives of the alcoholics. Over the seventeen months of the project, the mean number of interviews per client in the E group was 21.8 compared to 13.5 for the C group. E group caseworkers saw 51 percent of the husbands at least once, while C workers reported seeing only 29 percent. One hundred eleven (of the original 146) clients were eventually treated in the E group. The number of cases actually seen in treatment for the C and O group was not given although it was reported that C and O workers drew 10 percent less of their assigned clients into treatment than E workers. (Assuming each group was originally assigned 73, and the E workers involved roughly 76% of their clients—compared to the agency's overall discontinuance rate at intake of close to 50%!—this would mean roughly forty-one clients were seen in the C and O groups.) However, of the 111 E clients, apparently only seventy-four were evaluated at outcome introducing a potential serious bias. The direction of this bias is unknown but it is likely that the thirty-seven cases lost for research interviewing may have been among the least cooperative and least motivated; losing them for data analysis, therefore, potentially predisposes the E group toward more favorable results.

The focus of the project's outcome assessment was on reports of the husband's drinking behavior by the caseworker and the wife, and on the attitudes, emotional state and behavior of the wife. "The wife's anxiety, unhappiness, distressing irrationality, and life problems were the primary considerations in assessing the results of the project" (p. 122). Many of the battery of items used to assess outcome concerned feelings and mood and were to be answered by the client. A self-administered inventory to assess anxiety was also used, as was a scale measuring attitudes toward alcoholism. A large part of the outcome data was based on judgments by the workers themselves. Since the workers were also conducting the treatment, and the E group workers (and apparently the C group workers) knew about the nature of the study, this introduced a critical source of bias favoring the treated groups. Special research interviewers were also used to collect data, apparently from all four groups involved in the project. However, the researchers seemed to assume that these interviewers knew about the experimental program, because it was acknowledged that, "such knowledge could have introduced some bias in favor of the E group" (p. 134). Data were collected immediately after termination of treatment for all treated groups, and at intake for the untreated (P) group. (Only findings where comparisons were made between treated and untreated groups are reported here.) A six-month follow-up also was conducted for 63 percent of wives from the E and C groups, but since untreated wives were not included in the follow-up, those findings are not germane here.

The project caseworkers from both the E and C groups reported that 68 percent of their clients improved in their attitudes and perceptions about themselves. However, when data from the other groups, particularly the untreated group were added, the researchers were forced to conclude that there actually were no differences between the groups. Once again, this illustrates the dangers of relying only on caseworkers' judgments without use of a control group. Wives from the treated groups were on the average no less unhappy, anxious, or dissatisfied with themselves than wives in the untreated group. Thus, none of the treatment regimens notably altered self-appraisals or mood (p. 136). Even in their attitudes toward alcoholism, a major focus of treatment, the treated wives manifested no more understanding than did the untreated wives (p. 136). On the basis of this information, the researchers concluded that the experimental ". . . treatment regimen was not shown to have helped the wives of alcoholics feel better or relate to or act toward other family members in a better adjusted or more rational manner" than did the wives receiving conventional and less intensive treatment. Even more importantly, none of the treated groups of wives, ". . . testified to a better status in these respects than did the wives in the [untreated] group" (p. 137).

Two rays of hope were held out by the researchers. The first was that *de facto* separations existed in about 30 percent of the cases in the E and C groups but only 4 percent of the untreated group. This, the researchers concluded, possibly represents a gain in that wives were "emancipated" from their husbands. However, in view of the fact that these were all intact marriages to begin with (p. 7), and there were no differences between the treated and untreated wives on any of the mood, feelings or attitude scales, the positive benefit of such emancipation is open to questions; i.e. despite emancipation, treated wives report feeling no better than the less emancipated, untreated wives. Further, such emancipation may also reflect time differences rather than the effects of treatment. The untreated wives were only evaluated at intake, perhaps at a crisis point, while an average of several months had passed for treated wives since their application. Had both groups been evaluated over similar periods of time, it is possible these differences would have disappeared. The second presumed area of change favoring the treatment was that both E and C wives reported significantly fewer ways in which their husbands' drinking affected their families than did untreated wives. However, this may be an artifact of the fact that more treated wives were separated from their husbands, so they obviously would be less exposed to the effects of drinking.

Overall, the impact of the project treatment, both experimental and conventional, appeared minimal. This conclusion is bolstered by follow-up data for E and C wives which led the researchers to conclude that, "Even the advantages of the man's reduction in drinking and the wife's psychological emancipation seemed to have been lost several months after treatment ended" (p. 142).

A number of the problems inherent in this design have already been discussed in the body of the review. Briefly, these include: random assignment of the three treatment groups, but consecutive assignment for the untreated group; the fact that the untreated group apparently was selected and evaluated at a different time than the treated group, presenting a serious potential source of bias (in an unknown direction); the dramatic attrition rates for the experimental group, which introduced the possibility that only the more favorable cases were evaluated for that group; and the fact that treatment workers supplied a large amount of the data for the treated groups, thus introducing further potential bias favoring positive results for those groups.

Other flaws in this study included the facts that the methods of statistical analyses of data were not clear; attrition rates for the conventional treatment group were not reported, although the researchers imply they were even higher than for the E group; outcome data sometimes were presented for the untreated group in comparison with the treated group and, at other points, the untreated group was excluded, and it was not always clear as to why this was so; the reliability, validity and discriminability of the research instruments were unknown; and finally, in terms of comparisons between the different treatments, the real, operational differences between the forms of treatment appear to be rather murky.

The extent to which these flaws affected the results of this study remains unclear. Certainly, they point to rather cautious interpretation of findings. But, on the whole, apart from the fact that the project, ". . . was successful in developing and describing a method for more effectively engaging and holding in treatment the wives of alcoholics" (p. 142), no major beneficial effects can be ascribed to the treatment received by those wives.

THE SEATTLE DELINQUENCY PREVENTION EXPERIMENT
(Berleman, Seaberg & Steinburn, 1972)

This study was an outgrowth of the delinquency prevention project by Berleman and Steinburn (1967), which was described earlier in this chapter. The earlier study was considered a pretest phase for this study, and since most of the design and methodology characteristics of the two studies are similar, only a brief summary of those characteristics need be repeated here.

The population from which the samples for the study were selected was the entire male population entering seventh grade in two junior high schools in a predominantly black ghetto in Seattle. Weighted measures of previous school misbehavior, using teachers as judges, and weighted measures of community acting-out behavior, using police officers as judges, were used to develop a population of boys who were considered "high risk" for future acting-out. Of 421 boys in the total population, 105 fell into the high risk category. To meet the requirements of the research design which called for fifty-four boys each in the experimental and control groups, an additional twenty boys (to guard against attrition) were identified by teachers as potential problems in relation to future acting-out. The addition of these twenty boys constitute a defect in the design since they technically do not fit the definition of the target group for the study. However, since there were equivalent numbers of these boys in each group, the overall biasing factor likely is minimal.

Using randomization procedures, equal numbers of boys were assigned to experimental and control groups. This produced equivalence between groups in terms of categories of high risk ("severe" to "none"). The researchers also apparently assumed this produced comparability between groups on other dimensions as well (p. 330), but the small size of the sample precludes this assumption, although pretest statistical matching could have answered this question. A substantial number of boys (18) were lost to the experimental group through attrition; eight had moved or were committed to state institutions, five refused services and five withdrew after less than one year of service (it is questionable whether dropping out after a potential of several months of service justifiably can be called "attrition"; however, the researchers did not include those boys in their data analysis). A number of boys, for unspecified reasons, were also lost to attrition in the control group. The attrition in the experimental group did introduce some degree of bias in comparing the two groups. This is particularly so since a higher percentage of whites than nonwhites dropped out. Thus, by the time service was completed and data were analyzed, the experimental group had a significantly higher percentage of blacks than did the control group. The researchers acknowledge that this may have predisposed the experimental group to less favorable findings, since the higher percentage of blacks in the experimental group meant members of that group were more visible targets for traditional forms of discriminatory behavior.

The services were provided by male, M.S.W. social workers, each of whom had a caseload with a maximum size of eighteen. The orientation of those services was on the notion of the "client system," composed of the boy as the nucleus, plus all other persons who had a significant influence on him. Thus, any individual, or combination of individuals could be a primary recipient of services. "The workers were highly assertive in their delivery of service" (p. 332). They functioned as advocates, mustered resources, counseled individually and in groups, and served as discussion and recreation leaders. They focused on both the boy and his family, and used parent groups to some extent, although the details of such groups are not presented.

The services were indeed both intensive and extensive. Contacts were maintained for a period ranging from one to two years. The average number of contacts per client system was over seventeen per year, with number of hours of contact with each system averaging over 313 for the entire period of the project. While 77 percent of the total time exposure to the workers was with the boys in weekly group sessions, only 17 percent of all contacts occurred with the boys in the group sessions. This indicates both the intensity of the groups, and the broad range of other services provided.

As with the earlier study (Berleman & Steinburn, 1967), the dependent variable of acting-out behavior was operationalized by use of school-disciplinary and police-offense data. The researchers justified use of these indicators in terms of their desire to rely upon those measures commonly considered as reflective of youthful acting-out behavior. It was assumed that whatever biases exist in use of these data would be randomly distributed across experimental and control subjects. The data were collected eight times: once at preservice, every six months during service, and three times after service was terminated, the last posttest being eighteen months after the completion of service. Apart from the attrition in the groups mentioned earlier, there was additional attrition in data collection, so that the number of boys in the experimental group ranged from forty-two to fifty-two at different points in time, and from thirty-eight to fifty in the control group. The effects of these differences on the findings are unknown. The data were divided into four measures of acting-out: frequency and severity of school acting-out and frequency and severity of community acting-out. Data were presented both as raw scores and in terms of change scores adjusted for any preservice differences between the groups.

Of fifty-six comparisons made between the groups, ranging from the first service phase to the last postservice phase, there were no significant differences favoring the experimental group. Indeed, thirty-seven out of the fifty-six comparisons favored the control group, with the only five differences that did reach statistical significance also favoring the control rather than the experimental group. The research staff also followed the boys' attendance records, contacts with the guidance department, number of school suspensions and grades for citizenship and effort. On all of these secondary measures, the two groups were virtually indistinguishable, although comparisons apparently were made only during the service period. The dismal results of this project led the researchers to conclude: "Overall, the results of these analyses clearly support the rejection of the hypothesis that the services would significantly reduce the acting-out behavior of the experimental boys" (p. 341).

The major flaws in this generally well-executed study have already been discussed in the review. In sum, it is not clear that the groups were comparable on all dimensions at the outset of the project (although the researchers assumed that randomization provided comparability); there were high rates of attrition, and possible differential effects of this attrition were unknown; the experimental group had a significantly higher number of blacks, and this may have produced a bias in favor of the controls; and the use of only officially designated rates of acting-out behavior omits other, more subtle, measures of change. In addition, the range of Center services was available to control boys and this may have confounded results. Indeed, the researchers pointed out that on some occasions, project workers provided brief services to control boys, although contact was avoided whenever possible. Of course, the prolonged and intense efforts of project workers with experimental subjects were in no way duplicated with control clients.

The true effects of these problems can only be speculated upon, and perhaps, a degree of caution added to interpretation of the findings. However, like several previous studies in the area of child and adolescent behavior, this experiment, ". . . did not yield evidence that the rendering of a social service to carefully selected acting-out youths and their significant others was effective in moderating these youths' acting-out behavior" (p. 343).

SUMMARY

The twelve studies reviewed in this chapter examined the effectiveness of professional caseworkers by comparing outcome differences between clients who had received professional services with similar clients who received either no services at all or haphazardly selected or informal services. The services provided by the professional workers generally were both intensive and extensive; in most instances, the service programs lasted longer than a year, and in some, lasted several years. Despite these extended efforts, there is no evidence that they produced any measurable impact on the lives of the clients. Ten of the studies clearly showed no differences between the experimental and control groups, and two studies claimed positive results for experimental clients. However, one of these studies (Lehrman *et al.*, 1949) ignored much of its outcome data in making that claim; when all data were used there were no differences between the experimental and control groups. The second study claiming positive results (Most, 1964) contained such serious deficiencies in design that the only conclusion that could be drawn is that the results were inconclusive since alternative explanations for the findings could not be eliminated.

Almost all of the studies reviewed in this chapter concentrated on work with children and their families; seven of these focused on delinquents and "predelinquents," two on children in child guidance clinics and one on intellectually superior children in a "deprived" urban area. The other two studies focused on wives of alcoholics (Cohen & Krause, 1971) and women seeking marital counseling (Most, 1964). The services provided in most of the studies included a wide range of individual, group and environmental activities designed to modify the social functioning, feelings and attitudes of the clients either directly, or by affecting those in their milieu. The consistent negative results reported in these studies do not support the efficacy of professional casework methods in dealing with any of these problem categories. These conclusions are particularly apparent in work with children, especially those whose future behavior is likely to include acting-out or delinquent behavior. Unless far more effective methods of intervention can be developed than those provided in these projects, the wisdom of social workers intervening at all with such children must be seriously questioned.

The introduction to this chapter posed the question: Are the services of professional caseworkers more effective than either no services at all, or haphazardly received or informal services? The answer, supplied by the twelve studies reviewed in this chapter, is—NO.

CHAPTER 3 REVIEW OF STUDIES WITH OTHER-TREATED CONTROLS

ALL OF THE STUDIES reviewed in this chapter—in contrast to those in the previous chapter—include a "control" or comparison group which is formally acknowledged to be receiving services. The services to the control group generally are provided by nonprofessionals, particularly "caseworkers" without master's degrees such as are typically found in public assistance agencies and in many probation or parole agencies. Thus, the question this chapter seeks to answer is: Are services provided by professional caseworkers more effective than, or in any way superior to, services provided by nonprofessional workers, when the clients and problems are generally the same for both groups? It should be noted that since there are no untreated controls, demonstration of significant differences favoring either the experimental group or other-treated controls cannot be taken as evidence that those services were any better than no treatment whatsoever.

THE NEIGHBORHOOD IMPROVEMENT PROJECT
(Geismar & Krisberg, 1967; Geismar, 1968)

This study focused on low-income "multiproblem" families living in a housing project in what was described as "one of the most deprived areas" of New Haven, Connecticut. The overall goal of this action-research project was the betterment of neighborhood conditions, with particular concern about juvenile and adult delinquency rates, family dysfunctioning and economic dependency. On the assumption that the family was a "prime seed bed" for delinquency, the project focused on improving the social functioning of the residents of the housing project in general, and of the most disorganized families living in the housing project in particular. Social functioning, or more specifically, family functioning was defined as denoting, ". . . all behavior of family members, individually and collectively, which affects the welfare of the family group. Family functioning is made up of the diverse socially expected roles of family members which either contribute to the well-being of the family or threatens its existence" (Geismar, 1968, p. 445).

Potential cases for the treatment group were selected on the basis of the following criteria: (1) they had to be living in the target housing project—Farnam Courts—with school age children in "clear and present danger"; (2) they had to be known to at least three health or welfare agencies in New Haven; (3) they had to have, in the opinion of the project director, problems in areas of functioning sufficient in number and severity to warrant the appelation "multiproblem"; and (4) they had to be judged "unwilling or unable to accept help in the past" (Geismar & Krisberg, 1967, p. 70). Case records of community agencies were used for diagnostic purposes. Eventually, thirty-five families were selected as the initial treatment group. However, during the course of the project, a total of forty-five cases received services. The report was not clear about how the additional ten families were selected. These project families were predominantly white and were characterized as the "most seriously disorganized families" in the project. However, because of the nature of the selection process, there is no way of knowing the extent to which those families were really representative of any population—either of other families in the housing project, or even of "seriously disorganized, multi-problem" families in the Farnam Courts project or elsewhere.

To secure a control group, the research staff reviewed the State Department of Social Welfare records of families living in four other low income housing projects in New Haven. Seventy of the "most problematic" families were selected to serve as controls. All of these families were receiving A.F.D.C., including whatever services—presumably perfunctory according to the researchers— typically were provided such families. Only a modicum of success was achieved in matching the experimental and control groups which differed from each other on several potentially significant variables: The control group contained a far higher percentage of black families and families with absent fathers. The experimental and control groups also lived in different geographic areas. In addition, the treatment and control groups were interviewed prior to treatment to establish a quantitative measure of their social functioning. Unfortunately for the design of the study, the control group demonstrated higher levels of family functioning at pretest, so that the two groups were substantially different at the outset of the study on perhaps the most crucial dimension—the dependent variable of family functioning. In contrast to the experimental families, as a group, the control families were not even characterized as "multiproblem."

The core of services in the project was "reaching out-family-centered" casework. The researchers describe these services as "differing only in emphasis from the form of casework practiced in agencies in North America and taught in graduate schools of social work" (Geismar & Krisberg, 1967, p. 113). The caseworkers, with one exception, were part-time team members, volunteers from her community agencies. All had master's degrees; each carried a small caseload in the demonstration project.

Weekly seminars were held by the project director of services which were designed to teach the philosophy of intensive reaching-out casework and to ensure consistent application of the N.I.P. casework methods and techniques. These services are described in more detail in this study than in perhaps any of the other studies reviewed in this book. The casework services were based on the recognition of the critical interplay between the individual and his social circumstances, and hence, ran the gamut from intensive individualized services averaging over four direct contacts per month over the eighteen months of the project, to environmental manipulation to coordination of a range of other necessary services. Operational guidelines for the reaching-out family-centered casework could be summarized as follows: (1) going out to the client rather than waiting for him to come to you; (2) directness in dealing with clients; (3) supportive use of authority; (4) viewing and treating the family as a unit; (5) having the worker act as a coordinator of services; and (6) seeing the family and treating it within the context of a larger social system of which it is a part (Geismar & Krisberg, 1967, p. 115). In addition to these intensive casework services to the families in the experimental group, the Neighborhood Improvement Project, as a whole, offered a sweeping program of group services and community organization to the entire housing project; these services, of course, were available to the clients in the experimental group.

The goal of N.I.P. was to improve social functioning of the experimental families. The directors of the project considered it realistic to look for changes in such areas as family relations, child-rearing, social activities, health and economic practices, and so on. In line with their overall goals, the St. Paul Scale of Family Functioning was used as the main criterion measure. This instrument was designed specifically to measure the level of functioning of families, such as those in the project, and to measure the effects of intervention with such families. This instrument has been used extensively in numerous investigations, many of them conducted by one of the researchers in the N.I.P. (Geismar). The Scale consists of nine categories of family functioning (with 26 subcategories). The major categories are: family relationships and unity; individual behavior and adjustment; care and training of children; social activities; economic practices; home and household practices; health practices; relationship to social worker; and use of community resources. Each category of the Scale is measured by means of a seven-point Level of Functioning Scheme, ranging from Inadequate (1) to Adequate (7) as rated on the basis of several specific criteria. Judgments of level of functioning were made by three independent judges based on material collected from interviews with the families. For the treatment group, the material that formed the basis for the judgments was collected by the caseworkers involved with the respective families, in four interviews spaced six months apart over the course of the eighteen-month project. For the control group, their regular A.F.D.C. workers plus trained research interviewers collected data three times, at nine-month intervals.

This instrument has considerable face validity in that the categories of change are directly related to the targets for intervention. In addition, the reliability of the judges appeared satisfactory in that in a reliability test involving judgments on thirty cases, two out of three judges agreed and one checked the adjacent position in a minimum of 87.4 percent of the main categories of the Scale. However, the real power of this instrument to discriminate between different groups is unclear. Further, the fact that the judges appeared to know at what points in time the interview material was collected could tend to bias judgments at outcome in the direction of more positive findings. However, since the judges apparently did not know which cases were in the experimental and control groups, this bias presumably would be distributed equally between groups.

Overall indices of neighborhood changes, such as court and police records and public assistance records were used to compare the entire housing project with four other projects over several years to examine any overall effects of N.I.P. These were either inconclusive or revealed no differences in delinquency rates and economic dependency at the conclusion of the general project. Experimental and control families were compared on the Scale of Family Functioning. Unfortunately, by the conclusion of the Project, a considerable degree of attrition had occurred in both groups with fifteen of forty-five families lost to the treatment group for a variety of reasons (only two families rejected services), and nineteen of seventy families lost to the control group. This left an N of thirty for the experimental group and fifty-one for the control group. Any potential bias as a result of differential patterns of attrition was unknown. When scores on the St. Paul Scale of Family Functioning were compared at the end of the eighteen-month experimental period, the thirty families in the treatment group were demonstrated to gain an average of almost seven scale steps in family functioning, while the control families gained less than one scale step on the average. The difference in movement scores between the experimental and control groups was analyzed by chi square and was statistically significant, leading to a conclusion that this demonstrated a significant positive effect of treatment. Since the level of significance indicated the differences were not due to chance, the researchers rhetorically asked, "If not by chance, what else but intervention can explain their occurrence?" (p. 335).

Unfortunately, because of the nature of this design, alternative explanations cannot be ruled out. The initial differences previously noted between the experimental and control groups, involving several possibly crucial variables on which the two groups were not comparable, makes any conclusion of effectiveness or noneffectiveness potentially misleading. With neither matching nor the more preferable randomization of assignments to the experimental and treatment groups, and such obvious noncomparability, any gain for the experimental group can be explained as a "selection-maturation" artifact—the interaction that occurs when the selection of subjects for the experimental and control groups results in groups with different potential for rates of change. In fact, since the scores at pretest were more extreme in a negative direction for the experimental than for the control group, any positive change from pre- to posttest may be a product of statistical regression—the general tendency for those groups selected for treatment because of extremely negative scores to show evidence of improvement at a later point in time, irrespective of the treatment. As evidence of these problems, the mean total family functioning score for the experimental families at the conclusion of treatment was still more than three steps below the pretest scores of the control group. Although a design using analysis of covariance for equating experimental and control groups on pretest scores might have reduced uncertainty, such a design is hampered when the covariate is not perfectly reliable, and especially when the samples are drawn from such obviously disparate populations (Lord, 1960).

The scores themselves and their manner of collection also bear mentioning. The mean total family functioning score is actually a *summation* of movement on nine separate seven-point scales. Thus, the 6.93 step net change demonstrated by the experimental group is really a total of the changes on all the individual scales; on eight out of nine of these scales, the mean movement was less than one step. This is hardly a dramatic or even particularly encouraging sign regarding the effects of such intensive casework intervention. These results are further inflated by the scores of one family which moved a total of twenty-two steps over the course of the study. These gains were characterized by the researchers as the acculturation to living in an American urban community of a Spanish-speaking family. When this family is removed from the analysis, the mean total movement score of the experimental group drops over one point to 5.86.

The data for making the judgments on the Family Functioning Scale were supplied by two different groups of people; the treatment workers supplied information on the families' social functioning for the experimental cases, and a different group including trained researchers supplied this information for the control group. This introduced an obvious and critical source of bias. In the first place, two different groups supplying information could be using different criteria or observational methods for collecting data. Secondly, use of caseworkers to supply data on their own treatment effects could lead to some distortion of the data in the direction of more favorable reports. In addition, the experimental and control groups were measured at different times, with the experimental group receiving extra attention. The researchers justified the fewer observations of the control families partly on the basis of the desire to avoid the "Hawthorne Effect" or positive changes which are "likely to be produced by recurrent research interviews" (p. 328). The unstated but clear implication: Why was the "Hawthorne Effect" of such little concern for the *experimental* group?

Finally, there is a strong potential confounding effect between the efforts of the caseworkers in the experimental project, and the exposure of experimental clients to the range of other services in the overall N.I.P. Thus, it was impossible to sort out the influence these services—group and community—might have had on the experiment itself. Whatever effects were found, apart from all of the above flaws, might just as logically have been a result of the total group and community endeavor as the casework services. In all, the design of this study does not justify concluding that the experimental services had an effect on the families in the treatment program. It is possible that they did, but the great bulk of the evidence mitigates against such a conclusion.

This project has been widely hailed as an example of the positive benefits of casework intervention with multiproblem families. Apparently, this has occurred without careful analysis of the design of the study so that the researchers' conclusions are taken at face value. However, the fact is that the design flaws in this study are so numerous that no practical conclusions really can be generated. Indeed, the methodological deficiencies are so serious that there is little justification even for considering it an experimental design, despite its ostensible use of a "control group."

THE CHEMUNG COUNTY STUDY
(Wallace, 1967; Brown, 1968)

This project was intended to evaluate what had become almost a truism among public assistance experts in the 1960's: that if you reduce caseloads and provide skilled staff to counsel recipients, their chances toward self-sufficiency are increased (Wallace, 1967, p. 379). That assumption was tested in rigorous research by assessing the effects of intensive social casework with multiproblem families receiving public assistance (A.F.D.C.).

A pool of 195 A.F.D.C. families from varying ethnic groups was created from the Chemung County Department of Welfare (in and around Elmira, New York) using specific criteria for selection. These criteria included the following: the families must be receiving A.F.D.C.; there must have been a mother-figure and at least one child; the families must have been receiving services from at least two other agencies; and past agency service must have been over a period of three or more years prior to screening (Brown, 1968, p. 11). From this pool fifty families were randomly assigned to the treatment group and fifty to the control group. An excellent feature of this study was the creation of a "hidden control," fifty additional families randomly assigned to a third group to serve as a control against possible special attention to the regular control group. These families were known only to the research staff. Statistical analysis of demographic data and outcome measures showed the experimental group and primary control group to be comparable at the start of the program.

Services to the experimental families were provided by two M.S.W. caseworkers with reduced caseloads and "enhanced cooperation" from community agencies (the nature of this cooperation was not spelled out). The caseworkers were especially hired for this project after several months spent in recruiting and interviewing for the job. The casework was to be intensive, was to involve more than the usual "reaching-out," was to involve the whole family, and was to involve treatment goals that would be planned, articulated and systematically conducted. These conditions were tested on the basis of data kept by project caseworkers, and were found to have pertained during the thirty-one months of the project. Experimental families received a median of better than two contacts per month, with over 20 percent of the families seen once a week or oftener. While interpretation of this as "intensive" casework may be open to question, these services, plus contacts with "significant others," were substantially greater for the experimental than the control families who received whatever were the typical services of that public assistance agency.

The implicit dependent variable of "increased self-sufficiency" was defined in terms of the attempt to secure improvement in the adequacy of family functioning. Family functioning was operationalized on the St. Paul Scale of Family Functioning which was discussed in the summary of the previous study. A second instrument used as a form of cross validation was the Hunt-Kogan (Community Service Society) Movement Scale for which additional trained raters were especially hired. The first instrument focuses mainly on families and evaluates absolute level of family functioning at the beginning and at the end of treatment using pairs of judges. The latter scale focuses on changes in individuals and consists of single judges making a judgment of movement shown between opening and closing states, according to specified criteria. Data for both kinds of judgments were supplied by opening and closing summaries prepared by the research staff, who interviewed families in the experimental and primary control group prior to and after treatment (and interviewed the hidden control only at posttest), plus information drawn from outside records such as from schools, courts, and so on.

When opening and closing profiles for all groups were evaluated, there were 35,700 ratings available for analysis. These data were subjected to three rating attempts, one by the judges on the St. Paul Scale, one by the C.S.S. judges on the Hunt-Kogan Scale, and once by the C.S.S. judges using the St. Paul Scale. Careful evaluation of rating procedures was made, and although it was reported that no overall judging bias was apparent, this conclusion is contradicted by the fact that the experimental group clearly benefitted from whatever differential was indicated since the "higher rating" judges handled twice as many demonstration as control cases (Brown, 1968, p. 12).

The project, then, assessed the effects of intensive professional casework, with workers given full professional freedom to use their skills, under optimal conditions of having adequate time to spend with each case and with maximum cooperation of the community. At the conclusion of the project, however, on all of the outcome measures, and using all three sets of ratings, there were no significant differences between the experimental group and either of the control groups, nor were there any significant pre- to postchanges within the group. In addition, there were no major differences between the effects obtained by the two caseworkers. This led the researchers to conclude that, "Whatever was done by these workers for these clients cannot be demonstrated to have had a beneficial effect . . ." (Brown, 1968, p. 127), and, "In short, nothing much seems to have happened in the demonstration cases that did not also happen in the controls" (p. 123).

The research design for this study was a good one, so that the lack of differences between the groups, especially given the fact that a higher proportion of demonstration than control cases were rated by the "higher rating" judges, likely could not be ascribed to methodological deficiencies. The hypothesis that professional caseworkers working under optimal conditions would be more helpful to these clients than the services generally provided is based on a widespread belief among social welfare personnel, and was therefore appropriate for testing. The use of only two caseworkers, of course, limits the generalizability of the findings. Although there was turnover in one of the staff positions, 92 percent of the experimental families had the same caseworker throughout as compared to only 32 percent of the control families. Further, although considerable quantitative data were available on the nature of the casework, it is not clear that the casework methods and techniques were either well-defined for the study, or even appropriately modified for use with such "multiproblem families."

The concern with the quality of the casework, and with the notion that the reason nothing happened may have been that the casework was deficient, led to a *post hoc* analysis of that subject. Two casework professors examined the case records to judge the overall quality of the casework. They concluded that the casework was, ". . . slightly above average for regular public assistance workers and slightly below average for trained caseworkers" (Brown, 1968, p. 149).

However, the relevance of these judgments is open to question. In the first place, the overall negative results of the study apparently already were known and may have introduced bias in the two professors' evaluations. How could they consider casework that they knew to have failed as good casework? Second, the criteria used by the judges to evaluate the casework are both of undemonstrated and questionable relationship to effectiveness, including as they did such dimensions as, "description of the situation; adequacy of recording relevant facts in the opening situation," and, "adequacy in recording of the treatment process." In fact, the caseworkers were selected after several months of interviewing and apparently were considered the best people for the job. This suggests that, contrary to the two professors' evaluations, these caseworkers may have been well above average in their performance, a rather disturbing possibility. Be that as it may, however, the purpose of the study was not to assess the casework of a small minority of exceptional or outstanding caseworkers. Rather, it was to assess what would be reasonable and feasible expectations for the average quality of professional casework in similar circumstances around the country.

In sum, whatever was done by these professional caseworkers under these conditions in this situation cannot be demonstrated on the basis of the particular measures used in this study to have an appreciable effect. This was so when evaluating the effects of the professional casework on its own (changes within the experimental group), as well as in comparison with the lesser efforts of untrained workers.

PREVENTING CHRONIC DEPENDENCY
(Mullen, Chazin & Feldstein, 1970; 1972)

This was another study attempting to evaluate the effectiveness of intensive, professional casework with public assistance recipients. A key difference between this and the previous study was a focus on "newly dependent" families in this study. The key assumptions of the project involved the notion that many families receiving public assistance for the first time were in need not only of financial help but also of skilled individualized counseling. This was assumed because it was thought that many of these families would be applying for public assistance because of serious personal and social problems in addition to their economic situations, and would experience a general deterioration in functioning because of their inability to cope with the effects of "dependency." Based on this, it was held that professional caseworkers were especially equipped, through their dual skills in personal counseling and environmental intervention, to provide needed services (Mullen *et al.*, 1972, pp. 309, 310).

The design of the project involved collaboration between the Community Service Society of New York (C.S.S.), a private, nonsectarian social work agency, and the New York City Department of Social Services (D.S.S.). First-time applicants to D.S.S. who had at least a two-person family were randomly assigned to a demonstration (experimental) or control group. This assignment resulted in a total of 118 families in the experimental group and eighty-two families in the control group. The families in both groups were from several ethnic groups, with roughly 56 percent

black, 27 percent white, 15 percent Puerto Rican, and 12 percent
"other." Seventy-six percent of the female family heads were
under thirty-six years of age, and 66 percent were not living with
their spouses. Overall analysis of the demographic characteristics
of both groups revealed them to be comparable on all dimensions at the inception of the project.

The independent variable was initially identified as collaboration between the public sector (D.D.S.) and the private sector
(C.S.S.). The experimental families received regular public assistance services, defined as various kinds of financial services,
plus a limited number of home visits by a worker. They also
were to receive services from C.S.S. which included an M.S.W.
caseworker assisting the family through counseling and working
with community resources in the client's behalf. Details of these
professional services were not clearly spelled out. In addition,
C.S.S. and D.S.S. workers were to plan together for the general
welfare of each client. However, for a variety of reasons, this
did not work out as planned, so that the collaborative venture
was largely not implemented. Thus, the main independent variable was the effect of professional casework intervention in addition to the regular services of D.S.S. which were applied to both
experimental and control families. The length of professional
intervention ranged up to twenty-four months, although the
median length of time between application for assistance and
outcome evaluation for project families was 15.9 months. In addition to numerous collateral contacts, project families received
a median of fifteen direct contact interviews, although the number of direct contacts ranged from one to a maximum of 129.

Assuming that random assignment produced equivalence between groups (they were comparable on demographic characteristics at the outset of the study), the study employed a posttest
only design. Research interviewers conducted structured interviews with experimental and control families. The interviews
were designed to provide material which could evaluate the success of the project in achieving its objectives: preventing individual and family disorganization, and improvement of family
economic and psychosocial functioning. The content of the in-

terview was based on the objectives of the project which were presented in general terms such as improvement in economic, health, employment and housing conditions and personal, parental and family functioning. The research questionnaire was developed to obtain information on all areas that reasonably could be expected to be a target of the casework efforts. In addition, information was developed on the clients' own assessment of changes.

The questionnaire was highly structured and precoded with fixed alternative and short-answer questions. The items for the questionnaire were derived from numerous other measures such as the St. Paul Scale and the Hunt-Kogan Scale. The questionnaire was designed to provide information that would permit the assessment of all families in eleven general areas: (1) economic status of the family; (2) employment of family members; (3) socio-economic status of family; (4) family use of health facilities; (5) family's housing condition and practices; (6) family marketing and consumer practices; (7) family cohesion and relationships; (8) mother's functioning as a parent; (9) psychosocial functioning of children; (10) psychological functioning and status of female family head; and (11) helpfulness of collaborative service. For each of these areas, several questions were included on the schedules. Most of these were *ad hoc* items thought to have face validity. In addition, questions from six other scales were used including a "marketing" and a "child-rearing" scale and four subscales of the Parental Attitude Research Inventory. The overall validity, reliability and discriminability of the instruments used in this study is unknown, although such data were available for some of the subscales. Eventually, eighty-three questionnaire items were examined, including seventy-one dealing with family functioning, and twelve with clients' perceptions of whether they received help from organizations or professional workers (it was not clear whether this was intended to examine whether or not that "help" was helpful or whether it was simply received).

Of the 118 experimental families, ninety-seven were engaged at C.S.S., with the remaining twenty-one either refusing service or not located. Of the ninety-seven, eighty-eight had a research interview. Of the eighty-two control families, sixty-eight were seen in a research interview. The effects of this differential attrition on the eventual outcome are unknown, although the possibility of disrupting the randomization pattern are probably fairly slight since only 25 percent of the experimental group was lost over the course of the study as compared to 17 percent of the controls. Another problem involved in data collection was that the original plan for the project called for research interviews with all families fourteen months after engagement. However, for a small group of families, apparently fourteen, interviews came after seven or eight months of engagement, so that in some of the cases, treatment may not have been completed.

The prime area of investigation in this study, of course, was in the area of family functioning. Of the seventy-one items in this area (data are presented for each in the original text) only one indicated a significant difference ($p < .05$) between groups (more experimental than control families reported that a family member had complained to an authority other than the landlord or his agent about conditions of the building in which the family lived). Of course, the probability of finding one p-value significant at the .05 level out of seventy-one comparisons, in itself is likely a result of the multiple comparisons and therefore due only to chance (Wilkinson, 1951). Thus, it must be concluded that this finding does not reflect a true difference between the groups which can be attributed to the treatment. Three of the twelve "help received" questions resulted in statistically significant differences, in that more experimental families reported receiving organizational or professional help in getting medical services and with personal or family difficulties, and had a larger number of appointments concerned with personal or family problems. Data were reanalyzed dropping any families from the experimental group who either had no contact for one reason or another with C.S.S. workers, or who had not had at least five in-person interviews with C.S.S. workers. Three additional significant differences favoring the experimental group were found, but none of these were in the area of family functioning, i.e. they were in the area of "help received."

Overall, it is clear that while the experimental group reported to a greater extent than controls that they received help from organizational sources, differences between the groups in the area of family functioning are nearly indiscernible. Of the total eighty-three contrasts, forty-two favored the experimental group by at least 1 percent. However, eleven of these were in the area of "help received," so that only thirty-one of seventy-one family functioning comparisons favored the experimental group while forty comparisons regarding family functioning either were virtually identical or favored the control group.

There was some problem in this study with regard to the independent variable—the intervention. The collaboration efforts were not implemented as planned, and the professional casework services were not clearly specified. Further, the assumption of the study that application for financial assistance often is accompanied by a variety of other problems was not uniformly valid. Thus, families without the problems for which they were ostensibly receiving help could hardly be expected to improve on those dimensions. Similarly, although work with each family was individualized, the outcome instrument measured a variety of indicators, many of which may not have been problematic for some of the families; the researchers note this by stating that "not all goals would be appropriate for all families" (1970, p. 4).

The instrument itself is open to question since data on validity and reliability for the total instrument are unknown. Further, as mentioned in the summary, the effects of differential attrition may have produced some bias, although the direction of that bias (whether in favor of the experimental or control group) is not clear. Additionally, the fact that several families were measured within seven or eight months of engagement, and presumably for some, the treatment was not completed, may not have allowed the full effects of the treatment to be manifested. (The researchers noted that the small numbers in this group would not measurably affect outcome differences, 1970, p. 27, but such assurances cannot be made without supportive evidence.) Finally, families in both the experimental and control group reported receiving other help from friends, various nonprofessional community residents and existing community agencies, although no significant differences between the groups on this dimension were reported.

Two potential problems in the posttest only research design involve, first, the fact that the absence of preservice information prohibits the direct examination of pre- to post-changes, and allows only for posttest comparisons, and second, possible important differences between the groups on the dependent variables at the outset of the study are unknown. Group equivalence was assumed, and this conclusion was bolstered by the fact that the groups were comparable on demographic characteristics, so that it appeared as though the randomization pattern was effective in equating the groups. However, without a pretest, initial equivalency can only be assumed, not proven. On the other hand, Campbell and Stanley (1963) consider the posttest only design with random assignment to groups as a perfectly acceptable alternative to the traditional pretest-posttest design. In fact, they consider the pretest as not actually essential to true experimental designs since randomization, with a large enough sample, can adequately assure lack of initial biases (Campbell & Stanley, 1963, p. 25). Thus, on the whole, the posttest design probably did not produce harmful or biasing effects and allowed accurate and appropriate conclusions.

Overall, despite the problems described above, it is clear that the professional casework, whatever its nature, did little or nothing to facilitate the functioning of the families in the experimental group in comparison with families in the control group. This is apparent on almost every indicator of family functioning, including those that generally were appropriate for almost all members of the experimental and control groups, e.g. economic status of the family. There were no real trends showing that professional caseworkers have a differential or selective effect with specific problems, whether the problems are personal or environmental. Thus, this study, in combination with the previous two studies reviewed in this chapter (Geismar & Krisberg, 1967; Brown, 1968) raises serious questions about the need for, or value of, professional casework services in public **assistance** agencies over and above those services typically provided by non-professionals.

CASEWORK WITH FEMALE PROBATIONERS
(Webb & Riley, 1970)

The purpose of this study was to determine whether young women on probation can be successfully involved in a treatment program with an outside, voluntary casework agency, and whether the treatment program can significantly improve their "life adjustment."

The subjects for this study were drawn from the caseload of the Pasadena office of the Los Angeles County Probation Department. As women were placed on probation by the court, they were assigned to either treatment or control groups on a random basis. Thirty-four women were assigned to each group, although attrition "for a variety of factors" left an experimental group of twenty-six subjects and a control group of thirty-two. The probationers were all between the ages of eighteen and twenty-five, and there were no differences between the groups on any demographic variables, indicating some degree of comparability.

The project was conceived on the basis of a cooperative relationship between the probation department and the Foothill Family Service Agency of Pasadena. Conferences were held between probation workers and family agency caseworkers throughout the treatment program. Girls were referred to the agency by the probation officer; if the clients were reluctant to participate, the probation officer, ". . . became insistent and said that he wanted the subject to participate and that it was expected of the subject" (p. 567). The researchers note that, "No subject challenged this instruction overtly or flatly refused . . ." (p. 567). Further, if clients discontinued and the family service worker could not contact them, the probation officer was advised and attempted to reestablish contact between subject and worker.

The family service agency developed a special program (Goals for Girls) to work on this project. The primary treatment method consisted of individual casework involving psychosocial diagnosis, treatment plan and casework interviews. Psychological testing was also used to aid in treatment planning, and, often, other members of the family were seen (p. 567). No other details of the treatment were spelled out except to say that the course of treatment, beyond the degree of "outreach," was basically the same for the probationers as it was for other family service clients. The length of the project was one year, with 46 percent of the experimental group clients receiving between ten and forty-nine interviews, with a median level of six to nine interviews. Subjects in the control group received the typical services of the probation department.

The dependent variable of "life adjustment" was operationalized as scores on the M.M.P.I. and a form of semantic differential (SD). The M.M.P.I. has been used extensively in counseling research and several of its scales have repeatedly yielded evidence of the ability to detect client changes (Bergin, 1971). The researchers report no specific information of this sort on the form of semantic differential used in this study. These instruments were administered prior to and at the end of treatment. Further outcome data were obtained by constructing a set of "behavior correlates," an instrument on which subjects were rated by the probation officer before and after treatment. Rated behavior included conduct related to the following areas: probation record, employment, school, family, social life and emotional stability (p. 569).

Scores on the M.M.P.I. and SD were compared within the experimental group and within the control group. Six out of twelve of these comparisons showed statistically significant changes in the predicted direction for the experimental group and only one of twelve showed significant changes within the control group. In addition, five out of sixteen behavior correlates "reflected markedly improved ratings of the experimental group as compared to the control group" (p. 569). No statistics were presented to document this latter assertion. Based on these data, the researchers concluded that the demonstration project had a significant impact on the probationers in the treated group and was therefore a success.

Several design flaws, however, point to serious questions about those conclusions. The casework treatment—which was not clearly specified—really may have made an impact. On the other hand, since the ratings on the "behavior correlates" were made by the probation officers who presumably knew which clients were in the experimental program and which were not, a question of possible bias arises. The objectivity of these ratings may have been contaminated by such knowledge.

Further, the researchers on the psychological measures and apparently also on the "behavior correlates," did not use between-group statistical measures. They merely reported that the experimental group improved significantly on selected measures and the control group did not. This appears to have the ring of logic to it for developing a conclusion that a significant effect of the treatment was demonstrated. However, as pointed out previously, if the researchers had utilized a more appropriate statistical test—particularly an analysis of covariance to equate the groups on pretest scores, or even a t-test between groups if the pretest scores were equivalent—the difference *between* groups, which is the crucial measure in evaluating overall impact of an experimental variable, may not have been significant. This is particularly true in this study where, in several instances, the differences between the scores of the two groups were very slight.

The most crucial flaw in this study, though, is the problem involving differential mortality. Of thirty-four women randomly assigned to the treatment group, eight (23%) were lost to "attrition" (undefined), while only two clients of thirty-four (6%) were lost from the control group; this difference was statistically beyond the .001 level ($X^2 = 13.2$; 2 d.f.). This introduces an interesting question as to why clients are more likely to drop out of a program conducted by professionals than nonprofessionals (even with the "encouragement" of probation officers that they attend the family service agency program). More importantly, however, this differential mortality disrupted the randomization pattern with the probability that sufficient bias was introduced into the two samples so that they were no longer comparable. Although there is not clear evidence in the data, it is possible or even likely that the most difficult or most negative clients were the ones who dropped out, thus further biasing the data for the experimental group in a positive direction. In fact, even the conclusion of the researchers that the project was able to demonstrate successful involvement of clients who do not voluntarily initiate casework treatment seems unwarranted. That is for the obvious reasons that, first, the clients clearly were coming under duress, and second, the conclusion is based only on those clients who selected, for whatever reason, to enter and continue treatment, and ignores the fact that a substantial proportion of clients terminated before any "involvement" whatsoever could be demonstrated.

In all, the only conclusion that can be developed from this study is that the data do not justify any definite conclusion about the success of the intervention program.

PROTECTIVE SERVICES FOR THE AGED
(Blenkner, Bloom & Nielsen, 1971)

The last study to be reviewed in this chapter involves an evaluation of the effects of a demonstration program of protective services for the aged conducted in Cleveland, Ohio. The project was sponsored by the Benjamin Rose Institute, one of the few agencies in Cleveland providing extensive protective services to older people. The researchers recognized that persons judged to be in need of protective services—the mentally impaired aged living within the community outside of institutional walls" (p. 483)—are the concerns of a variety of professions. They aver, however, that there is ". . . general agreement regarding the need for aid and the fact that social work is the logical profession to assume primary responsibility" (p. 486). Hence, this project was developed to assess the effectiveness of intensive social casework services on behalf of aged persons deemed in need of protection.

The two basic components demonstrating the need for protective services were defective mental functioning and defective social resources. The project concentrated on the noninstitutionalized older person who was likely to come to the attention of welfare and health agencies that offered individual services. Over a twelve-month period, thirteen participating agencies referred 164 "protectives" to the project on the basis of the following criteria: (1) clients were to be sixty years of age or older; (2) behavior indicates that the person is incapable of caring for himself and his interests without serious consequences to himself and others; and (3) there are no relatives or private individuals able and willing to assume the kind and degree of support and supervision required to control the situation. Cases were randomly assigned to two groups as they were referred: (1) the experimental or demonstration group (N = 76); and (2) the control group (N = 88). The subjects for the study were predominantly over seventy-five years of age, female, white, native-born, and nonmarried. Most had only a grammar school education and median income was only $102 per month.

The project lasted one year. Persons in the control group were left with the referring agency to be served in the normal fashion of the agency. The bulk of these were economic assistance (public assistance and Social Security), housing and health agencies— the agencies with the highest proportions of non-M.S.W. staffs. For clients in the experimental group, social casework, provided by M.S.W. workers, all of whom had more than fifteen years of experience, was the core service. Two caseworkers were selected from the regular B.R.I. staff and two were specially recruited for the job. The key directive of the project was: "Do, or get others to do, whatever is necessary to meet the needs of the situation" (p. 489). These caseworkers were given extra funds to offer a wide variety of ancillary and supportive services, provided on an individualized basis depending on client needs. The main thrust of treatment was "a form of social therapy," enlisting environmental supports and restructuring the situation, in addition to direct counseling. The experimental services were indeed intensive —the average number of participant and collateral interviews was 31.8 per case.

To assess changes and evaluate the impact of the demonstration program, four broad aspects of the participants' lives were evaluated during the demonstration year: (1) competence, e.g. mental and physical functioning; (2) protection, involving evaluations of physical environment, concrete assistance, interested parties, "environmental protection-social"; (3) contentment, signs and symptoms; and (4) effect on others—collateral stress and comparative collateral stress. In addition, survival and institutionalization rates were collected. Data were obtained from highly structured research interviews by the research staff with participants and collaterals, and from observer ratings by the research staff (plus clinical ratings by the caseworkers for the demonstration project only). Multiple measures of mental functioning, physical functioning, physical environment, concrete assistance, interested parties, contentment, signs and symptoms of disturbance and collateral stress were derived and quantified to yield scores for statistical treatment. Data were collected at the beginning of the program, at regular intervals during the program, and at the one-year termination point.

Despite the intensive efforts of the project caseworkers, the data revealed few significant differences favoring the experimental group. The only statistically significant differences were in the areas of "protection" (regarding "physical environment" and "concrete assistance"), and "effect on others" (relief of collateral stress), both of which favored the experimental group. However, most of the effects on both dimensions were probably due to higher rates of institutionalization of demonstration clients (34% in the experimental group and 20% in the control group). The researchers note that there was no real impact on the participants themselves in terms of increased competence, or slowed deterioration, or greater contentment or lessened disturbance. In fact, after considering overall findings of the project, including higher death and institutionalization rates for experimental clients, the researchers were forced to consider the hypothesis that the intensive services actually accelerated decline.

This led the researchers, commendably, to conduct a five-year follow-up study of all experimental and control participants. The data revealed that both for institutionalization and death, the rates were persistently and consistently higher for the demonstration project clients than for the control clients. Thus, with survival being the ultimate outcome criterion, the results of this intervention program clearly favored the control rather than the experimental group.

The researchers carefully checked their data to see if there were any possible discrepancies between the samples that could account for these disturbing findings. They found that the comparability of the samples precluded such alternative explanations. Instead, they concluded that earlier institutionalization, while it provided some relief for collaterals, did not prove protective for the participants. Instead, the higher institutionalization rates led to higher death rates for the experimental group. However, even for noninstitutionalized participants, death rates were substantially higher for experimental clients than for control participants, although the reasons for this were not clear. The researchers also noted there was no evidence that experimental clients had "shorter lives but merrier ones" or "good deaths."

It is not clear how representative the clients in this sample were. A survey of the caseloads in participating agencies indicated that as many as 200 persons in need of protective services might be identified by the thirteen participating agencies in any one month (p. 487). The researchers did not describe how the specific 164 subjects for this study were chosen (although the two groups appeared to be equivalent at least to each other based on randomization and comparison of demographic characteristics).

The control group in this study received a fairly extensive amount of services during the course of the project. Almost half of the controls (as compared to one eighth of the demonstration group) were referred to other community agencies for services. While it appears that most of the services for the control group were provided by nonprofessionals, it also appears that those services were provided to a greater extent for this control group than for most of the other control groups in the studies reviewed in this chapter. The researchers note that the provision of services was primarily a reflection of continuing public housing and public assistance services that were supplied to demonstration and control subjects alike. And the data they report (p. 491) bear out that the experimental group did receive a far greater proportion of services on all dimensions except, perhaps, financial assistance. However, the extent of services provided to the control group in this study—even though most were provided by nonprofessionals —appears to add a slightly different perspective to the data. The researchers recognize this when they comment that, because of this fact, the demonstration services had to be a strong variable, providing considerably greater service of a more varied nature than is ordinarily available in the community, in order to obtain significant differences between the experimental and control groups.

The reliability and validity of the instruments used to measure outcome are unknown. In fact, details of the actual measures used were not presented. A further problem was that the number of subjects rated or interviewed was not uniform or consistent. Interview scores, for example, ranged from four-fifths on the Physical Functioning Questionnaire to three-fifths on the Mental Status Questionnaire. Fewer than 80 percent of the subjects had collaterals who could be rated on collateral stress. And it was not clear whether these inconsistencies were equally present in both the experimental and control groups.

On the whole, though, the carefully constructed nature of this study made it reasonably clear that the negative results for project clients were very likely a direct result of the intensive services provided by professional caseworkers, suggesting the proneness of these caseworkers to ". . . introduce the greatest changes in lives least able to bear them" (p. 493).

SUMMARY

The five studies reviewed in this chapter contrasted the intensive services of professional, M.S.W. caseworkers with the typical services (or nonservices) provided by nonprofessionals, mainly non-M.S.W. social workers. The professionals generally engaged in a far higher number of client and collateral contacts than the nonprofessionals. The professionals often worked under optimal conditions of reduced caseloads and increased budgets, and always provided more intensive and extensive services than the nonprofessionals. Despite those far greater efforts of the professionals, there is no evidence that they produced any significant impact on their clients. Two of the studies clearly showed no differences between the experimental and control groups; one study showed results favoring the control group; and two of the studies claimed positive results for experimental clients, but contained such serious flaws in design that the most optimistic conclusion that could be drawn from those reports is that their results are inconclusive since alternative explanations for the results could not be ruled out.

Most of the studies reviewed in this chapter, with the possible exception of the study on female probationers (Webb & Riley, 1970), concentrated on work with one or another population of low income and multiproblem clients. All of these studies recognized the importance of environmental factors and worked intensively to manipulate those factors, restructure environmental resources, and to provide direct casework counseling as well. The results of these studies do not support the efficacy of professional casework efforts in this regard, and point to the equally potent efforts of nonprofessionals in dealing with problems of low income clients. Further, the results of these studies cannot be ignored or refuted on the grounds that the caseworkers did not pay sufficient attention to social, situational or environmental factors (e.g. Meyer, 1972; Perlman, 1972). Indeed, these results point to serious questions about the wisdom of professional caseworkers being involved at all in providing direct services to the poor, unless far more effective intervention methods can be developed than were provided in these projects.

The introduction to this chapter posed the question: Are services provided by professional caseworkers more effective than services provided by nonprofessional workers? The answer, supplied by the five studies reviewed in this chapter, is—NO.

CHAPTER 4 DETERIORATION EFFECTS IN CASEWORK

So long as we suspect that a method we use has at least some potential for harming others, we are in the extremely awkward position of having to weigh the scientific and social benefits of that procedure against its possible costs in human discomfort (Erikson, 1967, p. 368).

IN ANALYZING THE GENERAL effects of casework, it is possible to overlook other trends in the data. For example, it might be shown that certain clients seen by certain caseworkers using certain methods may have improved, while other combinations of clients × caseworkers × methods may not have been successful. Reanalysis of the data in these seventeen studies does show such a secondary trend, but it is not an encouraging one. In twelve of the studies, almost three fourths of them, clients receiving services from professional caseworkers were shown to deteriorate over the course of treatment!

The deterioration found in these studies involved at least one of three types of phenomena, occurring on one or more of the outcome indicators used in the study: (1) clients in the experimental group fared more poorly than subjects in the control group, even though both groups were comparable at the beginning of treatment; (2) clients in the experimental group demonstrated improved functioning at a lower rate than control subjects, again with both groups equivalent at pretest; and/or (3) clients in the experimental group scored more negatively at posttest than they had at pretest. These were not readily observable findings, since these data were often buried in comparing general effects between groups. Similarly, the strength of the findings varied between studies; frequently the differences reached statis-

98

tical significance, while at other times, the deterioration became obvious only when analyzing trends in the data. The remainder of this chapter will briefly review in chronological order those studies in which deterioration of clients was present and the context in which it occurred. The primary issue, of course, is: Did the casework produce the deterioration? Based on the succeeding evidence, this issue will be discussed in the conclusion of this chapter.

Powers and Witmer (1951)

One of the earliest controlled studies of casework, this delinquency prevention project was also the first to demonstrate deterioration. While overall comparisons between experimental and control groups yielded no significant differences, the differences favored the control group. There were only 218 court appearances for control boys compared to 264 for treatment boys, a difference that approached statistical significance. In appearances before the Court Prevention Bureau, sixty-five treatment boys compared with only fifty-two control boys appeared two or three times (Teuber & Powers, 1953). Further, in careful analysis of individual cases, one of the authors (Witmer) concluded, ". . . that when the study services were effectual most of the boys did function better socially than their C-twins. This conclusion can be accepted, however, only if its opposite is also accepted: that some of the boys who were not benefitted may have been handicapped in social adjustment by the organization's efforts. If this is true, we can conclude that the apparent chance distribution of terminal adjustment ratings . . . was due to the fact that the good effects of the study were counterbalanced by the poor" (p. 455).

Apparently, then, there was a tendency for services to have a variable effect, with the good effects tending to cancel out the negative effects. When examining the data for a reason for this variability, the researchers concluded that, to a large extent, the major differences related to the initial degree of adjustment of the boy. Boys who tended to be aided by the project's efforts were those with minimal problems and fairly adequate homes, while those who deteriorated were more maladjusted from the outset. The question, of course, posed by such a finding, is: Which of these groups should be the priority target for casework services?

Levitt et al. (1959)

In this study of child guidance cases, differences consistently favored the control cases. Out of twenty-six initial comparisons, sixteen favored the controls and ten favored the experimental group. The probability value that this was due to chance was .21. On reanalysis, in which all treatment cases receiving less than ten interviews were dropped from the analysis, the differences still favored control cases by a ratio of 5:3.

Tait and Hodges (1962)

This delinquency study not only showed no positive effect of treatment, but produced a clear negative effect on the clients receiving services. Thirty-nine percent of the treated group compared to only 25 percent of the control group had police or court experience following treatment. This difference approached statistical significance ($X^2 = 2.8$; 1 d.f.; $p < 10$). The data were further reexamined for this analysis with regard to children who were known to both the police and the courts, presumably the outcome category involving the most severe and persistent delinquency indicators. These figures showed twenty-four children from the treatment group were known to both agencies compared with only three from the control group, a statistically significant difference ($X^2 = 6.5$; 1 d.f.; $p < .02$) clearly favoring the children who did not receive treatment.

Miller (1962)

This delinquency control project also showed evidence suggestive of this phenomenon. In several areas related to "trends in disapproved behavior," "trends in illegal acts" and "trends in court appearances," the experimental group showed increases rather than the hypothesized, desired decreases. Several of these increases approached statistical significance ($p < .10$). However, no comparable figures were reported for the control group (the data cited in Chapter 2 showing no differences between the groups were for different dimensions). Thus, there is no way of knowing whether such deterioration was an effect of treatment, or whether the treatment simply could not prevent what would have occurred anyway as a result of "natural" processes.

Most (1964)

This study of marital counseling reported that 20 percent of the treated group scored more negatively at posttest than on pretest on self-ratings of marital satisfaction. Of course, the remainder of the clients were reported to have improved, once again suggesting a variable effect for the treatment. In addition, an undetermined number of subjects receiving treatment who discontinued before five counseling sessions were excluded from the data analysis. Although it is not certain, these clients were likely also to have scored in a more negative direction had the marital satisfaction inventory been readministered to them when they terminated treatment.

Berleman and Steinburn (1967)

This study, focused on "acting-out behavior" of young boys, in reporting the percentage of boys with school disciplinary records, concluded that there were no overall differences between the groups. However, reanalysis reveals that, in the second postservice period, the percentage of boys in the experimental group (84.2%) with school disciplinary records was far higher than the percentage of boys in the control group (53.8%; X^2 was significant beyond the .01 level). Indeed, these figures showed the standing of the groups at posttest were actually reversed from the pretreatment phase where the percentage of boys in the experimental group with school disciplinary records was actually lower (by over 10%) than the percentage of boys in the control group.

McCabe (1967)

This study involving educationally superior children revealed several areas in which experimental group members declined at a higher rate than control group members, or in which control group members improved at a higher rate than experimental group members. On the overall index of outcome, 67 percent of the experimental cases improved, compared to 72 percent of the control cases. Perhaps even more importantly, 33 percent of the experimental group clearly declined in functioning over the course of treatment as opposed to 28 percent of the controls. When data were analyzed separately by ethnic groups, the greatest decline was found for black clients. On the overall index, eight out of twenty-two experimental clients declined as opposed to only one of fifteen control clients (this difference was significant at the .1 level). The outcome pattern was reversed for the Puerto Rican cases, so at least on the overall index, some variability of effects were present with the negative effects for the black clients apparently cancelling out the positive effects for the Puerto Rican clients so that no significant differences between the experimental and control groups could be observed.

Further analysis by ethnic group revealed similar findings on many of the fifty-eight outcome indicators used in this study. Generally, though, the findings showed more powerful deterioration for black experimental clients than it showed positive changes for Puerto Rican experimental cases. Puerto Rican experimental cases had higher means following treatment on 58 percent of all measures, as compared to increases on 30 percent of the measures for controls. This difference was statistically significant. However, while 76 percent of the measures showed increases for black experimental cases, 93 percent of the measures showed increases for black controls, again a statistically significant difference, but this time favoring the control group. Further, thirteen out of forty-two measures showed declines for black experimental clients, but only four out of fifty showed decline for black control families.

Thus, there was clear evidence of variability of effects in this study, with Puerto Rican cases tending to show some improvement, and black cases showing consistent deterioration. For these black cases, treatment, at worst, appeared to directly produce that deterioration, or, at best, retarded normal development.

Geismar and Krisberg (1967)

In this study with multiproblem families, 10 percent of the families receiving casework services deteriorated in family functioning over the course of the project. There apparently were some variable effects in this study since 60 percent of the rest of the experimental families were reported to improve and no change was demonstrated in the remaining family. Unfortunately, a comparable breakdown was not available to examine such possible decline in the control group, so it is difficult to draw any definitive conclusions about whether treatment actually produced the changes.

Brown (1968)

This study of multiproblem families revealed a somewhat different indicator of deterioration. In this project, 96 percent of the families in the experimental group remained on public assistance rolls during the entire period of time of the project— approximately two years. But in the control group, only 52 percent of the families remained on public assistance throughout the period of the project (the chi square for the difference between groups was significant well beyond the .001 level). Of course, remaining on public assistance, in and of itself, cannot be taken to be a sign of deterioration. But in this case, families remained dependent on public assistance presumably because of special help they were receiving. According to the remainder of the outcome indicators used in the study, that help never materialized. While different criteria for case closings were used in the two groups (closings in the experimental group occurred when the total family situation, rather than only the resolution of economic dependency, was perceived to be improved), it nevertheless appears as though the prolonged maintenance of the dependency of experimental families on public assistance for a far more extended period of time than control families was neither helpful nor justified in reality by any differential outcome in family improvement. Further, the implicit dependent variable in this study was "self-sufficiency" (Wallace, 1967, p. 379), and the goals of the study included the desire to reduce economic dependency (Brown, 1968, p. 121). Thus, using prolonged economic dependency as the measure of deterioration, it can be seen that the families in the experimental group fared more poorly than control families as a direct result of this project, according to the project's own outcome criteria.

Cohen and Krause (1971)

The casework conducted with wives of alcoholics in this project produced evidence suggesting that a deterioration process was at work for clients in the experimental group. On several outcome measures, wives in the primary experimental group, where "innovative techniques" were used by the workers, reported a more negative outlook at the conclusion of treatment than did wives who had not received treatment. Experimental group wives were significantly more negative about their own adequacy as parents after treatment than were untreated wives. The wives in the experimental group reported less sexual satisfaction after treatment than did wives in the untreated control. Finally, at the conclusion of treatment, *de facto* separations existed in about 30 percent of the treatment cases and in only 4 percent of the untreated cases. This is despite the fact that, ". . . any differential effect of the experimental regimen, which aimed by plan at such emancipation, was relatively small" (p. 137).

Of course, this separation rate could possibly be viewed as some form of benevolent emancipation for the wives. But several factors suggest this would not be an appropriate conclusion from those wives' points of view. In the first place, a major criterion for acceptance into the study was that the marriage had to be "intact" (p. 7), and the goal of the project was to retard or reverse disintegration of the family (p. 4), rather than facilitate it. Second, as noted above, the experimental group wives reported dissatisfaction in several other categories of functioning and relationship. Finally, a six-month follow-up revealed a general tendency for husbands' drinking to abate anyhow; wives to feel better adjusted to their families, less anxious and to have reconsolidated their family relationships; and, "Even the advantages . . . [in] the wife's psychological emancipation seemed to have been lost . . ." (p. 42). Thus, on balance, it would be difficult to conclude anything other than that treatment tended to have a pernicious effect.

Blenkner, Bloom and Nielsen (1971)

This study of "protective" services to the aged was reviewed in Chapter 3 with regard to the deterioration of clients in the experimental group. Again, when comparing experimental and control clients on an overall basis, experimental clients were shown to have substantially higher death rates. These were directly related to the casework intervention which had produced higher rates of institutionalization for experimental clients, which in turn, produced higher death rates. However, even for those subjects who were not institutionalized, control subjects had considerably lower death rates than experimental subjects. Thus, with survival being the ultimate criterion, findings in this study clearly favored the control group subjects.

Berleman, Seaberg and Steinburn (1972)

This delinquency prevention project focusing on "acting-out behavior" used school and police disciplinary contact data as criterion measures. Out of fifty-six comparisons between experimental and control groups, during and after treatment, using raw scores and data adjusted for preservice differences, thirty-seven (roughly two-thirds) favored the control rather than the experimental group. Most of the deterioration occurred in the area of school-disciplinary contacts, where twenty out of twenty-eight comparisons favored the control group, with five of these reaching statistical significance. On the whole, services to the boys in the experimental group appear to have produced, rather than prevented, more severe acting-out behavior.

CONCLUSION

The finding that deterioration of clients receiving professional casework services occurred in almost three fourths of these studies is perhaps even more serious and disturbing than the finding reviewed in the previous two chapters. It seems not only that professional casework, on the whole, is not helpful, but that, often, clients are actually harmed by casework services. Clearly, the fact that professional services may be harmful was not suspected by most caseworkers. Now that this fact is known, as suggested by the quote at the introduction of this chapter, caseworkers have to weigh the scientific and social benefits of what they do against the possible costs in human discomfort. This is an especially difficult challenge for caseworkers, whose *raison d'etre* is to alleviate, not produce, discomfort.

The deterioration observed in these studies involved children in six of twelve of the studies, and adults or families in six. Thus, the deterioration cannot be said to be merely a function of "normal" change patterns in children. Further, although deterioration appeared in some of the studies on some outcome criteria and not on others, this was expectable because, as discussed in Chapter 1, changes in personal and social functioning appear to be multidimensional, often appearing on some measures, and not at all on others. Indeed, such changes generally appear to have very low intercorrelations.

It is highly unlikely that this finding was due to chance. In the first place, it appears to be occurring on such a widespread basis, that it is unlikely to be happening only by chance. In this review, almost three quarters of the studies showed evidence of deterioration (in the remainder of the studies, either deterioration was not obvious, or data were not presented in a way amenable to such an analysis). In the second place, this apparently is a phenomenon not unique to social casework. In related areas such as psychotherapy and counseling, deterioration has been found in over thirty studies (Bergin, 1971). Thus, this finding has supportive, cross-validating evidence from related fields. Third, this finding is not a result of selection bias. Only two other studies are available involving professional caseworkers (Barron & Leary, 1955; Witmer & Keller, 1942), where the effects of services are compared against no treatment or nonprofessionally treated controls. (These studies were not included in this review because it was not clear that caseworkers provided at least 50% of the services since an undetermined proportion were provided by other clinic professionals.) In both of these studies, deterioration of experimental clients clearly was present. Thus, if they were included in the overall total, the number of studies involving professional caseworkers evidencing the deterioration effect would rise to fourteen out of nineteen.

It is extremely unlikely that the deterioration in all of these studies is simply due to such phenomena as measurement error, individual variation or regression to the mean. Obviously, if deterioration were simply an artifact of measurement error or individual variation, it would have appeared more widely in control groups, and not have been confined mainly to experimental groups. Indeed, the findings of deterioration reached or approached statistical significance in most of the studies, thus refuting the argument that they are likely due to chance variations. Further, since in these studies (with the exception of Most, 1964 and Geismar & Krisberg, 1967), experimental and control groups were equivalent at pretest on the outcome measures, this phenomenon could not have been simply a result of some differential regression operating in the experimental and not the control groups. In fact, what generally happened was the *opposite* of regression to the mean, with extreme negative scores becoming even more negative for experimental clients in many instances. This further diminishes the possibility of deterioration being some type of artifactual phenomenon.

Now, in some of these studies, some variability of effect apparently occurred (e.g. Powers & Witmer, 1951; Most, 1964; Geismar & Krisberg, 1967; McCabe, 1967). That is, some clients in the experimental group were reported to improve while others deteriorated. This raises the possibility that casework may be for better or for worse.

However, these studies were clearly in the minority. Further, the positive changes reported in those studies, as reviewed in the previous two chapters, were on the whole not particularly substantial. Thus, the key question is: Are the minimal benefits that may be attainable by caseworkers worth chancing the clear risks clients must take when they receive professional casework services?

It generally is important to examine outcome data for individual as well as group effects with the ultimate goal of attempting to isolate certain clients who may be more amenable to help by certain workers and/or methods. However, except for the few instances noted above, it is not clear that such individualized positive effects occurred in these studies. Indeed, even if some positive effects for a few individuals could be found, it would be difficult to isolate the reasons (such as the worker's methods, his "personality," his attention, the client's "personality," etc.) for those effects. Thus, except for the task this problem presents for future research, the possibility of finding some positive effects for a few individuals—no matter how the concept of accountability is stretched—in and of itself appears to offer scant justification for the mounting of the types of expensive, large scale intervention programs reviewed here. This is especially so given the generally null and negative effects of those programs for most clients.

In three of the studies where deterioration occurred (Miller, 1962; Most, 1964; Geismar & Krisberg, 1967), control procedures were so faulty as to make any definitive conclusions regarding the cause of the deterioration suspect. However, in the remaining nine studies, control group procedures make it appear likely that the deterioration in the experimental group could be attributed to some aspect of the casework program, *per se*, rather than to some chance or outside occurrences.

There are several ways in which the caseworkers in these programs may have been implicated. The first, and probably least threatening possibility, is that in some of these instances, deterioration may have occurred naturally or spontaneously, i.e. without treatment. The fact that it occurred *with* professional intervention, however, suggests that caseworkers provided for these clients a "zero factor"—no impact whatsoever. In such instances, the caseworkers were not even capable of controlling perhaps randomly occurring or even predictable fluctuations, so that it was as if the caseworkers were not even there. This is the least likely possible explanation of deterioration, however, since, if deterioration had been occurring "naturally," it is unlikely to have occurred to a higher degree in the experimental than the control groups as it was shown to do.

Another explanation for deterioration has to do simply with the ineptness or lack of competence of professional caseworkers in attempting to help their clients. This could have appeared in many ways. For example, by the very fact that the clients were involved in a formal intervention program, the illusion may have been created that the clients actually were receiving help, thus preventing them from seeking help from other sources, even from people in the natural environment with "naturally therapeutic" personalities (Bergin, 1971). Thus, for some of these clients, the deterioration may have been reversed had they used other resources, since the caseworkers in their program were ill-equipped to do this.

Another possibility is that the activities the caseworkers performed in and of themselves directly caused the deterioration. Perhaps this occurred by disturbing an already established equilibrium; by encouraging clients to engage in behavior that might have been destructive for those specific clients, e.g. "bringing up feelings," when that may have been dysfunctional and harmful for certain individuals; or by engaging in inappropriate situational manipulations (as was clearly the case in the Blenkner *et al.*, 1971, study on "protective" services for the aged). Further, there is some cross-validational evidence supporting the notion that deterioration is worker-induced. Research has been able to operationalize and measure specific behaviors of professional helpers that significantly correlate with improvement or deterioration in clients (e.g. Truax & Carkhuff, 1967; Truax & Mitchell, 1971).

Despite the lack of clarity over what exactly causes deterioration—indeed, the causes are probably multifactorial—the evidence on the presence of deterioration among clients of professional caseworkers is strong enough to justify the warning that professional casework may be hazardous to our clients' well-being.

CHAPTER 5 SUMMARY ANALYSIS OF STUDIES

THE EFFECTIVENESS of professional casework services has been examined in seventeen controlled studies. Of these seventeen studies, when all data were considered, fourteen showed that professional caseworkers were unable to bring about any overall positive changes in their clients beyond those that would have occurred with no treatment at all, or that could be produced by nonprofessional workers. In the additional three studies, clear conclusions could not be drawn because of major deficiencies in research methodology. Further, in three quarters of these studies, clients receiving professional casework services were shown to deteriorate. These are, to say the least, disturbing findings for the profession.

Now obviously, a tremendous amount of information was accumulated in those seventeen studies, some of which may help clarify these discouraging results. Thus, in order to place that information in perspective, and to facilitate drawing general conclusions regarding the studies, and, hence, the current state of effectiveness of professional casework practice, this chapter will present a summary analysis of the key points of all the studies. Tables 5-I and 5-II provide a summary and side by side comparison of the major features of the seventeen studies. Those features will be discussed in the text in the following order: (1) Research Methodology; (2) The Clients and Problems; and (3) The Workers and Methods.

RESEARCH METHODOLOGY

The major categories of research methodology that will be discussed here include the type of design used, the outcome criteria that were used to measure success and the use (or nonuse) of a follow-up.

TABLE 5-I. SUMMARY OF STUDIES REVIEWED: UNTREATED CONTROL GROUPS

Author & Year	CLIENTS			CASEWORKERS				Length (L) & Amount (A) of Contact	ASSESSMENT PROCEDURE		Outcome
	No.	Characteristics	Method of Selection	Orientation	Major Approach	Setting for Services			Dependent Variable	Criterion Measures	
Lehrman et al. (1949)	E=196 C=110	Children with median age of 10 to 15 years; 2.5 to 1 ratio of boys to girls; all cases closed at child guidance clinic for period of one year.	Matching; "Defector" control	Psychoanalytic	Direct individualized services	Office		L= median of 12-23 months A= unclear (75% had more than 30 interviews)	Adjustment	Clinical ratings from parent & child interviews; one year follow-up	No overall difference between E & C groups; E group had higher percentage of "improved" than C group
Levitt et al. (1959)	E=237 C=93	Children of both sexes and their parents; all cases seen at child guidance clinic for 10 years.	Matching; "Defector" control	Undefined, presumably psychodynamic	Direct individualized services	Office		L= unclear A= 18 interviews per case	Adjustment	Psychological tests; objective facts; parents' evaluations; childrens' evaluations; clinical judgments; 5-year follow-up	No significant difference between E & C groups
Powers & Witmer (1951)	E=325 C=325	Predelinquent boys age 10-17 screened through teacher reports and test data; mixed SES and ethnic groups	Matching; Random	Dynamic psychology	Direct individualized services	Homes, school, office		L= 8 years (mean of 4 years, 10 months per boy) A= 27.3 contacts per year	Frequency & seriousness of delinquency; social adjustment	Court records, police statistics; ratings of seriousness of offenses; ratings of social adjustment	No significant difference between E & C groups

TABLE 5-I cont.

Author & Year	CLIENTS			CASEWORKERS			Length (L) & Amount (A) of Contact	ASSESSMENT PROCEDURE		
	No.	Characteristics	Method of Selection	Orientation	Major Approach	Setting for Services		Dependent Variable	Criterion Measures	Outcome
Tait & Hodges (1962)	E=108 C=57	Pre-delinquent elementary school children, male & female, referred by teachers, with high scores on Glueck Scale. Mixed ethnic background; lower SES	Unclear; presumably matching	Psychodynamic	Direct individualized services	Homes, office	L= 3 years (mean of 11 months) A=10.9 interviews per parent, 4.5 interviews per child	Delinquency rates	Court and police records	No significant difference between E & C groups
Miller (1962)	E=205 C=172	Low SES gang members; mixed ethnic background; mixed sex	Matching	Psychodynamic; group dynamics	Group and individualized services	Streets, homes, schools	L= 3 years A= 3.5 contacts per week	Law-violating behavior (delinquency)	Number of court appearances	No significant difference between E & C groups
Most (1964)	E=20 C=20	Middle & upper middle class women voluntarily seeking marital counseling; predominantly white; under 28 years of age	Apparently post-hoc matching	Undetermined	Individualized counseling	Office	L= average 3 months A= unclear; 5-13 contacts	Marital satisfaction	Client self-ratings	Greater movement in E group. E & C groups not comparable; no between-group statistics
Craig & Furst (1965)	E=29 C=29	First grade boys rated as "probable delinquents" on Glueck Social Prediction Scale	Matching	Undetermined; possibly psychodynamic	Intensive child guidance therapy	Child guidance clinic	L= 5 years (median 50 months) A= unknown	Delinquency rates	Teachers' behavior reports; delinquency records	No significant difference between E & C groups

TABLE 5-I cont.

Author & Year	CLIENTS		Method of Selection	CASEWORKERS			Length (L) & Amount (A) of Contact	ASSESSMENT PROCEDURE		Outcome
	No.	Characteristics		Orientation	Major Approach	Setting for Services		Dependent Variable	Criterion Measures	
Meyer, Borgatta & Jones (1965)	E=189 C=192	High school girls; mixed race & SES; identified as "potential problems"	Random	Ego psychology; diagnostic casework	Group services; individualized services	Office	L=1 contact to 3 years A=median—17 contacts	School behavior, social functioning	Client & worker ratings; school grades; school-related behaviors; teacher ratings; personality & attitude inventories	No significant difference between E & C groups
Berleman & Steinburn (1967)	E=21 C=26	Black 7th grade boys with school disciplinary problems & police records	Matching; Random	Undetermined	Intensive, direct individualized & group services	Settlement house, home & school	L=5 months A=median—75 hrs per client	Acting-out behavior	School disciplinary records; police records	No significant difference between E & C groups
McCabe (1967)	E=42 C=25	Mainly black & Puerto Rican children; relatively "intellectually superior, socially disadvantaged"	Matching; Random	Ego psychology	Groups, some individual services	Office	L=3 years overall A=67.5 meetings (median attendance)	Intellectual functioning of children; parental functioning; family functioning	Intelligence tests; school achievement; behavior rating scales; ego functioning scales; ratings of parental & family functioning	No significant difference between E & C groups
Cohen & Krause (1971)	E₁=74 E₂=41 E₃=41 C=23	Wives of alcoholics voluntarily seeking help. Mixed SES & ethnic background	Random; post hoc matching	Experimental; presumably psychodynamic	Direct individualized services	Office	L=17 months A=21.8 interviews	Wives' anxiety; unhappiness; life problems	Structured interviews; client evaluations; attitude questionnaire	No significant difference between E & C groups

TABLE 5-I cont.

| Author & Year | CLIENTS | | | CASEWORKERS | | | | Length (L) & Amount (A) of Contact | ASSESSMENT PROCEDURE | | |
	No.	Characteristics	Method of Selection	Orientation	Major Approach	Setting for Services			Dependent Variable	Criterion Measures	Outcome
Berleman, Seaberg & Steinburn (1972)	E=52 C=50	7th grade boys screened by school & police records as high risk for future acting-out. Lower SES; mixed ethnic status; predominantly black	Random	Undetermined	Intensive, individual, group and family services; advocacy	Home, office		L= 1 to 2 years A=171 contacts per client system per year	Juvenile delinquency; acting-out behavior	School disciplinary records; police records	No significant difference between E & C groups

TABLE 5-II. SUMMARY OF STUDIES REVIEWED: OTHER-TREATED CONTROL GROUPS

Author & Year	CLIENTS			CASEWORKERS				Length (L) & Amount (A) of Contact	Dependent Variable	ASSESSMENT PROCEDURE	
	No.	Characteristics	Method of Selection	Orientation	Major Approach	Setting for Services	Control Group Workers			Criterion Measures	Outcome
Geismar & Krisberg (1967)	E=30 C=51	Low-income multiproblem families; predominatly white	Unclear, mainly *post hoc* matching	Reaching-out, family-centered	Intensive direct services; use of environmental resources; multimethod	Office, home, neighborhood	Public assistance workers—B.A.'s	L=18 months A=mean of 4.4 direct contacts per month	Family functioning	Geismar Scale of Family Functioning	Major movement within E group. Major differences between E & C groups at pretest not handled statistically; other design flaws uncontrolled
Brown (1968)	E=50 C₁=50 C₂=50	Multiproblem families receiving ADC	Random	Multiproblem, family-centered	Intensive direct services; use of environmental resources	Office and home	Public assistance workers—B.A.'s	L=31 months A=median of 2+/month	Family functioning	Geismar Scale of Family Functioning; Hunt-Kogan Movement Scale	No significant difference between E & C groups
Mullen, Chazin & Feldstein (1970; 1972)	E=88 C=68	Newly dependent public assistance recipients; mixed ethnic group; families with at least 2 members	Random	Psychodynamic	Direct individualized services	Undetermined, probably office, home	Public assistance workers—B.A.'s	L= up to 2 yrs A= median of 15 direct interviews	Individual & family disorganization; family functioning	Ratings of structured interview with clients in 11 areas of family functioning	No significant differences in family functioning between E & C groups

TABLE 5-II cont.

| Author & Year | CLIENTS | | | CASEWORKERS | | | | Length (L) & Amount (A) of Contact | ASSESSMENT PROCEDURE | | |
	No.	Characteristics	Method of Selection	Orientation	Major Approach	Setting for Services	Control Group Workers		Dependent Variable	Criterion Measures	Outcome
Webb & Riley (1970)	E=26 C=32	Female probationers aged 18-25; variety of ethnic groups	Random	Psychodynamic	Direct individualized services	Office	Probation workers-B.A.'s	L= 1 year A= median of 6–9 interviews	Life adjustment	M.M.P.I: Semantic Differential; behavior ratings	No between-group measures given. Reported "improved" scores on 5 of 16 ratings favoring E group, and on 5 of 12 psychological measures favoring E group
Blenkner, Bloom & Nielsen (1971)	E=76 C=88	Mentally impaired aged in need of protective services; noninstitutionalized	Random	Social therapy; possibly also psychodynamic	Intensive direct services; use of environmantal resources	Office and home	Variety of community workers; generally non-social work or non-M.S.W.	L= 1 year A= mean of 31.8/case	Competence; environmental protection; affect; effect on others	Ratings from structured interviews; observer ratings; clinical ratings; death & institutionalization rates	Experimental group had higher death and institutionalization rates. Also higher on "physical environment," "concrete assistance" and relief of collateral stress

Design

All of the studies used, or claimed to use, one of two forms of experimental design, utilizing either an (ostensibly) untreated control group (summarized in Table 5-I), or an other-treated control group, contrasting the effectiveness of the services of the professionals with the services of nonprofessionals (summarized in Table 5-II). The importance of using a control group for comparison purposes cannot be overemphasized. Frequently, services to a treatment group appear to be effective until findings for a control group are examined. For example, in the studies reported by Powers and Witmer (1951) and Cohen and Krause (1971), caseworkers reported improvement rates for their clients of roughly two-thirds. However, when the results for the control group were added to the picture, it was clear that as many clients improved in the control as the experimental groups. Indeed, in studies where client's subjective assessments of improvement were utilized (e.g. Levitt *et al.*, 1959; Meyer, Borgatta & Jones, 1965; Cohen & Krauss, 1971) "improvement" was reported as frequently by clients in the control groups as in the treatment groups. These findings point to the serious deficiencies in those studies purporting to examine effectiveness without using control groups (e.g. Beck & Jones, 1973). Without a control group, no real conclusions about effectiveness are possible; control group data add absolutely essential, and often shocking, information to the findings of a study.

None of the studies reviewed here revealed perfect or flawless designs. However, as Perlman (1972) notes: "Although technical flaws may be found here and there in these studies, nevertheless, it is clear that each was individually and carefully designed, according to preconceptions and hypotheses regarding the particular problem to be tackled, the maximal conditions of testing, and the expected outcomes" (1972, p. 194). Ten of the studies used the highly desirable form of assignment to groups of randomization, and of these, four utilized the even more optimal combination of randomization plus matching. The remainder of the studies used some form of matching of experimental and control groups, matching either prior to assignment to groups (e.g. Tait & Hodges, 1962; Craig & Furst, 1965), or on a *post hoc* basis in which an experimental group is identified and then the researcher sets out to find a group that can be used for comparison purposes (e.g. Levitt, 1959; Most, 1964; Geismar & Krisberg, 1967). Of the two forms of matching, the former is clearly preferable. That is because the latter form often is not successful, and the researcher is left with a control group that is not comparable to the experimental group on crucial dimensions, thereby raising serious questions about any conclusions (e.g. as in Most, 1964; Geismar & Krisberg, 1967).

It is clear that the lack of positive findings cannot be attributed to inadequate research methodology. In a review of over 180 experimental studies in fields related to casework, Mann (1972) found no relationship between the quality of the methodology in the research design and positive findings of change. In other words, positive findings do not appear more frequently in well-designed research than in poorly-designed research. In fact, out of the seventeen controlled studies of casework, the only studies to report positive results were the three with the most serious design flaws and/or inadequate methodologies (Most, 1964; Geismar & Krisberg, 1967; Webb & Riley, 1970). A fourth study claiming effectiveness (Lehrman *et al.*, 1949), which also had serious design flaws in use of possibly noncomparable experimental and control groups, was shown to be making this claim on the basis of limited use of outcome data. When all data were included, there were no differences between the experimental and control groups.

It is important to note, though, that even serious design flaws do not always and necessarily prevent drawing accurate conclusions from a study. The nature of each methodological problem must be examined within the context of a given study. As an example of this, the study evaluating the effectiveness of casework services for the aged in England (Goldberg, 1970) was heavily biased toward findings which would favor the group receiving professional services, a serious design flaw (or, more accurately, combination of several design flaws; Fischer, 1972). Despite this bias, no significant differences between experimental and control groups were found. Thus, in that instance, the design flaws actually added weight to the conclusion that treatment had no effect.

If flaws in design and methodology invalidate conclusions in studies that report positive results, why do not similar flaws invalidate findings in studies with null or negative results (where there are no differences between the groups)? In other words, is it a sign of bias to accept on face value the conclusions of studies that claim professional services were not effective, while disputing claims of effectiveness on the grounds of inadequate methodology?

In the first place, none of the claims made by any of the researchers have been accepted at face value; as many flaws as could be detected were identified for all the studies, and cautions about unwarranted or over-enthusiastic interpretations suggested where indicated. Second, although some of the studies with null and negative results had flaws similar to those claiming positive results, the flaws in the latter group were consistently of a far more serious and disruptive nature. For example, when noncomparability between experimental and control groups was found in any of the studies with null results, it was nowhere near as extensive as the noncomparability reported in the Most (1964) and Geismar and Krisberg (1967) studies (each of which reported positive results). Similarly, differential mortality reported in any of the studies with null results did not reach the extent of the differential attrition rates found in Webb and Riley (1970), which reported positive results. That study had an attrition rate of 24 percent for the treatment group compared with less than 6 percent for the control group, a difference which was statistically significant beyond the .001 level, thus ruining the randomization pattern established at the outset of the study.

Finally, and perhaps most importantly, studies utilizing experimental designs, by definition, are set up on the basis of an assumption that the groups under investigation are not significantly different (Edwards, 1972). The claim of significant differences —rejection of the null hypothesis of no differences between the groups—means that the researcher must document, first, that the difference is a true difference, and second, that major possible alternative explanations for the results can be ruled out. In most of the seventeen studies of casework, no claims were made that there were significant differences between the groups (i.e. that the professional casework was effective); thus, there were no assertions to dispute. On the other hand, the studies that claimed effectiveness—declaring in effect that professional casework intervention brought about some positive change in clients—must be able to demonstrate, if not prove, or at least give substantial reason for inferring, that any differences found were indeed a product of the treatment experience. These studies must also show that the findings are not explainable on the basis of flaws or inadequacies in the research design which would allow the occurrence of chance or spurious relationships, or effects due merely to the passage of time, and so on. In essence, as Jones and Borgatta (1972) note, the rules of science place the burden of proof on the person who makes the assertion of a relationship, not upon the person who challenges the assertion.

In sum, then, for the several reasons detailed above, there is no reason to believe that the nature of the research designs, *per se,* used in these studies caused the numerous findings of no significant differences between experimental and control groups. Nor is there reason to believe that major alterations in those designs would in any way change the results.

One final point should be made on research design. Even finding significant differences favoring the experimental over the control group, when all methodological conditions are perfect, does not establish what actually produced the changes. When findings favor the experimental clients, a common assumption is that the treatment must have produced (or caused) the effects. But the most that can be assumed from such a result is that *something* in the experience of the experimental clients led to the observed changes. It may have been mainly the effects of attention ("placebo effect"), the effects of being in an experiment (the "Hawthorne effect"), certain personality characteristics of the workers, or their techniques or methods. The list could be extended indefinitely. Thus, finding differences favoring the experimental clients in no way validates the theoretical system, or even the treatment procedures, of the workers. What such findings do establish is that further research into the factors possibly accounting for this finding likely would be worthwhile.

Outcome Criteria

The seventeen studies of casework effectiveness demonstrated great diversity in use of criterion measures. Table 5-III summarizes the types of outcome measures that were used and the number of studies that used them. The measures ranged from subjective to objective, dealing with numerous aspects of both personal and social functioning of the subjects. Judgment, descriptive and performance data were utilized and collected in a variety of ways including psychological questionnaires and inventories, worker, client and independent ratings; evaluations by "significant others," e.g. parents and teachers; structured interviews by trained researchers; observed behaviors; and official records. Together, these measures provide a wealth of intervention about the effects of professional casework services. In twelve of the studies, at least two formal instruments were used as outcome measures. In every study, as clearly as could be determined, including those where only one major instrument was used, more than one source of data was used to provide information for that instrument, (e.g. the clinical judgments of "adjustment" described in Powers

TABLE 5-III

SUMMARY OF OUTCOME MEASURES

Type of Measure Used	Number of Studies
Pscyhological Tests	4
Specially-designed inventories and structured interviews	7
Evaluations of significant others	6
Formal client evaluations	4
Objective performance data	11
Clinical judgments by independent researchers	6
Movement scales (St. Paul and Hunt-Kogan)	2
Number of studies using more than one measure	12
Number of studies using more than one source of data	17

and Witmer, 1951, utilized data from schools, interviews with children and interviews with parents). Thus, the uniformly negative results of these studies can hardly be seen as a result of insufficient diversification of outcome measures. And, as discussed in Chapter 1, since change in clients is often multidimensional, the use of more than one measure considerably enhances the possibility of detecting any changes. Clearly, in these studies, the outcome eggs were put in more than one basket.

Several of the studies used instruments designed specifically to measure the effects of casework (e.g. Geismar & Krisberg, 1967; Brown, 1968). Other studies (e.g. McCabe, 1967; Mullen *et al.*, 1970, 1972) used instruments specially constructed to measure the specific changes expected in those particular studies. In most of the studies, the outcome measures used were specifically related to the goals of the casework intervention in that study. For example, when the goal was to reduce the incidence of juvenile acting-out behavior or delinquency, as it was in several studies, specific indicators of acting-out behavior and delinquency were used; when the goal was to produce greater client understanding of alcoholism (Cohen & Krause, 1971), a questionnaire measuring attitudes toward alcoholism was used; when the goal was to improve ego functioning (McCabe, 1967), an instrument designed to measure changes in ego functioning was used; when the goal of the study was to enhance family functioning (e.g. Geismar & Krisberg, 1967; Brown, 1968), instruments designed to measure changes in family functioning were used; and so on. This is not to say that every instrument in every study was perfect. In some of the studies, the reliability and true validity of the instruments, especially the newly constructed ones, were unknown. On the other hand, most of the instruments had a considerable amount of face validity, i.e. the relevance of the measuring instrument to what the researchers were trying to measure was apparent "on the face of it" (Selltiz *et al.*, 1962, p. 165). As Meyer (1972) notes regarding many of these same studies, in most instances, ". . . the researchers . . . got their cues from casework practitioners" (p. 162). In many cases, selection and development of outcome measures was the result of collaboration between agency, workers and researchers.

In several of the studies, the focus was on prevention. However, while these studies were *conceptualized* as preventive efforts, the outcome indicators, e.g. personality measures, school achievement, behavioral measures, often were the same as would be used in evaluating the effectiveness of remedial or rehabilitative efforts. Thus, whether the ostensible focus was on prevention or remediation, there appears to be substantial justification in most cases for extrapolating from one to the other, and for deriving more general conclusions about effectiveness.

In at least two of the studies (Powers & Witmer, 1951; Cohen & Krause, 1971), when caseworkers were asked to make judgments about their own effectiveness, they concluded that roughly two-thirds of their clients had benefitted from treatment. However, in neither case were these results borne out when more objective measures were used, and more importantly, were shown to be completely erroneous when results for the control group were evaluated. Clearly, reports of effectiveness based only on the perceptions of the workers involved are open to serious question; they almost inevitably are liable to severe distortions in favor of inflated rates of effectiveness.

One popular argument (e.g. Beck & Jones, 1973, p. 13) about outcome research such as reviewed here is that "meaning" is often sacrificed for rigor, and "hard data" or objective outcome measures are used which are insensitive to subtle changes or ignore the central importance of such dimensions as the client's feelings. Indeed, it is difficult to understand the rationale of some caseworkers that goals too subtle to measure are too significant to discard. However, in those studies where the "subtle measure" of changes in client feelings was one of the outcome measures (Cohen & Krause, 1971; Levitt *et al.,* 1959; Meyer, Borgatta & Jones, 1965) almost exactly the same proportion of clients in the experimental and control groups reported they "felt better." This suggests two possibilities. Either the use of client feelings as an outcome measure is unreliable, or the myth that clients receiving casework treatment, if nothing else, tend to feel better, has been effectively refuted.

Overall, the measures used in the seventeen studies tap almost every conceivable effect of casework intervention—psychological, behavioral, social, performance—as rated by clients, workers, research teams, independent judges, and as obtained through objective data, e.g. school, police or court records. When there are potential limitations in the data (e.g. police and court records are widely thought to be biased against particular individuals and groups), the limitations were minimized by being uniformly distributed in the experimental and control groups so that any effect of the bias apparently was present in equal proportions in both groups. Clearly, it cannot be argued that the broad range of criterion measures used in these studies did not give the effects of social casework a fair chance to be displayed, or were on the whole somehow insensitive to the kinds of changes that might be expected. Again, this is not to say that every instrument was ideal. But it is highly unlikely that use of other or different instruments would have altered the results shown in these studies. That is for two reasons. First, there was no indication that any of the instruments or measures were differentially sensitive to change; there were no tendencies for certain kinds of measures, including even the most subjective such as the clients' feelings, to reflect changes while others did not. Second, a recent analysis of over 180 experimental studies (Mann, 1972) showed that all types of instruments—psychological, social, behavioral—demonstrate the existence of change with approximately the same frequency.

Follow-up

A common myth about the effects of casework intervention is that, while they may not show up immediately, they often show up long after the study is over, and therefore go undetected. The rationale for the assumption that social casework may only have long range effects is unclear, but presumably it has to do with the notion that long periods of time are necessary for clients to integrate their new learnings and new understanding into their patterns of functioning. This perhaps is related to the fairly common assumption that since most problems took a long time to develop, it will also take a long time for them to change. For example, apparently dismayed at the lack of short-term effects in her study, McCabe (1967) speculates that, ". . . the method of intervention used in this study Project may, in the long run, have much more impact than was immediately apparent" (p. 289).

Fortunately, these studies provide ample information to check the validity of these assumptions about the potential long-range effects of social casework. At least ten of the seventeen studies used follow-ups in which outcome was compared for experimental and control groups (Lehrman *et al.*, 1949; Powers & Witmer, 1951; McCord & McCord, 1958; Levitt *et al.*, 1959; Miller, 1962; Tait & Hodges, 1962; Craig & Furst, 1965; Berleman & Steinburn, 1967; McCabe, 1967; Blenkner *et al.*, 1971; Berleman *et al.*, 1972). The length of these follow-ups ranged from six months to eight years (McCord & McCord, 1958).

In no instance did any differences between the experimental and control groups appear, for all intents and purposes refuting the myth about the potential long-range effects of casework. Both short- and long-term effects of professional casework were noticeably absent in these seventeen studies.

THE CLIENTS AND PROBLEMS
Clients

A truly impressive range of clients/subjects were involved in the seventeen studies. Both sexes were represented, with some studies focusing mainly on females (Cohen & Krause, 1971; Webb & Riley, 1970; Most, 1964; Meyer, Borgatta & Jones, 1965), some focusing largely on males (Berleman *et al.*, 1972; Berleman & Steinburn, 1967; Craig & Furst, 1965; Powers & Witmer, 1951), and the remainder of the studies (N = 9) focusing largely on members of both sexes. A broad range of ethnic and racial groups were also involved, including blacks, whites and Puerto Ricans. As best as could be determined from the data presented in the original reports, clients were of mixed racial and ethnic groups in eight of the studies, predominantly black in two of the studies, and predominantly white in seven studies. A broad range of age groupings were spanned in the studies, with nine out of the eleven studies using untreated control groups focusing on children as their primary clients; several studies centering around work with young and middle-aged adults (e.g. Webb & Riley, 1970; Cohen & Krause, 1971; Mullen *et al.*, 1970, 1972; Most, 1964); and one study concentrating on work with the aged.

Most of the studies focused on individuals as their primary clients both singly and in the context of groups but in a number of studies, families were the target of the workers' efforts (e.g. Geismar & Krisberg, 1967; McCabe, 1967; Mullen *et al.*, 1970, 1972; Brown, 1968). Indeed even in the studies where individuals, usually children, were the primary targets of intervention, other family members often were involved (e.g. Cohen & Krause, 1971; Berleman *et al.*, 1972; Levitt, 1959; Tait & Hodges, 1962; Berleman & Steinburn, 1967). In all, over 3,300 separate cases were involved in these seventeen studies. However, since many of these cases were families with multiple members, ultimately, in terms of absolute numbers of people, several times that 3,300 figure were involved in these studies, as primary or secondary targets for intervention, as sources of data or subjects for evaluation, or both.

At least nine of the studies focused predominantly or totally on lower income clients (Tait & Hodges, 1962; Miller, 1962; Geismar & Krisberg, 1967; Brown, 1968; Mullen *et al.*, 1970; Berleman & Steinburn, 1967; McCabe, 1967; Blenkner *et al.*, 1971; Berleman *et al.*, 1972). In the other eight studies, either the data were not clear on this matter, or the clients were of mixed socio-economic status or predominantly "middle class" (e.g. Most, 1964; Cohen & Krause, 1971; Lehrman *et al.*, 1949; Levitt, 1959). This heavy, but by no means exclusive, concentration on lower income clients has been seized on by some (e.g. Beck & Jones, 1973; Perlman, 1972) as a limitation on the generalizability of the findings of these studies, and as an explanation for the consistently negative findings, the argument being that, for a variety of reasons, success cannot be expected with low income clients.

However, the services *were* offered, and the purpose of conducting research was to evaluate their success. *Post hoc* explanations, based on that very research, that success never should have been expected in the first place, are of little help, or comfort, to the people—caseworkers, researchers, and most importantly, clients—involved in those projects.

Moreover, it is perfectly clear that a large proportion of the studies did not deal exclusively or even mainly with low income clients. Perhaps even more importantly, the consistency and uniformity of negative results across all studies strongly suggests that there was no differential effect of client social class, i.e. effective results were no more apparent in studies with mixed or predominantly middle income clients than they were in studies concerned with lower income clients. Thus, the extent to which the inclusion of several studies focusing on low income clients produced any meaningful limitation on either outcome or potential for generalization appears to be minimal.

There are two important implications of having such a broad range of clients represented in these studies. The first is that generalizations are facilitated. The second is that such diversity allows the effects of casework intervention to be differentially examined. If, for example, professional caseworkers' efforts were shown to be more or less effective with one type of client-group (children), and more or less ineffective with another group (the aged), there would be some basis for at least limited optimism. However, such differential effectiveness clearly was not demonstrated for any particular group. Across the board, for all groups, outcomes tended to be negative.

Now, the extent to which the client samples in these studies are truly representative of the populations from which they were derived is not absolutely clear. Some of the studies (e.g. Geismar & Krisberg, 1967; Miller, 1962; Most, 1964; Webb & Riley, 1970) either selected samples of convenience or were unclear about the matter of representativeness. But most of the studies, as Geismar (1972) has indicated, ". . . clearly went beyond the techniques—widely employed in practice research—known as convenience or accidental sampling and selected fairly representative study groups" (p. 36). This was demonstrated either through selection of the sample in a way to insure representativeness, or comparing the characteristics of the sample with a set of known characteristics about some population. This, of course, enhances the generalizability of the conclusions.

Problems

Several different types of problem categories were included in the seventeen studies. Two studies (Lehrman *et al.,* 1949; Levitt, 1959) focused on general child guidance clinic cases, discussed in terms of traditional diagnostic categories (e.g. psychoneurotic, primary behavior disorder, etc.). One study was concerned with the "readjustment" of probationers (Webb & Riley, 1970). One study dealt with protective services for the aged (Blenkner *et al.,* 1971). Two studies were concerned with "multiproblem families" receiving public assistance (Geismar & Krisberg, 1967; Brown, 1968), while a third also dealt with public assistance recipients, this time "newly dependent" families whose problems largely were unknown in advance, but assumed to include crisis overtones (Mullen, Chazin & Feldstein, 1970). One study was concerned with "socially disadvantaged, intellectually superior" children whose problems were assumed to relate, in part, to overcoming the effects of a "pathological environment" (McCabe, 1967). Two studies were concerned with marital problems (Most, 1964; Cohen & Krause, 1971), and one of these focused on concomitant problems of the spouses' alcoholism (Cohen & Krause, 1971). The remainder of the studies, seven in all, were concerned with problems variously called delinquency, "potential or predelinquency," "acting-out behavior" or "potential deviancy" (Meyer, Borgatta & Jones, 1965). Each of these seven studies, of course, dealt with children and adolescents as primary subjects.

The range of problems which these seventeen studies addressed certainly seems to accurately reflect the range of problems with which caseworkers are (and have been) concerned and involved in practice. There perhaps may be somewhat disproportionate concentration (7 studies) on the area of "delinquency." And the negative results in all seven of these studies presents very clear, but unfortunately negative, implications for social work programs with "pre-delinquent" or delinquent children. Moreover, when the results for those seven studies are compared with the results in the remainder of the studies, no differential outcome patterns based on the nature of the problem category emerged. In addition to the null or negative findings for all seven delinquency studies, no definitive patterns of success were apparent for any other specific problem category. Thus, there is little reason to believe caseworkers are any more effective with any of the other specific problem categories involved in these studies than they are with "delinquency." The overall uniformity and consistency of results across all problem categories, on balance, appears to aid, rather than in any way hinder, the potential for generalizations.

Several of the seventeen studies reviewed in this book involved the provision of services to clients who did not seek help voluntarily. This fact has been grasped by some writers as another explanation of the uniformly negative results found in these studies. For example, Beck & Jones (1973) state that ". . . [an] adverse influence on the results in these . . . studies stems from the use of cases that did not seek counseling on their own initiative. . . . The result is inevitably a sample with low average motivation" (p. 13).

Several factors tend to minimize the viability of that argument, however. In the first place, the traditional emphasis of social casework and social work as a whole, has been on reaching-out to populations in need. This may be one of the key factors distinguishing our profession from other professions where the tendency is to wait more or less passively for the "highly motivated" client to initiate contacts.

Second, in almost every one of the seventeen studies, once the worker initiated contact, clients were given the option of refusing services. This was less evident in the Webb and Riley (1970) study where duress was used with probationers, and also may not have been the case for the children in the child guidance clinic cases (Lehrman *et al.,* 1949; Levitt 1959), although certainly the parents in those studies sought out treatment. In the majority of the remainder of the studies where agencies initiated contact, the researchers reported that most subjects willingly cooperated, or were grateful for the opportunity, and in at least one of the studies (McCabe, 1967), subjects were reported to be pleased to receive the special attention.

Third, the "real" distinctions between clients who seek out treatment on their own and those where treatment is initiated by the agency are unknown. The process of becoming a client is a complex one, involving personal, social and cultural factors, not to mention the simple availability and accessibility of services. Indeed, the majority of people experiencing serious self-perceived social and/or psychological distress do not seek professional help for their problems (Bergin, 1971). Only a small proportion of such people ever reach professional help, and even a smaller percentage of these ever see a caseworker. Further, there is no evidence that people who seek out treatment are substantially more susceptible to help than those who are the recipients of agency-initiated help. In fact, when people who have sought and received treatment are compared with both early terminators and people with similar problems who never sought out treatment, the evidence is that none of the groups on the whole fare any more poorly in the short or long term (Bergin, 1971; Garfield, 1971).

Finally, though, assuming for the moment that "voluntary" initiation of treatment *is* a key variable explaining success, it would be logical to expect that studies where clients sought out treatment would demonstrate a higher degree of success in comparison with those studies where contacts were initiated by the workers. In fact, that was not the case. Across all of the studies, ranging from the extremes of duress (Webb & Riley, 1970) to client-initiated treatment (e.g. Cohen & Krause, 1971), there are no differences in outcome which could distinguish the studies in terms of whether treatment was client- or agency-initiated.

Indeed, if the effectiveness of professional casework is contingent mainly upon the client being one of the tiny proportion of people who completely on their own initiative, voluntarily seek out and find treatment, and all other factors including the competence of the worker are secondary or irrelevant, there would appear to be very little justification for the continued existence of the professional endeavor called social casework.

THE WORKERS AND METHODS

Perhaps the most crucial variable to examine in these studies is the caseworkers themselves and the nature of the services they provided. When all is said and done, any generalizations from these studies are about casework and caseworkers. Hence, the validity of the generalizations depends at least in part upon the extent to which the services provided in these seventeen projects accurately reflect what caseworkers as a whole do. Indeed, it is in this area that casework apologists have been most vociferous in denouncing the adequacy of the studies. Their objections can be considered by examining each as a separate speculation on the reasons for the consistency and uniformity of the null and negative results in the seventeen studies.

The quality of the casework(ers) was substandard

Dozens of caseworkers were involved in these studies. And the most likely possibility regarding their performance is that it was biased in favor of superior, rather than inferior quality, or, at least, was better than could be expected from the typical or average professional caseworker. This is for two primary reasons. First, many of the projects took place in agencies that generally are recognized as outstanding by the standards of the profession Such agencies as the Jewish Board of Guardians (Lehrman *et al.,* 1949), the Institute for Juvenile Research (Levitt *et al.,* 1959), the Community Service Society of New York (Mullen, Chazin & Feldstein, 1970), the Youth Consultation Service (Meyer, Borgatta & Jones, 1965) and the Benjamin Rose Institute of Cleveland (Blenkner *et al.,* 1971) have national reputations as representing the epitome of quality in social casework. Other agencies providing services in these studies, while perhaps less well-known nationally, all maintain particularly high professional standards for their workers, and include family service agencies (e.g. Cohen & Krause, 1971; Webb & Riley, 1970), and settlement houses (e.g. Berleman *et al.,* 1972).

A second reason for considering the services provided by the workers in these studies to be above average is that in several of the remainder of the studies, workers were hired specifically for the project (e.g. Brown, 1968; Powers & Witmer, 1951; Tait & Hodges, 1962). Each project recruited extensively for workers, and employed only those workers they thought most capable.

This combination of services provided by workers either in agencies with particularly high professional standards or recruited specifically for the project points to an overall level of service that is probably the best the profession has to offer. Thus, the only limitations on generalizations here would be that services provided by the vast range of caseworkers not included in these studies could probably be expected to be even less successful. The only other possibility is that the dozens of workers involved in this study happened to be—somehow just by chance—a totally nonrepresentative sample of incompetents. Of course, if professional education cannot be expected to produce a minimum level of practice competence in all its graduates, it is not at all clear what *can* be expected.

The casework practiced in these studies was outmoded or outdated

The seventeen studies do indeed span a broad range of time—from 1949 (Lehrman *et al.*) to 1972 (Berleman *et al.*). However, of the seventeen studies, twelve were reported in 1964 or later, and, of these, five were reported in the 1970's. It is difficult to determine at what point one form of casework becomes outmoded, and another becomes *avant-garde*. However, it is clear that whatever the nature of the casework provided, it leans toward relatively more recent forms.

Casework cannot solve social problems

This criticism is levelled most directly at studies dealing with low income "multiproblem families," and juvenile delinquency. Its most typical form is that casework oversold itself, and either simply cannot be expected to help people living in "multideficit environments" (e.g. Perlman, 1968, 1972; Beck & Jones, 1973), or cannot be sufficient unless services, ". . . include clients' impinging environment" (Meyer, 1972, p. 161).

In the first place, several of the studies did indeed attempt to "include the clients' impinging environment," by dealing with significant others, providing broker and advocacy services, providing concrete, material aid where necessary and in some instances, even community-oriented programs (e.g. Geismar & Krisberg, 1967; McCabe, 1967; Berleman *et al.*, 1972; McCabe, 1967, Mullen *et al.*, 1970; Miller, 1962; Blenkner *et al.*, 1971). These projects were no more successful in achieving effective outcome than projects that presumably ignored environmental factors.

In the second place, none of the projects presented their goals as in any way trying to solve or affect social problems. Instead, many attempted to provide individualized services to individuals and families to help them cope with the effects of an oppressive environment. This is the essence of social casework as noted by Perlman (1972): ". . . the casework process does not even scratch a social problem. It affects only this person or that family victimized by the social problem" (p. 196). Unfortunately, as the results of these studies show, not only were social problems not scratched, but it was difficult to discern any distinct benefits for the individuals and families who had received professional casework services.

The casework was not defined specifically enough or in relation to outcome

Part of this issue was discussed previously in relation to outcome criteria. Both Meyer (1972, p. 162) and Perlman (1972, p. 194) have acknowledged that the researchers got their cues from casework practitioners and also frequently specified expected outcomes. Thus, in most of the studies, the researchers were distinctly not under the impression that, ". . . casework was a coherent system of operations" (Meyer, 1972, p. 162). Accordingly, in most of the studies, a variety of outcome measures were used in the event that some of the less coherent casework operations produced multidimensional or differential effects.

The second aspect of this issue relates to specification of inputs. In most of the studies, the casework was individually designed to meet the needs of the client or client-group. This seems to be at the heart of casework as an individualizing process. The workers in most of the projects were expected to provide whatever services were necessary to enhance the functioning of their clients. And these services did indeed range from intensive, individualized, therapeutic counseling to environmental manipulation. The specific nature of the client population was also a key factor in designing many of the service programs. Many of these included experimental, extensively prepared projects related to special problems (e.g. regarding alcoholism in Cohen & Krause, 1971; multiproblem families in Brown, 1968 and Geismar & Krisberg, 1967; the aged in Blenkner *et al.,* 1971; "predelinquents" and gangs in Miller, 1962 and Berleman *et al.,* 1972; and so on). No differential effects appeared for any of these specially designed programs. But the definition of social casework as "the services provided by professional caseworkers" certainly seems justified by the presumably varied nature of the programs in these seventeen studies.

Implicit in the criticism that input was not sufficiently specified seems to be the hope that further identification of the exact nature of the services would somehow change the overall results. This, of course, is impossible. Merely specifying the nature of the input to a greater extent cannot change the output. Overall results in these studies are based upon comparisons between groups and would have remained the same no matter how specifically the input—or services—was identified. Indeed, the absence of any definitive patterns of positive outcome (except for the few instances cited in the previous chapter) for certain kinds of clients with certain kinds of problems receiving certain types of services from certain kinds of workers suggests the potential futility of attempting to ferret out just what it was these caseworkers were doing.

The casework methods used were too dissimilar to generalize about them

The preceding discussion noted several examples of specially-designed programs in the seventeen studies. Further, the workers in these studies provided a wide range of services—material, individual therapeutic, group, environmental and so on. Were these services therefore, noncomparable? This is a crucial point because if it is clear that the specific individual services provided from study to study were in every instance completely distinct from each other, any generalization from these studies would be suspect. It would, then, always be possible to say that the "real" casework had never been examined.

For example, because in several of the studies (particularly Miller, 1962; Meyer, Borgatta & Jones, 1965; McCabe, 1967) group methods, usually defined in broad terms, were a primary thrust of the intervention program, it might be argued that casework was not really tested in those studies. However, there is increasing recognition that if casework is indeed an individualizing process, then the practitioner is not confined to separate use of specific "methods"—e.g. work with individuals and work with groups (Meyer, 1972, p. 186; Perlman, 1974, p. 2). Thus, any method might be applied depending upon the needs of the case. In fact, in discussing many of these same studies, Meyer (1972) has acknowledged that they, ". . . are prototypical of the traditional casework method" (p. 160). Indeed, it traditionally has been recognized that casework intervention should not be equated with the one-to-one interview, and that casework treatment refers to treatment conducted through individual interviews, multiple-client interviews, family sessions, plus a whole range of environmental services (Family Service Association of America, 1964).

Further, other factors suggesting comparability of services would tend to facilitate generalizations derived from these studies. There appeared to be considerable uniformity among the studies in terms of the core theoretical orientation of the services provided. In most the orientation was clearly specified as "psychodynamic" of one form or another. (The terms used in the "orientation" column in Tables 5-I and 5-II were quoted directly from the original reports when possible, accounting for the varying descriptions of basically similar orientations, such as "dynamic psychology," "psychoanalytic," "ego psychology," "psychodynamic," etc.). In those studies where the orientation was unspecified, the period of time during which the study occurred plus the general descriptions of the services in those studies (e.g. "child guidance psychotherapy" in Levitt *et al.,* 1959), also suggest a psychodynamic orientation. This is because virtually every model of social casework up until very recently was derived from some form of psychoanalytic theory. Indeed, by far the most prevalent theoretical orientation underlying most approaches in present-day social casework is psychodynamic (Roberts & Nee, 1970; Turner, 1974), again facilitating generalization to social casework practice in general.

A final justification for considering as basically similar the core of the services offered in these several studies is derived from research on the *process,* as opposed to the outcome, of casework (e.g. Hollis, 1968; Mullen, 1968, 1969a & b; Reid, 1967; Fischer, 1970; Reid & Shyne, 1969). This research, carried out in agencies similar to many of those in the seventeen studies, has produced remarkably consistent results. In these studies, no matter what the nature of the clients' problems, no matter how unique they were, caseworkers tended to do the same thing: They *talked* to their clients, and they did so within a very narrow range (e.g. in every study where this was measured, 80 to 85% of worker communications fell within only two of seven possible categories). Thus, within the general classes of client-problems that were studied in this process research—including marital, parent-child, family and psychiatric problems—and across all differences between individual clients, caseworkers offered almost no differential intervention procedures whatever. These process findings pertain largely to examination of direct contacts between workers and clients. Since the core activities of the programs in these seventeen studies involved worker-client interviews, the generalizations to these programs seem appropriate.

Actually, this should not be an unexpected finding, given the theoretical orientations which inform the practice of most caseworkers (Roberts and Nee, 1970; Turner, 1974). Not one of the major, traditional models of social casework, which largely are based on psychodynamic formulations, provides clear prescriptive statements—procedures or techniques—regarding what caseworkers actually should do with their clients (Fischer, 1972a). So caseworkers have always done whatever seemed to be a good idea at the time, and that essentially has involved talking to their clients. Again, a major reason for defining casework as the services of professional caseworkers.

This may clarify the problem of lack of specification of input that was discussed previously. It is likely that specific procedures of intervention were not reported in many of the studies because there were very few such procedures. And, of course, this can hardly be viewed as a fault of the research or the researchers. Instead, it is clearly a result of the imprecision and vagueness in the theory and practice of social casework.

In sum, despite their ostensible differences on the surface, there appear to be basic underlying similarities in the actual services provided in most of the projects. In large part, these commonalities lie, first, in similar theoretical orientations, and second, in the documented tendency for caseworkers to treat all clients virtually the same way, regardless of the nature of the clients' problems. The services provided in these projects, then, were above all else, clearly social casework.

A CONCLUSION ON EFFECTIVENESS

Seventeen controlled studies have been conducted in which professional caseworkers provided services to clients in the experimental group. Changes in social and psychological functioning of those clients were compared with changes in similar subjects who received either no services, or services from nonprofessional workers in less intensive service programs. The results are consistent across all types of services programs, all types of clients, all types of problem categories and no matter what the outcome indicator or criterion measure. In none of the studies was there clear evidence that professional casework produced results superior to no treatment at all, or in any way better to the minimal services provided by nonprofessionals. Thirteen of the studies clearly showed no differences between the groups. Four studies claimed success for the professional caseworkers, but either were operating on the basis of incomplete reporting of data (Lehrman *et al.*, 1949), or contained such serious design flaws that those conclusions could not be sustained. Moreover, in almost three quarters of the studies, clients receiving professional services were shown to deteriorate, faring more poorly on at least one outcome dimension either than they had prior to treatment, or in comparison with subjects in the control group.

These results are all the more amazing in that in almost every study, special conditions pertained for the professional caseworkers which alone might be expected to enhance success rates (the "Hawthorne effect"). The professional caseworkers usually were aware of the fact that they were participating in an experiment and that their work would be carefully evaluated. (In the studies where nonprofessional workers were used for comparison purposes, the nonprofessionals generally were not informed about the study.) Thus, the professionals likely worked particularly hard and with enthusiasm to enhance outcome. Further, the professionals usually had reduced caseloads, special training or supervision and/or extra funds to expend on their clients. Every effort was made to provide special advantages for the professional caseworkers that might not be available in everyday practice, and, still, overall results were negative.

Further, these results cannot be attributed to lack of inclusion of all available studies. Only two other studies comparing the effects of professional casework with untreated or nonprofessionally treated controls are available (Witmer & Keller, 1942; Barron & Leary, 1955). Both of these studies were excluded because other professionals also provided services to clients in the experimental group, and it was not clear that caseworkers provided at least 50 percent of the services, thus hampering potential conclusions. However, in both of those studies, negative or null results also were demonstrated, a fact bolstering the conclusion derived from the seventeen studies reviewed in this book.

As indicated in the preceding sections, there is little reason to believe that the caseworkers, clients and problems in these studies were not representative of typical conditions in practice, thereby enhancing the possibilities for generalizations. The one possible exception to this might be that the caseworkers were generally operating under more or less optimal circumstances, and may have been above average in competence level. Further, evidence was cited in this chapter suggesting the likelihood that the core of services in most of the studies was basically similar, thereby enhancing comparability and, hence, generalizations. However, even assuming for purposes of discussion that each program supplied substantially different, independent methods of services, it is clear that not one of them is superior to the others since definitive positive results were achieved by none. Thus, no matter what the nature of the casework, the client, the problem or the program goals, professional casework not only has failed to demonstrate effectiveness, but lack of effectiveness clearly is the rule rather than the exception. Indeed, when the evidence on overall outcome is coupled with the evidence on deterioration, it appears not only that professional casework is not helpful, but that clients clearly would have been better off in a large percentage of these projects had they never received professional casework services.

CHAPTER 6 IMPLICATIONS*

How could this incredible situation have come about? The bulk of practitioners in an entire profession appear, at worst, to be practicing in ways that are not helpful or even detrimental to their clients, and, at best, operating without a shred of empirical evidence validating their efforts.

It is difficult if not impossible to explain unequivocally all the reasons for this situation. However, in examining some of the factors that may be related to this lack of success in demonstrating effective practice, the most reasonable hypothesis seems to be that the theories and methods most caseworkers traditionally have been using are deficient in so many critical areas, that the outcome in practice and research hardly could have been expected to be any different. Some of the most salient of these deficiencies can be summarized briefly as follows. Since the early 1920's, caseworkers largely have been enamored of a single model of practice—the psychodynamic model (or one of its several variations); in fact, this was the major theoretical orientation of the services in most of the seventeen studies. This has produced a long-lasting overdependence on a narrow and unitary conception of social casework that not only led caseworkers into the blind alley of ineffective practice, but by and large precluded the systematic and objective evaluation and selection of new, potentially more effective approaches as they appeared. A variety of practice problems—many of which were demonstrated in the seventeen studies reviewed in this book —can be traced to use of psychodynamic perspectives: a focus on internal, intrapsychic phenomena and client self-understanding and insight at the expense of the crucial area of social functioning; lack of development of principles and procedures of socio-environmental change and situational manipulation; an assump-

---

* This chapter is based upon, and expanded in, *Effective Casework Practice: An Eclectic Approach* (Fischer, 1976).

tion that all clients, regardless of their problems, can benefit from esoteric, verbal discussions about those problems, thereby focusing on "talk" as the main therapeutic mechanism; an imprecise and vague professional jargon; a focus on theories that help workers understand their clients but not change them, emphasizing study and diagnosis at the expense of intervention; and an almost complete lack of systematic ways for caseworkers to implement their theories, so that techniques or procedures of intervention— what the workers actually are to do—either were given scant attention or ignored almost altogether. Indeed, every study examining the *process* of social casework (some of these were reviewed in the previous chapter) shows that caseworkers operate largely on the basis of individual "style"—idiosyncratic, largely intuitive ways of dealing with clients. As Meyer (1972) has noted, such findings make a mockery of social work education. But, of course, without techniques to implement in practice, caseworkers have no specific ways of influencing their clients, so the findings that "style" is the major variable affecting practice could hardly be unexpected.

The plain facts are that the original psychodynamic theories from which the major casework systems are derived have never demonstrated their own practice effectiveness in research (Eysenck, 1966; Rachman, 1971), a fact increasingly recognized even by psychoanalytic theorists and practitioners (Marmor, 1968). Thus, not only is there little or no reason—on both empirical (lack of research evidence of effectiveness) and conceptual (critical theoretical deficiences such as lack of techniques) grounds— to expect that the traditional approaches used by most caseworkers would result in effective practice, but there is also little reason to believe that revisions of these models, or continuing research on them, would validate their use.

Of course, it would be both simplistic and inaccurate to conclude that the psychodynamic approaches themselves are responsible for all of the current problems in casework or even that all of casework is psychodynamically-based. While most of the major casework approaches do owe considerable allegiance to the psychodynamic model, casework has made tremendous strides in broadening its knowledge base in the 1960's and 1970's. This can be seen in increasing attempts to utilize role theory, systems theory, communication theory, and to develop approaches such as family therapy (Strean, 1971; Turner, 1974).

Unfortunately, the extent to which utilization of these theories has benefitted the *interventive practices* of caseworkers is unclear. For example, role and systems theory, and to a lesser extent communication theory, do add substantially to caseworkers' ability to assess and understand situations. But these approaches rarely go beyond understanding to provide specific techniques of intervention—guidelines as to just what caseworkers should *do* after they understand the problem (see Turner, 1974). Similarly, family therapy, at least as viewed by caseworkers (Scherz, 1970; Sherman, 1974) seems to consist of a loose conglomeration of principles derived from a psychodynamic base on one hand and communication theory on the other hand. Thus, it is not clear what family therapy offers beyond conventional casework practice except that, with family therapy, the major focus of the caseworker's verbal procedures tends to be on communication patterns rather than on intra-psychic phenomena. Even more importantly, despite caseworkers' increased use of family therapy, there is not a single controlled study of any of the communication-based approaches to family therapy demonstrating effective outcome with clients (Wells *et al.*, 1972).

How is it possible that caseworkers were not more alert to these deficiencies in their practice? As discussed in Chapter 1, since all of the "experts," plus one's own colleagues, agreed that practice was effective, there was little reason to question those judgments. Further, over the years, caseworkers appear to have developed a pronounced tendency to discount the importance of evaluative research, especially when the results of that research were not to their liking. Thus, when warnings were available, such as could be found in negative findings in individual studies, they were ignored. Instead, caseworkers became devoted to the "art" of practice at the expense of scientific input. For example, Hollis (1968), in discussing her own research on casework communication, avows that, "Casework is in essence an *experience* between two people . . . that can only be described as art rather than science" (p. 7). A recent nationwide study of professional social workers bears out the prevalence of this attitude: over 40 percent believe that casework *should* be more art than science (Kirk & Fischer, 1974). In fact, over a fifth of the respondents in that study were not persuaded that scientific research is very useful at all in generating social work knowledge.

IMPLICATIONS FOR THEORY AND PRACTICE

Given the disastrous results found in these studies, it would be reasonable to conclude that social casework is no longer a viable enterprise. On the other hand, saying the services in those studies were not effective is not to say that some services were not indicated or necessary. The question is, what services, and how can they most effectively be utilized?

As should be clear from the results of those seventeen studies, over a period of forty years and apparently including use of even the most modern methods (which bear considerable similarities to the least modern methods), caseworkers have been achieving, at best, unspectacular results. And unless radical and deepseated changes are made in both casework theory and practice, there would indeed appear to be little justification for the continued existence of the institution of social casework.

Now the purpose of this chapter is not to explore and develop all angles of the kinds of changes necessary to justify casework. But some features do bear noting, including those which appear to be most worthy, if not noble, about social casework: a value system centered on the importance and dignity of the individual; a commitment to countering the increasingly dehumanizing forces of modern society as they impinge upon the functioning of individuals; a recognition of the critical interplay between societal and individual functioning; a commitment to meeting the diverse needs of individuals by providing a wide range of services; a willingness to serve as the crucial link between individuals and their environment; a commitment, as shown by many of the seventeen studies, to serving the most stigmatized groups in society; in short, a recognition that without primary attention to the individual, the entire society suffers.

Unfortunately, the studies reviewed here bear witness to the fact that these commitments were not always implemented, certainly not effectively implemented, in practice. For example, caseworkers have long acknowledged the necessity of providing a range of services, including environmental manipulation, tailored to meet the needs of clients. However, while in many of the seventeen studies some environmental activities were undertaken, by far the most prevalent form of activity, no matter what the nature of the clients' problems, involved the direct interview, i.e. the clinical role. The facts are that until recently, explication of the requisite knowledge for functioning in a nonclinical—but still casework—capacity virtually has been ignored by the field. Thus, one area where caseworkers might begin to act to meet their commitments is an expanded focus on development of more adequate knowledge for such role clusters as educator/consultant and broker/advocate.

The functions inherent in these roles include the provision of a broad range of services, and engaging in numerous activities, most of which do not involve direct contact with the primary clients. Actually, such activities may mark a good deal of what is most distinctive about social casework—involving a balance of individual and system-oriented perspectives—with every activity differentially performed depending on, and tailored to, the needs and priorities of the client.

Unfortunately, the research reviewed in this book plus that conducted elsewhere (e.g. Goldberg, 1970), points to a critical dilemma involved in having professional caseworkers provide indirect or environmentally-oriented services. To date, there is no evidence that professional caseworkers can provide those services more effectively than nonprofessional workers. But the point of refocusing attention on these services as one priority for professionals is that such concentration may force development and enhancement of the knowledge needed to effectively deliver those services.

Further, there are indeed pressing reasons for integrating such expanded functions into every professional caseworker's basic repertoire. In the first place, these services, complementing the more direct or clinical activities, add the range, breadth and comprehensiveness which ostensibly is the trademark of social casework, and distinguish the activities of caseworkers from those of other professionals working in related fields. Second, and even more importantly, such services are desperately needed by a substantial part of the clientele of caseworkers, particularly those from lower income and disadvantaged groups. Precisely because of this, these services should be integrated into every caseworker's practice, and differentially and systematically employed as part of an overall comprehensive intervention plan for each client.

A further and substantial part of the problem with the theory and practice of casework is that the methods and theories of casework have become confused with casework, *per se*. This book has utilized as an operational (and realistic) definition of social casework—"the services provided by professional caseworkers." As illustrated in Chapter 1, this definition is derived from the notion that casework is simply one branch of the social work profession, the branch that concentrates on the provision of individualized services. In other words, casework is a *professional* rather than theoretical or methodological designation.

Thus, the issue can be viewed not so much as whether or not casework is effective. Rather, the issue is, are the methods used by caseworkers effective? While the answer, to date, is clearly in the negative, this does not necessarily add up to a denunciation of the need for a branch of social work to focus on case by case helping. Instead, it points to the need to develop those methods of practice that offer the greatest promise of being translated into demonstrable positive gains for clients, i.e. into effective practice.

Casework can and must be independent of any specific theoretical orientation. Casework is not synonymous with "ego psychology" or "a problem-solving process" or "crisis intervention." Caseworkers may *use* various theories, but there must be a clear demarcation between the professional function, and the theory or knowledge used by the professional. The overidentification of casework with psychoanalytic theory, and the disastrous results of that union, speak for itself. The very existence of casework is now in jeopardy because its main methods have been found wanting.

The point is that caseworkers, if they will, can turn from pre-occupation with psychodynamically-based methods of practice developed solely by other caseworkers, to a careful examination of all available sources—whether within or outside the profession—for knowledge that could lead to greater effectiveness in practice. This must be done whether or not that knowledge easily fits into the traditional theoretical molds of casework. Further, instead of relying on faith, the word of "experts" or other nebulous or even nonexistent criteria, carefully considered criteria—particularly focused on assessing research evidence of effectiveness—must be used to select the knowledge for practice that shows the greatest potential for translation into measureable, constructive benefits for clients.

Overall, a commitment such as this to what is primarily an empirically-based practice points to the need for an open-ended stance toward decision-making for practice, proceeding on the basis of the best available current knowledge. This must include the understanding that such knowledge rarely, if ever, is conclusive, and is subject to revision when new or better evidence appears. It means being alert and open to new ideas and emerging developments in practice, a flexibility and openness which has been conspicuously absent in the past, as witness caseworkers' long-time infatuation with psychodynamically-oriented approaches. It means being directed in knowledge-selection by what is effective for the client, and not by devotion to any single theory or method.

Hopefully, this can have a liberating influence in that it divorces casework from the unnecessary constraints of any theoretical orientation that happens to be in vogue. Professional caseworkers simply cannot afford premature closure around one approach, expecting to use it indefinitely, without either awareness of new approaches, or willingness to examine and use new approaches with the potential for (or demonstrated) greater effectiveness when they become available. In essence, the primary task for social caseworkers, indeed, for members of any profession, is to be constantly searching for more effective methods of practice.

Now such a discussion would be largely irrelevant if there *were* no potentially more effective methods of practice available. But, in fact, there are already at hand several approaches that show promise for considerably increasing the effectiveness of caseworkers over their present levels. Elsewhere (Fischer, 1976) a variety of criteria have been presented to aid in evaluating and selecting knowledge derived from diverse sources, and a model presented for integrating and implementing that knowledge in practice, and these need not be repeated here. It also should be pointed out that while the approaches to be mentioned here appear to be the major current thrusts in the literature of interpersonal helping, new research may either invalidate some of this material, or validate different, more effective procedures that deal with similar human problems. Thus, the job of the caseworker is to be open to these new developments as they appear.

In fact, what is presented here is intended only to be illustrative of the currently available approaches that appear to have the potential for enhancing the effectiveness of social casework if incorporated into practice. The intent is neither to review the entire literature nor even discuss these approaches in depth. Thus, only brief mention of each shall be made here. It should be pointed out that no single approach that is currently available has demonstrated unequivocal effectiveness across the complete range of clients and problems. However, the approaches to be touched on below do contain, in one or more ways and in varying degrees, both within and between each of them, at least a modicum of empirical evidence pointing to effective results when they are implemented in practice. Further, and of major importance, each approach contains reasonably clear guidelines for implementation—i.e. specific techniques for both training and practice—features that are clearly missing in most traditional approaches to social casework.

The three major thrusts presented here as currently available for practice are: first, use of structure; second, behavior modification; and third, the therapeutic conditions of empathy, warmth and genuineness.

The first of these, *use of structure,* is perhaps the least familiar of the three since it is comprised of a synthesis of several procedures, all of which appear to have at least one distinct underlying commonality: they all involve an attempt to offer more structure to the interaction between worker and client. This material is based on the observation that whenever a formally structured approach to helping is compared with an unstructured approach, research tends to show more favorable outcome for the structured approach. Structure, as used here, includes not only a number of specific procedures, but a perspective on intervention that can provide a framework for *implementing* those procedures. Structure essentially involves such dimensions as careful planning of intervention, introducing as much certainty as possible into the client's situation, a commitment to action—rather than to dynamic passivity—on the part of the worker; use of direct influence, and above all else, being systematic (Phillips & Wiener, 1966). In addition to the general framework, there are several concrete ways in which structure either is pertinent for practice, or can be used in the form of specific procedures (each of these is detailed in Fischer, 1976). These would include the following: first, in utilizing a variety of measures for structuring the "intake" process; second, in applying material derived from the vast amount of research on social-psychological principles (Goldstein & Simonson, 1971); third, in the use of a number of types of structured role playing (Goldstein, 1973); fourth in the use of time limits to shorten the intervention process; and finally, in the termination process to enhance the transfer of positive change from the office or agency to the natural environment.

A second and probably more familiar major thrust in the literature involves the huge amount of work on *behavior modification* (Fischer & Gochros, 1975). Many of the procedures of behavior modification show considerable promise of bringing to social casework a number of previously missing dimensions: principles of environmental change; a range of specific techniques for implementation in practice; a clear connection between assessment and intervention; greater efficiency, clarity and susceptibility to research evaluation; several methods for determining effectiveness with each and every case; broad applicability to clients and problems; and communicable concepts so that principles and procedures can be readily taught to nonprofessionals and mediators in the natural environment (such as parents and teachers). Finally, and most importantly, increasing use of behavior modification is likely to considerably enhance the effectiveness of casework practice, as attested to by some 200 group experimental studies demonstrating the effectiveness of several of the behavioral procedures with a range of clients and problems (Morrow, 1971; Rimm and Masters, 1974; O'Leary and Wilson, 1975).

The third and final area to be discussed here involves the core conditions of *empathy, warmth and genuineness.* These are the first and only clearly operationalized dimensions of relationship to be successfully related—in extensive research with a variety of clients and problems—to effective helping (Truax & Carkhuff, 1967; Truax & Mitchell, 1971). While these conditions bear some surface similarity to the traditional social work emphasis on the importance of "relationship," in both substance and empirical evidence, the differences are considerable (see Fischer, 1976, Part III for elaboration of this point). Further, these are the dimensions mentioned in Chapter 4 as being significantly correlated with both improvement and deterioration, with clients seen by workers providing low levels of these conditions frequently shown to deteriorate in functioning. However, since there is considerable research showing that helpers can be trained to communicate higher levels of empathy, warmth and genuineness, it may be possible to avoid many of the deterioration effects described in Chapter 4, by guaranteeing that workers are trained to provide at least minimal levels of those conditions. While many of the seventeen studies reviewed in previous chapters did not attempt to control for various characteristics of the caseworkers, e.g. "style," when this *was* examined (e.g. Brown, 1968), no differences in outcome were found. Indeed, at this point, such examination may prove fruitless since research has revealed that the existence of high levels of empathy, warmth and genuineness, even among experienced practitioners, is relatively infrequent. This has led to the estimate that, on these dimensions alone, the only measures that are predictive of success in interpersonal helping, up to two thirds of professional helpers may be practicing ineffectively (Truax & Mitchell, 1971).

This section has attempted only to highlight some of the potential ways in which changes in social casework could be made in the direction of an empirically-based, outcome-oriented approach to practice. The necessity for these changes is based on the grounds that the negative findings in the research on the effectiveness of social casework appear to be largely a result of the tendency of most caseworkers—both educators and practitioners—to cling to the use of outdated, ineffective methods of practice. These are major and substantial changes for the field. But these changes in many caseworkers' typical orientation to practice—and the methods of practice themselves—are not intended to be viewed either as a panacea or as a way of insuring guaranteed effectiveness with all problems and all clients. Further, they should not be viewed in isolation from other necessary, basic, structural changes in the field such as in patterns of service delivery, reassessment of priorities regarding selection of client groups, education and so on (Fischer, 1976).

Again, the three areas presented as major "thrusts" in the literature were discussed only to illustrate that, if caseworkers are willing to make major and drastic revisions in their practice methods, all may not be lost. Further, the suggestions here were intended neither as the "last word" nor the "ultimate" in interventive practices. But each does contain considerably more evidence of effectiveness, and potential for increasing that evidence, than any of the approaches currently being used by the vast majority of caseworkers. The point is that caseworkers no longer need be caught in the bind of defending the use of methods—such as the psychodynamically-based approaches and communication-based family therapy—that contain little or no scientifically acceptable research evidence supporting their use, while virtually ignoring other approaches such as those described here that contain literally scores of studies attesting to their effectiveness.

It is, of course, likely that new and different approaches will be developed in the future and perhaps validated in research, and these too will be candidates for adaptation for casework practice.

Indeed, future research may find such new approaches to be even more effective, hence, more suitable for casework, than the approaches suggested here. But if approaches such as those described here, already available, continue to be ignored, there is little reason to believe that *any* new approaches with evidence of effectiveness would be incorporated into practice either. And then, assuming the casework enterprise would even endure, practice would, at best, continue to be largely ineffective, and at worst, harmful.

IMPLICATIONS FOR RESEARCH

In Chapter 1, it was suggested that the conceptual and definitional vagueness that plagues social casework may have produced some secondary benefits, in that differences in practice and new practice modalities could more readily emerge and be considered by practitioners. Unfortunately, as the preceding discussion has pointed out, such benefits never materialized. It would thus behoove caseworkers to begin to be far more specific about: (1) objectives and goals; (2) methods of practice; and (3) evaluation of results. This might be called "the movement away from vagueness" (Briar, 1973), and would include defining what caseworkers are attempting to accomplish in particular situations or cases in terms that have tangible, observable referents to those situations. This would then allow caseworkers to identify exactly what it is they are doing, toward what ends, and allow the determination of whether or not those ends were reached.

Definitional specificity of this nature requires the use of terms that lend themselves to such precision. The point is not to sacrifice meaning for measurement, but to turn to use of concepts or propositions that will not only lend themselves to measurement, but also will be meaningful in that they will lead to the provision of more effective services to clients. This has numerous implications. Use of objectives that are stated behaviorally, for example, means that goals for clients will be clear, specific, observable and measurable. Client and worker will know when they are achieved. Specification of objectives will also allow greater precision in selection of intervention procedures, as well as the selection of appropriate indicators of outcome. And the relationship between use of specific techniques and specific outcomes can be more clearly evaluated.

But specification of terms and objectives is only one step in the overall process of moving toward increased effectiveness. It is not a magical solution and clearly not an end in itself as implied by Newman and Turner (1974): "Defining goals more vigorously is so large a step . . . that a concerted effort to do so would probably satisfy critics for a while" (p. 14). But obviously, it is equally as possible for caseworkers to be ineffective using measurable techniques and objectives as it is using the murky concepts of today. Thus, specificity is only intended as a way of opening the door to promote the use of research to move toward demonstrated effective practice.

And the current state of the evidence on casework effectiveness does suggest some research priorities. It is time to call a moratorium on gross evaluative research of traditional casework methods, such as the type of research reviewed in this book, wherein large groups of clients are assigned to experimental and control groups and studied for long periods of time. Such research is not only time consuming and extremely expensive, but the research evidence on those methods of casework currently in vogue, and the conceptual evidence about the models and theories from which they are derived, suggest that such research would have little or no palpable return. Even one or two studies with findings favoring the treated group would be insufficient to overcome what is already known, and could logically be predicted, about the direction of the casework enterprise. The assumption that underlies this research—that caseworkers *must* be doing something effective—is no longer viable. The vast majority of caseworkers are not only practicing ineffectively, but many are engaged in practices harmful to their clients. There are no substantial research or theoretical reasons to believe otherwise.

Now the reason for calling a halt to the conducting of controlled research is *not* that it cannot be accomplished. Most of the studies reviewed in this book were very well done, and had adequate methodologies. And this is not to say that the numerous studies of the effectiveness of practice that *have* been performed to date have not been enormously productive. They have, although in a "negative" way. They have clearly illustrated the inappropriateness of many of the activities that we are currently performing; they have clearly illustrated the lack of potential of most of our current systems of practice; they have pointed to the need for new directions and the utilization of different approaches to practice; in short, they have identified the need to begin a process of knowledge-building, starting with the development of specific techniques, their application to selected practice problems and the evaluation of their effectiveness with individual clients.

The purpose of the remainder of this discussion is to focus on this process of *technique building and validation* in practice with individuals. As an alternative to group experimental designs, and based on clear identification of techniques and their methodical selection by empirical means as suggested in the previous section, caseworkers can begin research programs based on the systematic investigation of the success of individual procedures with individual clients, using rigorous case study methods of evaluation. Once sufficient evidence is accumulated through rigorous and widespread investigation of individualized procedures, *then* more broadly based, controlled, group experimental studies can be undertaken. These studies can be conducted both to ascertain the effectiveness of any given procedure or procedures in comparison to no formal intervention at all, but can also be used to compare the effects of two or more competing procedures (for an example of this type of study, see Paul, 1966).

Single-case study designs are not suggested here as ends in themselves, but as primary sources of data for the formulation of hypotheses for testing in group experimental designs, which can provide far more sophisticated evidence regarding the effectiveness of any given intervention procedure or set of procedures. But such research can best proceed by being informed *in advance* by the results of numerous single case study designs—by testing hypotheses based on solid facts rather than hunches, speculation or guess work. The essential difference between such a research program and that which has been conducted previously in social casework is that this research will be guided by hypotheses based on information gained directly from the demonstrably successful application of interventive procedures, and can therefore proceed at a geometrically faster and more efficient pace. In other words, researchers will no longer be hypothesizing the success of methods where there is not only a serious problem in defining just what those methods are, but where there is little reason to expect that success in the first place.

The essence of this point is that research can and should be built right into practice in order to study the relationships between the processes of intervention and the outcomes. Several different strategies—in essence, a new and developing technology of evaluation—are available for conducting such evaluations, and four of these will be briefly described here to illustrate the potential that such methods have for use in practice (each is elaborated, both in terms of strengths and weaknesses, in Fischer, 1976). These methods vary considerably with regard to design and to rigor, and none of them can do more than, at best, demonstrate that a particular worker using a particular technique with a particular client produced successful outcome. But all provide at least a minimal degree of systematization and objectification to practice. Further, each moves toward clearer identification of techniques of intervention in relation to specified problems, that is, they focus on the crucial task of technique-building and development. And each of these strategies presents a different method for observing, collecting data about, and evaluating the effectiveness of practice with each and every client. Again, the purpose of this discussion is not to explore each in depth, but only to highlight the fact that such strategies are indeed available and, in large part, feasible for incorporation into everyday practice.

The first strategy for building research into practice involves the "experimental investigation of single cases." Developed to its highest degree of rigor by researchers and practitioners with a behavioral orientation (e.g. Bushell & Burgess, 1969; Howe, 1974) this method requires objective identification of techniques, objective identification of the behaviors which it is desirable to change, and a method of observing and recording those be- haviors. Several variations of this design are available, but the basic method common to all involves collecting data on the oc- currence of the target behavior prior to intervention (the base- line), applying the intervention technique while still collecting data on the behavior and evaluating any changes that come about with intervention in comparison to the baseline. The interven- tion can also be withdrawn to see whether the frequency or duration of the behavior changes, and then reapplied to insure the stability of the desired changes.

These designs allow the worker to determine whether the use or nonuse of his techniques are objectively related to observed changes in target behavior. The criterion for success—the change in behavior—is clearly identified for both worker and client and is built right into the research design; it is possible to tell with each case whether or not a technique works. The data collected give ongoing evaluative feedback to the worker as to the effects of what he is doing, and provide the basis for making changes in the intervention program if such changes are necessary.

Of course, such a design is not the end product of research into practice effects, since techniques cannot be validated *in toto* with this design. Only specific effects with specific clients and spe- cific workers can be determined. Thus, information obtained from numerous replications of such designs can provide the raw data for the development of hypotheses for testing in more so- phisticated and rigorous group experimental designs.

The second method for building research into practice in- volves "objectified case studies." Based on the work of Chassan (1967), these procedures may lack some of the rigor of experi- mental investigations of single cases, but they do offer consider- able advantages over traditional case studies where a poorly de- fined intervention is applied to a nebulously defined problem with inadequately defined outcome criteria. In "objectified case studies," intervention techniques are systematically varied and results carefully recorded. With a client with "known character- istics," e.g. problem, demographic, etc., two or more specific tech- niques are selected, a relevant criterion measure is identified, and then a specific order of application of techniques is selected in advance, e.g. technique A for two weeks, technique B for two weeks, technique A again for two more weeks, and so on. This order is adhered to over a period of time during which data are consistently collected on the outcome instrument (s). At the end of intervention, a statistical determination of the effects of one technique versus the other can be made. Then, once a technique has been demonstrated to have a particular effect, it can be used again with another client, perhaps with similar characteristics, and the order of its application can be varied, or it can be applied in combination with different techniques.

Using this design, techniques can be studied with one client, and, if verified, replicated with other clients. As systematic variations in both clients and techniques are introduced, their effect upon outcome can be observed; thus, the value of the technique in contributing to overall effectiveness can eventually be specified. Both this and the previously described strategy are not simple undertakings, but in terms of both technique-building and outcome evaluation, are both feasible and necessary.

The third method of building research into practice is the *"a priori* model." This is a considerably different strategy from the two previous approaches, involving as it does the determination *in advance* of the stages through which an entire interventive process will pass. These stages can include a number of specific techniques applied within each stage. But the key ingredient in this method is that the worker and client cannot progress from one stage to the next unless certain specific criteria are met. In other words, methods of evaluating outcome are built right into the interventive process, and their achievement is the criterion for moving to a subsequent stage of intervention.

There is a crucial and perhaps obvious problem with such a model. It requires specifying in advance the types of clients and problems that presumably are suitable for such intervention. In fact, no models such as this, with empirical evidence of success, are currently available. Perhaps the closest that any approach comes to this *"a priori* model" is the integrative model of marital therapy developed by Tsoi (1972). This approach consists of four stages of therapy, each of which includes operationalized guidelines for moving from stage to stage, and is currently being tested in controlled process and outcome research.

The development of an *"a priori* model," of course, is a major task. But such a model, if developed and validated in research, would offer a number of advantages, in that both client and worker would have clear guidelines for success built right into the process; if a client achieves the final stage by negotiating all of the stages successfully, positive outcome could be established. Further, other independent measures of success can be used to cross-validate the accuracy of the in-process criteria.

The fourth and last method for building research into practice to be discussed here involves "systematized recording." This method centers around the attempt to introduce more systematic ways of recording pertinent information on the process and effects of intervention than are currently being used in most agencies. It is clearly the least rigorous of all of the models described here since, first, intervention is not preplanned in a specific, systematized fashion; and second, data-gathering is largely reliant on the caseworker's estimation of his own efforts and the client's reports of success (both of which can be supplemented by more objective means of data collection). Indeed, this method may best be considered as a preliminary step to the use of the other methods described here.

The overall procedure of systematized recording simply involves building into on-going practice more or less objectified forms of reporting what is (or appears to be) occurring. These processes, and the client's report of their effects, are then noted on a brief recording card or sheet, according to preset categories, and perhaps according to some system of codification of client problems, techniques and so on (such an instrument is presented in Fischer, 1976). What actually is recorded, though, is a function of the specific interactions between each client and worker, the specific problem-configuration, and the specific techniques selected by the worker.

The use of such methods would impel workers to try to more objectively identify just what it is they are doing, and just what the outcome is in relation to each technique used. While un-equivocal evidence of effectiveness is clearly impossible using such recording methods due to the lack of any systematic control of variables, they do present a way of gathering data about prac-tice for further testing in more rigorous forms of intensive, and ultimately extensive designs. They also comprise a way of keep-ing practitioners both constantly oriented to outcome and to evaluating the effects of their interventions. Further, there is some evidence that such recording can produce significant gains in efficiency, since the elimination of extensive summary or pro-cess recording can free up a considerable amount of time for the practitioner (Seaberg, 1965). In essence, such recording methods offer the potential for a major increment in the knowledge gained about patterns of service delivery, techniques used by workers in relation to specific problems, and, even with crude measures of outcome, in developing hypotheses for further test-ing regarding the effectiveness of casework services.

The purpose of this section was to suggest a number of differ-ent possibilities for building research into practice. These meth-ods vary considerably with regard to design, to rigor, and to level of evidence produced, but they all point in a similar direction: toward clearer identification of techniques of intervention in re-lation to specified problems and to their effects on those prob-lems. Thus, they each provide an empirically-focused orientation to, and on-going data about, outcome. Such data of course form the basis for eventually establishing a foundation for effective practice.

Most of the evaluative methods presented here appear to be both already available and feasible for implementation by case-workers in actual practice. They can and should be part of prac-tice, consistently maintained and integrated into the activity of every agency. Together, they provide a variety of means for case-workers to begin both the evaluation of the success of their own practice and the laborious, but absolutely essential (and long overdue) process of technique-building and validation. Further, these research methods also can be used to inform more broadly-based, rigorous research, so that, ultimately, if caseworkers are willing to make basic revisions in their practice, a greatly expanded repertoire of effective practice techniques can be made available to every caseworker.

CONCLUSION

The current state of research and practice in social casework appears to bear numerous similarities to a state described by Kuhn (1962) regarding the structure of scientific revolutions. Kuhn argues that most of "science" is governed by overriding models or paradigms that guide and structure scientific research and theorizing. These models prescribe the kinds of questions that scientists raise, provide rather rigid guidelines for the nature of the solutions to be sought, bias scientists' perceptions of phenomena and insure that research will not raise serious questions about the validity of the model. Thus, when anomalies, or deviations from the common rule arise, or are discovered in research, scientists attempt to account for these anomalies with the vocabulary and perceptions of the superordinate model. However, only after a series of such anomalies appear and a crisis occurs is any new model seriously examined and accepted; hence, the scientific revolution.

It appears as though a directly analogous situation has occurred in social casework. The major belief system of caseworkers has impeded them both from recognizing the substantial negative evidence about the effects of their work that has been documented in this book and from searching for new knowledge and new models. Clearly, though, the crisis in casework has already developed. The question is, will caseworkers face the necessity for "the revolution?"

REFERENCES—PART I

Barron, F. and Leary, T. F. "Changes in Psychoneurotic Patients With and Without Psychotherapy," *Journal of Consulting Psychology*, Vol. 19, 1955, pp. 239-245.

Beck, D. F. *Patterns in Use of Family Agency Service.* New York: F.S.A.A., 1962.

Beck, D. F. and Jones, M. A. *Progress on Family Problems.* New York: F.S.A.A., 1973.

Behling, J. H. *An Experimental Study to Measure the Effectiveness of Case-work Service.* Columbus, Ohio: The Ohio State University, 1961.

Bergin, A. "Some Implications of Psychotherapy Research for Therapeutic Practice," *Journal of Abnormal Psychology,* Vol. 71, 1966, pp. 235-246.

Bergin, A. E. "The Evaluation of Therapeutic Outcomes," in *Handbook of Psychotherapy and Behavior Change: An Empirical Analysis.* Bergin, A. E. and Garfield, S. L. (eds.) New York: John Wiley and Sons, Inc., 1971.

Berleman, W. C., Seaberg, J. R. and Steinburn, T. W. "The Delinquency Prevention Experiment of the Seattle Atlantic Street Center: A Final Evaluation," *Social Service Review,* Vol. 46, 1972, pp. 323-346.

Berleman, W. C. and Steinburn, T. W. "The Execution and Evaluation of a Delinquency Prevention Program," *Social Problems,* Vol. 14, 1967, pp. 413-423.

Blenkner, M., Bloom, M. and Nielsen, M. "A Research and Demonstration Project of Protective Services," *Social Casework,* Vol. 52, 1971, pp. 489-506.

Blenkner, M., Jahn, J. and Wasser, E. *Serving the Aging: An Experiment in Social Work and Public Health Nursing.* New York: Community Service Society of New York, 1964.

Briar, S. "The Current Crisis in Social Casework," in *Social Work Practice.* New York: Columbia University Press, 1967, pp. 19-33.

Briar, S. "The Casework Predicament," *Social Work,* Vol. 1, January, 1968, pp. 5-11.

Briar, S. "Effective Social Work Intervention in Direct Practice: Implications for Education," Briar, S. *et al. Facing the Challenge.* New York: C.S.W.E., 1973.

Briar, S. "Family Services," *Five Fields of Social Service: Reviews of Research.* New York: N.A.S.W., 1966.

Brown, G. E. (ed.). *The Multi-Problem Dilemma.* Metuchen, New Jersey: The Scarecrow Press, Inc., 1968.

Bushell, D. and Burgess, R. L. "Characteristics of the Experimental Analysis," Burgess, R. L. and Bushell, D. (Eds.), *Behavioral Sociology.* New York: Columbia University Press, 1969, pp. 145-174.

Campbell, D. T. and Stanley, J. C. *Experimental and Quasi-Experimental Designs for Research.* Chicago: Rand McNally and Co., 1969.

Chassan, J. B. *Research Design in Clinical Psychology and Psychiatry.* New York: Appleton-Century-Crofts, 1967.

Cohen, P. and Krause, M. S. *Casework with Wives of Alcoholics.* New York: F.S.A.A., 1971.

Craig, M. and Furst, P. W. "What Happens After Treatment? A Study of Potentially Delinquent Boys," *Social Service Review,* Vol. 39, 1965, pp. 165-171.

Edwards, A. L. *Experimental Design in Psychological Research.* (4th ed.). New York: Holt, Rinehart and Winston, 1972.

Erikson, K. T. "A Comment on Disguised Observation in Sociology," *Social Problems,* Vol. 14, 1967.

Eysenck, H. *The Effects of Psychotherapy.* New York: International Science Press, 1966.

Eysenck, H. J. "The Effects of Psychotherapy: An Evaluation," *Journal of Consulting Psychology,* Vol. 16, 1952, pp. 319-324.

Family Service Association of America. *Group Treatment in Family Service Agencies.* New York: F.S.A.A., 1964.

Fellin, P., Tripodi, T. and Meyer, H. J. (eds.). *Exemplars of Social Research.* Itasca, Illinois: F. E. Peacock, 1969.

Fischer, J. "The Relationship Between Personal Value Orientations, Client Diagnostic Variables and Casework Treatment Decisions." Unpublished Doctoral Dissertation, University of California, Berkeley, 1970.

Fischer, J. "Helping the Aged: A Review," *Social Work,* Vol. 17, 1972, pp. 106-107.

Fischer, J. "Is Casework Effective? A Review," *Social Work,* Vol. 18, 1973, pp. 5-20 (a).

Fischer, J. "Has Mighty Casework Struck Out?" *Social Work,* Vol. 18, 1973, pp. 107-110 (b).

Fischer, J. *Analyzing Research: A Guide for Social Workers.* Honolulu, Hawaii: University of Hawaii, School of Social Work Research Monograph, 1975.

Fischer, J. *Effective Casework Practice: An Eclectic Approach.* New York: McGraw-Hill (in press), 1976.

Fischer, J. and Gochros, H. *Planned Behavior Change: The Application of Behavior Modification to Social Work Practice.* New York: Free Press, 1975.

Forstenzer, H. M. "Discussion of a Follow-up Evaluation of Cases Treated at a Community Child Guidance Clinic," *American Journal of Orthopsychiatry,* Vol. 29, 1959, pp. 347-349.

Garfield, S. "Research on Client Variables in Psychotherapy," Bergin, A. and Garfield, S. (Eds.). *Handbook of Psychotherapy and Behavior Change.* New York: John Wiley, 1971, pp. 271-298.

Geismar, L. and Krisberg, J. *The Forgotten Neighborhood.* Metuchen, N.J.: The Scarecrow Press, Inc., 1967.

Geismar, L. "The Results of Social Work Intervention: A Positive Case," *American Journal of Orthopsychiatry,* Vol. 37. 1968, pp. 444-456.

Geismar, L. "Implications of a Family Life Improvement Project," *Social Casework,* Vol. 52, July 1971, pp. 455-465.

Geismar, L. *et al. Early Supports for Family Life: A Social Work Experiment.* Metuchen, N.J.: Scarecrow Press, 1972.

Geismar, L. "Thirteen Evaluative Studies," Mullen, E. J. and Dumpson, J. R. (eds.), *Evaluation of Social Intervention.* San Francisco: Jossey-Bass, 1972, pp. 15-38.

Goldberg, E. *Helping the Aged.* London: George Allan and Unwin, 1970.

Goldstein, A. P. *Structured Learning Therapy.* New York: Academic Press, 1973.

Goldstein, A. P. and Simonson, N. R. "Social Psychological Approaches to Psychotherapy Research," Bergin, A. E. and Garfield, S. L. (eds.), *Handbook of Psychotherapy and Behavior Change.* New York: John Wiley, 1971, pp. 154-195.

Gurin, G. *et al. Americans View Their Mental Health.* New York: Basic Books, 1960.

Hartman, A. "But What Is Social Casework?" *Social Casework,* Vol. 52, 1971, pp. 411-419.

Hays, W. L. *Statistics for the Social Sciences.* New York: Holt, Rinehart and Winston, 1973.

Herzogg, E. *Some Guidelines for Evaluative Research.* Washington, D.C.: U.S. Department of Health, Education and Welfare, 1959.

Howe, M. W. "Casework Self-Evaluation: A Single Subject Approach," *Social Service Review,* Vol. 48, 1974, pp. 1-23.

Hollis, F. *A Typology of Casework Treatment.* New York: Family Service Association, 1968.

Hyman, H. H. *et al. Applications of Methods of Evaluation: Four Studies of the Encampment for Citizenship.* Los Angeles: University of California Press, 1962.

Jones, W. C. and Borgatta, E. J. "Methodology of Evaluation," Mullen, E. J. and Dumpson, J. R. (eds.), *Evaluation of Social Intervention.* San Francisco: Jossey-Bass, 1972, pp. 39-54.

Kahn, A. J. "The Design of Research," Polansky, N. (ed.), *Social Work Research.* Chicago: University of Chicago Press, 1960, pp. 48-73.

Kirk, S. and Fischer, J. "Can Social Workers Understand Research?" Paper presented at Annual Meeting of Council of Social Work Education, Atlanta, Ga., 1974.

Kuhl, P. M. *The Family Center Project and Action Research on Socially Deprived Families.* Copenhagen, Denmark: The Danish National Institute of Social Research, 1969.

Kuhn, T. S. *The Structure of Scientific Revolutions.* Chicago: University of Chicago Press, 1962.

Lang, P. "The Mechanics of Desensitization and the Laboratory Study of Human Fear," Franks, C. (ed.), *Behavior Therapy: Appraisal and Status.* New York: McGraw-Hill, 1969, pp. 160-191.

Langsley, D. G., Pittman, F. S. III and Flomenhaft, K. "Family Crisis Therapy—Results and Implications," *Family Process,* Vol. 7, 1968, pp. 145-158.

Lehrman, L. J. *et al.* "Success and Failure of Treatment of Children in Child Guidance Clinics of the Jewish Board of Guardians," Jewish Board of Guardians, *Research Monograph* No. 1, 1949.

Levitt, E. E., Beiser, H. R. and Robertson, R. E. "A Follow-up Evaluation of

Cases Treated at a Community Child Guidance Clinic," *American Journal of Orthopsychiatry*, Vol. 29, 1959, pp. 337-347.

Levitt, E. E. "The Results of Psychotherapy with Children: An Evaluation," *Journal of Consulting Psychology*, Vol. 21, 1957, pp. 189-196.

Lindsay, R. P. "Comments on Accountability in Social Work Education," Oviatt, B. (ed.), *Evaluation and Accountability in Social Work Education*. University of Utah, 1973, pp. 15-22.

Loavenbruck, G. "N.A.S.W. Survey Finds Increase in Pay for Most Members," *N.A.S.W. News*, March, 1973, pp. 10-11.

Lord, F. M. "Large-Sample Covariance Analysis When the Control Variable Is Fallible," *Journal of the American Statistical Association*, Vol. 55, 1960, pp. 437-451.

MacDonald, M. E. "Reunion at Vocational High: An Analysis of *Girls at Vocational High: An Experiment in Social Work Intervention*," *Social Service Review*, Vol. 40, 1966, pp. 175-189.

Mann, J. "The Outcome of Evaluative Research," Weiss, C. (ed.), *Evaluating Action Programs*. Boston: Allyn and Bacon, 1972, pp. 267-282.

Marin, R. A. *A Comprehensive Program for Multi-Problem Families: A Report on a Four Year Controlled Experiment*. Rio Riedras, Puerto Rico: Institute of Carribean Studies, University of Puerto Rico, 1969.

Marmor, J. *Modern Psychoanalysis*. New York: Basic Books, 1968.

McCabe, A. *The Pursuit of Promise*. New York: Community Service Society, 1967.

McCord, J. and McCord, W. "A Follow-up Report on the Cambridge-Somerville Youth Study," *Annals of American Academy of Political and Social Science*, Vol. 322, 1959, pp. 89-96.

Meehl, P. E. "Psychotherapy," *Annual Review of Psychology*, Vol. 6, 1955, pp. 357-378.

Meltzoff, J. and Kornreich, M. *Research in Psychotherapy*. New York: Atherton, 1970.

Meyer, C. "Practice on Microsystem Level," Mullen, E. J. and Dumpson, J. R. (eds.), *Evaluation of Social Intervention*. San Francisco: Jossey-Bass, 1972.

Meyer, H., Borgatta, E. and Jones, W. *Girls at Vocational High*. New York: Russell Sage Foundation, 1965.

Miller, W. B. "The Impact of a Total Community Delinquency Control Project," *Social Problems*, Fall, 1962, pp. 168-191.

Morrow, W. R. *Behavior Therapy Bibliography*. Columbia, Missouri: University of Missouri: University of Missouri Press, 1971.

Most, E. "Measuring Change in Marital Satisfaction," *Social Work*, Vol. 9, 1964, pp. 64-70.

Mullen, E. "Casework Communication," *Social Casework*, Vol. 49, 1968, pp. 546-551.

Mullen, E. "The Relation Between Diagnosis and Treatment in Casework, *Social Casework,* Vol. 50, 1969, pp. 218-226 (a).

Mullen, E. "Differences in Worker Style in Casework," *Social Casework,* Vol. 50, 1969, pp. 347-353 (b).

Mullen, E., Chazin, R. and Feldstein, D. *Preventing Chronic Dependency.* New York: Community Service Society, 1970.

Mullen, E. J., Chazin, R. M. and Feldstein, D. M. "Services for the Newly Dependent: An Assessment," *Social Service Review,* Vol. 46, 1972, pp. 309-322.

Mullen, E. J. and Dumpson, J. R. (eds.). *Evaluation of Social Intervention.* San Francisco: Jossey-Bass, 1972.

Nagel, N. "Methodological Issues in Psychoanalytic Theory," Hook, S. (ed.), *Psychoanalysis, Scientific Method and Philosophy.* New York: N.Y. University Press, 1959, pp. 38-56.

Newman, E. and Turem, J. "The Crisis of Accountability," *Social Work,* Vol. 19, 1974, pp. 5-16.

O'Leary, K. D. and Wilson, G. T. *Behavior Therapy: Application and Outcome.* Englewood Cliffs, N.J.: Prentice-Hall, 1975.

Paul, G. "Behavior Modification Research: Design and Tactics," Franks, C. M. (ed.), *Behavior Therapy: Appraisal and Status.* New York: McGraw-Hill, 1969, pp. 29-62.

Paul, G. "Outcome of Systematic Desensitization, I and II," Franks, C. (ed.), *Behavior Therapy: Appraisal and Status.* New York: McGraw-Hill, 1969, pp. 63-159.

Paul, G. *Insight vs. Desensitization in Psychotherapy.* Stanford, California: Stanford University Press, 1966.

Perlman, H. H. "Can Casework Work?" *Social Service Review,* Vol. 42, 1968, pp. 435-447.

Perlman, H. H. "Once More with Feeling," Mullen, E. J. and Dumpson, J. R. (eds.), *Evaluation of Social Intervention.* San Francisco: Jossey-Bass, 1972, pp. 191-209.

Perlman, H. H. "Confessions, Concerns and Commitment of an Ex-Clinical Social Worker." University of Chicago, School of Social Service Administration. Occasional Paper Number 5, March, 1974.

Phillips, E. L. and Wiener, D. N. *Short-term Psychotherapy and Structured Behavior Change.* New York: McGraw-Hill, 1966.

Polansky, N. A. (ed.). *Social Work Research.* Chicago: University of Chicago Press, 1960.

Poser, E. G. "The Effect of Therapists' Training on Group Therapeutic Outcome," *Journal of Consulting Psychology,* Vol. 30, 1966, pp. 283-289.

Powers, E. and Witmer, H. *An Experiment in the Prevention of Delinquency —The Cambridge Somerville Youth Study.* New York: Columbia University Press, 1951.

Rachman, S. *The Effects of Psychotherapy.* Oxford: Pergamon Press, 1971.

Reid, W. "A Study of Caseworkers' Use of Insight-Oriented Techniques," *Social Casework,* Vol. 48, 1967, pp. 3-9.

Reid, W. and Shyne, A. *Brief and Extended Casework.* New York: Columbia University Press, 1968.

Rimm, D. C. and Masters, J. C. *Behavior Therapy: Techniques and Empirical Findings.* New York: Academic Press, 1974.

Ripple, L. and Alexander, E. "Motivation, Capacity and Opportunity as Related to the Use of Casework Service: Nature of the Client's Problem," *Social Service Review,* Vol. 30, 1956, pp. 38-54.

Roberts, R. and Nee, R. (eds.). *Theories of Social Casework.* Chicago: University of Chicago Press, 1970.

Rogers, C. R., *et al. The Therapeutic Relationship and Its Impact: A Study of Psychotherapy with Schizophrenics.* Madison: University of Wisconsin Press, 1967.

Rosenthal, R. *Experimenter Effects in Behavioral Research.* New York: Appleton-Century-Crofts, 1966.

Scherz, F. H. "Theory and Practice of Family Therapy," in R. W. Roberts and R. H. Nee (eds.), *Theories of Social Casework.* Chicago: University of Chicago Press, 1970, pp. 219-264.

Schwartz, E. E. and Sample, W. C. "First Findings from Midway," *Social Service Review,* Vol. 41, 1967, pp. 113-151.

Seaberg, J. "Case Recording by Code," *Social Work,* Vol. 10, 1965, pp. 92-98.

Segal, S. P. "Research on the Outcome of Social Work Therapeutic Interventions: A Review of the Literature," *Journal of Health and Social Behavior,* Vol. 13, 1972, pp. 3-17.

Selltiz, C. *et al. Research Methods in Social Relations.* New York: Holt, Rinehart and Winston, 1962.

Sherman, S. N. "Family Therapy," in F. J. Turner (ed.), *Social Work Treatment.* New York: Free Press, 1974, pp. 457-494.

Shirley, M., Baum, B. and Polsky, S. "Outgrowing Childhood's Problems: A Follow-up Study of Child Guidance Patients," *Smith College Studies in Social Work,* Vol. 11, 1940, pp. 31-60.

Siegel, S. *Nonparametric Statistics for the Behavioral Sciences.* New York: McGraw-Hill, 1956.

Simon, J. *Basic Research Methods in Social Science.* New York: Random House, 1969.

Stamm, A. "1967 Social Work Graduates: Salaries and Characteristics," *Personnel Information* (N.A.S.W.), Vol. 11, March 1968, pp. 1, 50-54.

Strean, H. S. (ed.). *Social Casework: Theories in Action.* Metuchen, N.J.: Scarecrow Press, 1971.

Stuart, R. B. "Research in Social Work: Social Casework and Social Group Work," Morris, R. (ed.), *Encyclopedia of Social Work,* Vol. 2, 16th issue. New York: N.A.S.W., 1971, pp. 1106-1122.

Suchman, E. *Evaluative Research.* New York: Russell Sage Foundation, 1967.

Tait, C. D. and Hodges, E. F. *Delinquents, Their Families and the Community.* Springfield, Illinois: Charles C Thomas, 1962.

Teuber, H. and Powers, E. "Evaluating Therapy in a Delinquency Prevention Program," *Psychiatric Treatment,* Vol. 21, 1953, pp. 138-147.

Tripodi, T., Fellin, P., and Meyer, H. S. *Assessment of Social Research.* Itasca, Illinois: F. E. Peacock Publishers, Inc., 1969.

Tropp, E. "Expectation, Performance and Accountability," *Social Work,* Vol. 19, 1974, pp. 139-149.

Truax, C. and Carkhuff, R. R. *Toward Effective Counseling and Psychotherapy.* Chicago: Aldine, 1967.

Truax, C. and Mitchell, K. "Research on Certain Therapist Interpersonal Skills in Relation to Process and Outcome," Bergin, A. and Garfield, S. (eds.), *Handbook of Psychotherapy and Behavior Change.* New York: John Wiley and Sons, Inc., 1971, pp. 299-344.

Tsoi, L. "Marital Therapy: An Integrative Model" (mimeo), Honolulu: University of Hawaii, 1972.

Turner, F. J. (ed.). *Social Work Treatment.* New York: Free Press, 1974.

Ubell, E. "Social Casework Fails Test," *New York Herald Tribune,* October 4, 1964.

Wattie, B. "Evaluating Short-Term Casework in a Family Agency," *Social Casework,* Vol. 54, 1973, pp. 609-616.

Webb, A. P. and Riley, P. "Effectiveness of Casework with Young Female Probationers," *Social Casework,* Vol. 50, November, 1970, pp. 566-572.

Weiss, C. (ed.). *Evaluating Action Programs.* Boston: Allyn and Bacon, 1972.

Wells, R. A., Dilkes, T. C. and Trivelli, N. "The Results of Family Therapy: A Critical Review of the Literature," *Family Process,* Vol. 11, 1972, pp. 189-207.

Wilkinson, B. "A Statistical Consideration in Psychological Research," *Psychological Bulletin,* Vol. 48, 1951, pp. 156-158.

Wilson, R. "An Evaluation of Intensive Casework Impact," *Public Welfare,* Vol. 25, 1967, pp. 301-306.

Witmer, H. L. and Keller, J. "Outgrowing Childhood Problems: A Study of the Value of Child Guidance Treatment," *Smith College Studies in Social Work,* Vol. 13, 1942, pp. 74-90.

Zax, M. and Klein, A. "Measurement of Personality and Behavior Changes Following Psychotherapy," *Psychological Bulletin,* Vol. 57, 1960, pp. 435-448.

PART II DISCUSSION

The central finding of a social research
study has a disturbing effect when at variance with commonly accepted values. For
some, the finding then becomes a challenge
to be disputed phrase by phrase; for others,
a challenge to reexamine assumptions on
which the values rest.

—GORDON BROWN
The Multi-Problem Dilemma

CHAPTER 7 A CAUTIONARY CHEER:
Some Reservations Regarding the Interpretation of Findings

WILLIAM C. BERLEMAN

Associate Professor
School of Social Work
University of Washington
Seattle, Washington

O NE GOOD THING about having amassed a body of research findings which cumulatively depict social work services to be ineffective is that we have, at the very least, something tangible at which to look. Granted, in overall configuration the spectacle is dismal, as Fischer makes painfully clear. Nonetheless, it was not too long ago that students of social work research had to content themselves primarily with the study of models for the conducting of evaluative research because, with some few exceptions, little rigorous research had actually been carried out. The "affluent" 1950's and 1960's witnessed an enthusiasm for social services of all types and a more subdued but not insignificant passion for evaluative research that put some of the services "to the test." The indifferent results of these tests—that is, the tested services could not be shown to enhance the social performance of experimental, or "treated" populations, over that of matched control, or "untreated" populations—have thrown professional social work into a querulous funk. In the thin gray light of the 1970's, social workers are now wrestling with the dispiriting but altogether necessary questions: Are these results to be believed? And if so, where do we go from here?

The first question is largely technical in nature, the second prophetic. In restricting his review to those studies which employed rigorous methodological standards in the assessment of the tested services and the care with which he points out possible pitfalls even where this methodology was employed, Fischer adequately answers the technical question: Yes, the findings are to be believed if one has faith that rational processes are appropriate in the evaluation of social work services. Most of Fischer's effort here is directed toward answering the technical question, but he is not at all indifferent to the second, or prophetic question: If we accept the findings, then where does social work practice go from here?

Unfortunately, the author provides us with little more than a hint or two. This is a pity, because intruding in this much needed review is an overweening desire to make a case against "social casework." Perhaps if the author had stated clearly the service mode that he predicts will lead to an era of successful service outcomes, the reader could better understand his wish to do in "social casework" so thoroughly. In any event, his eagerness to construct an altogether damning case against "social casework" runs counter to a purely dispassionate appraisal of the accumulated evidence, and the reader is disserved in not having brought to full view the object of the author's ardor for which he makes questionable sacrifices. In reading Fischer's review as in reading the research itself, the reader must, therefore, assess "the extent to which the bias of the investigator . . . his or her desire to prove or demonstrate some point . . . distorts the conclusion. . . ." The words are Fischer's own, and like most of us, he appears to have some bias.

A more even-handed review would probably have led readers to reach on their own much the same conclusion toward which he so eagerly pushes them. After all, the outcomes of most of the experiments he reviews clearly support the contention that many social work services are indeed ineffective. Apparently, however, this finding is not sufficient, for in addition the author would persuade us on two additional points: (1) All seventeen of the studies reviewed employed a similar treatment methodology, and (2) on balance this treatment produced detrimental results.

Fischer's argument suffers as he strains to document these two final contentions.

Taking first his assertion that there is "justification for considering as basically similar the core of the services offered in these several studies"; that the "studies suggest a psychodynamic orientation"; that this eventuates in "the documented tendency for caseworkers to treat all clients virtually the same way," namely "social casework"; ergo, that "the services provided in these projects . . . were above all else, clearly social casework." Considering the stern caution with which Fischer admonishes his researchers to make step-by-step inferences, it is curious that he can so quickly collapse the services of all of these studies into a single "no-matter-how-you-cut-it-it-still-comes-out-psychiatric-casework" category. Actually social casework arising from psychoanalytic theory did not significantly characterize the services of a number of these projects, particularly the "delinquency" studies.

Cambridge-Somerville, for example, was the conception of Dr. Cabot, whose orientation to service rested upon "moral suasion" transmitted through "the contagion of the highest personalities," who recognized, among other things, "our dependence on God" (Powers & Witmer, 1951, p. 94). While workers for the project could be, and many were, professional social workers, this was not a prerequisite for employment; foremost was the requirement that the worker show "enthusiasm and zeal for helping others" and had the capacity "to be a friend." Each counselor was permitted to follow his or her persuasion, which included "the most modern development of social work . . ." for some workers, but certainly not for others. Witmer, an evaluator of the program and an exponent of psychiatric casework, characterized the service as the provision "of an adult 'friend' who will stand by . . . through thick and thin" (Powers & Witmer, 1951, p. 573). If service so described can be brought under the umbrella of casework resting upon psychoanalytic theory—and clearly Witmer does not shelter it there—then psychoanalytic theory and techniques have even more of a rubbery reach then generally believed.

In Miller's Mid-City Project, the service orientation was derived largely from the sociological tenets of Thrasher and Shaw upon which were grafted the *"ad hoc"* procedures arising from the New York City Youth Board's "Street Clubs" programs. As Miller, an anthropologist, wrote, "By 1957 the corner-group worker method as a distinctive technique was being employed as a major feature of over twenty-five delinquency control programs in about a dozen American cities," and this "technique" characterized the service in his project (Miller, 1957). During the 1950's it was generally conceded that psychiatric casework, with its introspective client ruminations transpiring in the quiet cubicles of passive therapists, was unlikely to flourish amid the noisy bustle, deceptive gamesmanship and occasional calls to arms that distinguished adolescent gangs claiming street corner "turf."

Finally, in neither of the Atlantic Street Center studies was a psychiatric orientation of any consequence. The views of such sociologists as Sutherland, Reckless, Merton, and particularly, Cloward and Ohlin were far more influential (Berleman, Seaberg & Steinburn, 1972). When in describing the service of these studies it was said that "insight-oriented discussions of the problem situations various members had been involved in during the week," insight referred to teasing apart situational configurations (not personality configurations) and to exploring ways the situation could be manipulated to realize different outcomes.

In sum, the collapsing of disparate service modes into a global category labeled "social casework," and claiming that in turn this category rests exclusively upon psychoanalytic tenets does violence both to the facts and to the very discriminatory functions research is meant to serve. Fischer is too quick to characterize any service having a reliance upon "talk" as "social casework"; talk is a medium that can be put to many distinctive uses; "social casework" implies talk, but talk does not necessarily imply "social casework." The sheer probability of having all seventeen of these studies fall neatly within his single service mode is unlikely in the extreme given the many different factors—settings, client populations, worker idiosyncracies, and the like—that distinguished the studies one from another.

Nonetheless, the reader is to be persuaded on this score, and to be convinced further that this single service mode produced detrimental results. Again there is a straining to make this point, and I will cite only an instance. In the first Atlantic Street experiment (1967), Fischer's "reanalysis" of the data relating to frequency of school disciplinary offenses reveals that the control subjects were performing significantly better than the experimental subjects, and indeed the data provided by the researchers show this to be so. But what is omitted in this reanalysis is the fact that each occurrence of a disciplinary offense is unlikely to be as severe in nature as every other disciplinary offense. To accept only the frequency of disciplinary contacts without reference to the severity of those contacts means that "chewing gum and eating candy" is indistinguishable from "breaking or damaging school property." Such a proposition is tenuous. Severity and frequency should be considered together in an adequate analysis of the data.

Now in constructing a simple 2-by-2 matrix in which frequency is one axis and the weighted severity scores is the other, it can be seen that in addition to low frequency/low severity and high frequency/high severity that low frequency/high severity and high frequency/low severity are logical possibilities. In fact, these latter possibilities were observed outcomes in the first Atlantic Street Center experiment: in school disciplinary matters control subjects had low frequency but high severity while experimentals had high frequency but low severity. Users of research should ponder the question: Is it "better" to have the severity of a group's disciplinary contacts lowered when the number of disciplinary contacts for that group will increase or to have severity increase though the frequency of contacts is reduced? At the very least, the question is ambiguous, and can be argued convincingly either way. Certainly the outcome does not lend clear-cut evidence buttressing the indictment against "social casework," which, in any event, the Center did not see as its predominant service mode.

Conclusion

The foregoing is not meant either to make a brief for "social casework" as Fischer defines it, for the findings arising from studies utilizing this service mode are not encouraging, nor to discredit the thrust of much of his analysis, for his standards for evaluation are high. These standards are, however, compromised to the extent he is bent upon making a devastating attack upon "social casework," an attack that a more temperate assessment of the accumulated evidence shows to be without the power with which he would invest it.

Also, it tends to obscure some of the more telling arguments he makes in regard to the services evaluated in these studies. Whatever the theoretical views informing the services tested, the services actually given clients are poorly documented. Because theories favored by social workers have usually been those which purport to explain the wellsprings of client behavior, these theories have had little to say concretely about how one intervenes to modify that behavior. As the sociologist Albert Cohen put it: ". . . it does not necessarily follow directly, from a unified theory of deviance and control, how one goes about deliberately structuring the interaction process so as to manipulate, in the desired way, the variables affecting the production and reduction of deviance" (Cohen, 1966, p. 114).

This difficulty is not peculiar to the psychoanalytic theory underlying "social casework," but pertains as well to a range of sociological theory stressing social, rather than personality, configurations as the true locus of "the problem." The considerable fuzziness surrounding the components of social services can more adequately be explained by the fact that the theories social workers rely upon permit by inference so much latitude in their responses. While "social casework" derived from psychoanalytic theory exhibits this difficulty, it does not monopolize it, and Fischer could have aided his readers in showing how pervasive the difficulty is regardless of theoretical orientations. Even simple division of the services tested into "social casework" and "others" would have brought this out.

I assume Fischer will address at another time the question of where these discouraging research findings point. His glancing reference to Paul's elegant bit of research relating to the significant reduction of anxiety associated with public speaking through the use of behavioral learning techniques (specifically, desensitization) probably gives some hint as to his idea where social work ought to be headed. Unquestionably behavioral techniques begin to meet the serious problems traditional social work services have posed for the conducting of rigorous evaluative research. Moreover, as Fischer's review of the research shows, social workers should not be reluctant to incorporate behavioral techniques, for social workers appear to have little to lose.

It is to be hoped that social workers employing behavioral techniques will soon submit their efforts to the kind of testing Fischer outlines. His argument for the superiority of experiments utilizing matched experimental and control groups over such evaluative procedures as single-case, before-after studies is to my mind convincing. Whatever quarrel I have with Fischer's quarrel with "social casework," I do not question his procedural guide for conducting research of the highest order and his contention that *all* modes of service must come under these strict procedures if we are to discover which among them is truly beneficial.

REFERENCES

Berleman, W. C., Seaberg, J. R. and Steinburn, T. W. "The Delinquency Prevention Experiment of the Seattle Atlantic Street Center: A Final Evaluation," *Social Service Review*, Vol. 46, no. 3, September 1972, pp. 325-328.

Cohen, A. K. *Deviance and Control.* Englewood Cliffs, New Jersey: Prentice-Hall, Inc., 1966, p. 114.

Miller, W. B. "The Impact of a Community Group Work Program on Delinquent Corner Groups," *Social Service Review*, Vol. 31, no. 4, December 1957, p. 406.

Powers, E. and Witmer, H. *An Experiment in the Prevention of Delinquency: The Cambridge-Somerville Youth Study.* New York: Columbia University Press, 1951, p. 94.

CHAPTER 8 A BRIEF COMMENT:
Evaluating the Effectiveness of An Unspecified "Casework" Treatment in Producing Change

JEROME COHEN

Professor, School of Social Welfare
University of California, Los Angeles
Los Angeles, California
with the assistance of Dolores Barnes, Rose Cohn and Alice Trevedi*

JOEL FISCHER has again suggested the importance of the need for evaluation of social casework practice. In calling for commitment to evaluative research which uses scientific method and experimental design to judge the success or failure of social work intervention, he voices the desire of many in the social work profession to increase professional competence by systematically evaluating treatment methods. He asks, "Can a caseworker's commitment be demonstrated in practice?" This is not a frivolous question, but one with enormous potential impact and implication for the profession and for the programs in which casework services are offered to those who experience serious life problems. In order to evaluate the effectiveness of casework, considerable attention has been paid to issues of scientific rigor in the design, methodology and analysis used in the relatively few experimental studies which met a specified set of re-

* The reanalysis of the studies first identified in the original Fischer article (Fischer, 1973) was carried out during a doctoral seminar on evaluative research at the University of California, Los Angeles, School of Social Welfare with the three students and Professor Cohen.

quirements. Fischer then carried out a secondary analysis of the reported research.

I am in general agreement with Fischer's stated goal. In order to satisfy my own notions of experimental design, I accepted this opportunity to examine the studies used in Fischer's analysis and further, to comment upon the adequacy of the conclusions regarding the important issue of casework effectiveness. The introduction recognizes that social casework comprises the largest segment of the social work profession and practice. The analysis therefore bears the burden of a particularly heavy responsibility for careful conclusions.

1. Did the majority of the social work research examined by Fischer meet the criteria of experimental methodology?
2. Do the majority of studies, therefore, provide valid data for Fischer's secondary analysis?
3. Did Fischer apply to his own analysis the rigor he requires of the investigators whose work he examined?

Prior to examining seventeen experimentally "controlled" studies, Fischer presents a well-developed formulation of the necessary conditions to determine effectiveness relating a specific treatment to a specific outcome. Treatment and outcome here are presumably related to each other by some theoretical formulation. In this section he is concerned with the various technical aspects of the application of rigor to experimental design, and especially with the frequently repeated injunction to use appropriate control groups and to insure that measures of *between* group differences are used rather than measuring differences *within* groups. Frequent mention of this injunction appears to indicate that Fischer believes this is the most fundamental issue of experimental rigor. It is evident that the research which is cited too frequently dealt with these concerns inadequately. However, I would argue that Fischer has avoided mention of some more critical issues concerning the fundamental nature of experiments and has thus failed to apply to his own analysis the same rigor which he demands of the research which he examined.

A small section in the latter part of the book attempts to deal, but quite unconvincingly, I believe, with some basic criticisms of his analysis by others. These are mainly concerned with the *other* conditions necessary to carry out *rigorous* experimental design. The most important of these conditions are that the treatment or independent variable be clearly defined and that the nature of the outcome variable (s) be theoretically possible of achievement through the manipulation of the treatment variable. Without such conditions, there is no basis for experimentation leading to acceptable conclusions about the effectiveness of a given treatment. The claim that a lack of significant change in outcome measures makes the specification of more precise inputs unnecessary is unwarranted. An unspecified and inconsistent treatment may negate or prevent any possible changes which might, with more precise measures, have resulted. It is not enough to say, "Well, that is the best we can do right now because of the limitations of the state of the treatment variable at the moment." The book relies heavily upon scientific method and presumably wishes to avoid polemics and personal values committed to the use or rejection of any particular approach to social work practice.

The introduction states, "Hundreds of agencies across the United States, employing thousands of people, expending millions of dollars, are engaged in countless man-hours of effort to bring casework services to those who need and desire them." Given this condition, it is unquestionably true that there exists a responsibility for evaluating the outcomes of these services. Ultimately it is the research expert upon whose shoulders the responsibility for accuracy in evaluative research must lie. In collaboration with a *willing* professional community, the investigator must assure effective conceptualization and operationalization of both the treatment and the outcome to be evaluated by creating a research design which demands such rigor and can be satisfied with no less. The period of "wild analysis" in casework should not be repeated by "wild analysis" in research. Reaching conclusions about casework effectiveness from the existing data as presented comes close to that style.

While appropriate statistical analyses applied to research results and the inclusion of randomly designed control groups are extremely important, there is still room for variation and approximation as exemplified by the quasiexperimental designs suggested by Campbell and Stanley (1969). However, in my opinion, there is *no* possibility of any experiment at all if there is not a consistent controlled treatment ingredient which can be characterized as a similar class of events to that later identified in multiple studies. This condition is particularly important in the present case since this series of experimental studies is used to characterize in firm and conclusive terms the effectiveness of all casework.

There were differences in the kind of casework treatment used in the various experiments as described in the studies under examination. Some involved all professionally trained social workers while others included some untrained social workers or representatives of other professions. The acceptance of a standard that professionally trained social workers be responsible for "at least 50 percent of the treatment" is inadequate, particularly when not separating the results and effects of each "unspecified" input. This can only compound the possible errors in conclusions about effectiveness. And when Fischer gives up on evaluating casework itself and uses the studies to evaluate professional caseworkers, he is in even greater difficulty. The methods of choosing these particular caseworkers seriously affects any generalizability of the results. Throughout the book, Fischer moves back and forth on this issue trying to justify the applicability of the chosen studies as legitimate examples from which to conclude that "casework" or "caseworkers" have not been proven effective. For me, at least, he has not made his case. I am in agreement with Fischer that "the emphasis on objectively assessing the effects of practice is at the core of professional accountability." Permitting the treatment which is being evaluated to be so loosely defined is questionable research practice and itself raises the issue of professional accountability.

Not only were most of the practices poorly defined, which Fischer viewed as an advantage in terms of the flexibility thus afforded the profession, but the outcome measures, with a few exceptions, were unrelated to any theoretical framework suggesting the positive effect of such practice upon a predicted outcome. As an example, most of the studies attempt to evaluate the reduction of "delinquency" through "casework treatment." Research in the field of juvenile delinquency during the past twenty years has demonstrated that most delinquency cannot be reduced through casework intervention since delinquent behavior in large part is related to social structural factors as well as to different ways of defining, observing and counting delinquent behavior.

The heart of my argument, then, questions the conclusions as well as the not so rigorous method of this study of existing experimental research into casework effectiveness. I am in opposition to Fischer's willingness to evaluate these experiments by applying vague and differing definitions of the independent variable—casework—and dependent variables or outcome measures which are associated with behaviors frequently theoretically impossible to change through casework because of more powerful social forces which affect the outcomes. It is the responsibility of the professional, as research critic, to identify such problems and to suggest ways in which limitations in method and definition may be overcome. There is a need for clarification of method integrated with theory which suggests goals which can be reached with a specified mode of treatment. Without these conditions, evaluation based upon experimental method is meaningless, for the essence of experimentation is lacking—*control* of the treatment and the intervening conditions which affect the outcome. It would have been more logical and responsible, I believe, for Fischer to have pointed out that an experimental evaluation of casework is not possible until these criteria are met. There are components of professional casework methodology which can, at present, be clearly articulated and theoretically explicated in regard to changes which can logically be related to casework intervention. In terms of design, Briar (1973) has recently suggested the use of research designs utilizing the case as its own control rather than comparing group means in relation to various movement scales or other changes in behavior identified as the dependent variables. And it may well be that this approach will be most fruitful at present.

Finally, it is the willingness to accept and indeed, apparently to justify the lack of clarity in definition of professional social casework as exemplified in these studies that is primarily at issue. Our understanding of the control necessary for experiments is quite different. I believe that Fischer has accepted at face value many studies which illustrate a broad and poorly defined treatment; offered by "a *majority* of people with professional social work education"; and a set of dependent variables or outcomes which the treatment under investigation cannot produce, even if more clearly identified. It is not his concern about evaluation that is the basis of our difference of opinion. I share with him that ambition. However, there is no advantage to be gained by prematurely concluding that rigorous experimental research has evaluated casework and found it to be an ineffective method of treatment. The evidence simply does not warrant this conclusion. It is also true that the opposite conclusion has not yet been proven either, except through what has been termed by some, the "practice wisdom" of the profession and by others, its "folklore."

Before reviewing some of the experimental studies reported in both the earlier article and this book, it seems appropriate to identify several other issues of concern related to the conditions under which the reported research is reflective of "ineffectiveness." First, Fischer reports his observation that caseworkers seem to have developed a rather widespread lack of appreciation for scientific study and research, especially when results of that research are "not to their liking." In this light it is interesting to note that among the seventeen studies reported, Fischer found that the four which claimed effectiveness had "serious design flaws" in respect to *possible* noncomparable experimental control groups and poor statistical procedures, mainly in the use of limited outcome data. The other thirteen studies showing negative results regarding casework effectiveness were not identified as having *design problems* or *analysis problems* or *instrument problems* or *conceptual problems serious enough to suggest great caution* in accepting their results and conclusions about casework effectiveness. I wonder what the probability is of finding such a perfect correlation between "poor" research and positive effectiveness and "good" research design and negative effectiveness results. Could it be that positive results were not "to the author's liking"?

In the section on "Defining Casework" Fischer correctly identifies the key problem for experimental design and notes that the existence of vagueness of definition of casework is potentially dysfunctional for social work as a professional endeavor. He further recognizes that it "precludes caseworkers, and correspondingly, casework researchers, from specifying the methods and techniques of practice, and hence expectable outcomes and goals." He later shifts to a position of noting the "advantages" of such vagueness and once again, when the moment is suitable, at the end of the book, returns to the prior position—*it is not so good to be so vague.* Unfortunately, the important work that Fischer is engaged in is marred by such obvious use of the data to make one's own point.

Fischer has an interesting manner of evaluating the research designs used in this book. When the results are positive, he cautions against accepting the intervention as the basis of the improvement. However, even when the outcome instruments' reliability and validity are unknown factors, he is willing to accept face validity. When prevention was the goal and outcome indicators were evaluated in the same manner as remedial or rehabilitative efforts would be, Fischer still "feels comfortable" in accepting that as valid indicators. The converging evidence seems to indicate that Fischer is setting up the justification for the negative effectiveness results he later finds.

There is little question that Joel Fischer's work has stimulated interest in the conduct of evaluative social work research aimed at a better understanding of the conditions under which casework is or is not effective. He concluded that the studies he reviewed demonstrated the ineffectiveness of casework. His claim to have used methods of analysis based upon canons of scientific rigor which provide validity for his conclusions is what is being questioned.

SOCIAL WORK AND SCIENCE

The field of social work as a professional activity must ascribe to the methods of science in developing and evaluating its practice and knowledge. It is that commitment which distinguishes social work as a helping profession from other types of helping. The commitment to science has been described by Briar and Miller (1971) as more than an attitude of mind, but a *commitment to a methodology of inquiry*. The paradigm or assumptions under which social work has practiced since the turn of the century is that of observation, diagnosis and treatment, which Briar suggests is derived from the paradigm of science—observation, hypothesis and experiment (Briar & Miller, 1971, p. 81).

Scientific inquiry implies a rational process for gathering knowledge, which is held to be tentative and subject to revision. Basic to most scientific thought today is Empiricism, the philosophical doctrine that all human knowledge is derived from experience. In science, this doctrine is interpreted to mean that generalizations about the world can be considered to be valid only after being tested by objective techniques and verified by sense experience, using research designs which permit specific conclusions as a result of *strict* adherence to the rules of inquiry used.

Social work's commitment to the methods of science carries a commitment to empirical research and an elaboration of theory, implicit or explicit, underlying the research questions or hypotheses being tested. Fischer's conclusions regarding casework effectiveness were based on his analysis of studies which met his minimal design criteria. In order to be included in his sample, the studies must have:

a) control procedures so that causal inference can be made;*

b) the service must have been provided by professional caseworkers.

The focus of the remainder of this chapter is a reanalysis of the research design and methodology of ten of the eleven studies selected by Fischer and used in an earlier article and this book. In

---

* The effect of these controls is to guard against threats to *internal validity* . . . which affects the confidence with which one may assert that the intervention did, in fact, produce the observed effects . . . and *external validity* . . . which affects the confidence with which one may generalize from the results of study to a specific population. (Stuart, 1971) .

this way, we can examine the conclusions drawn by Fischer of the studies from which he generalized as to the effectiveness of social casework.†

Due to the dearth of experimental research in the field of social casework, it is not surprising that so few studies were uncovered by Fischer which met his minimal criteria for inclusion. He rightly pointed out that experimental rigor was the exception rather than the rule. However, once he accepted a reduction in rigor in the criteria, the validity of his findings are similarly reduced. Research rigor functions to strengthen the findings for purposes of explanation and generalizability. If design rigor is weak, so too are the findings and the secondary analysis of these evaluations should so indicate.

RESEARCH DESIGNS

Kahn describes a research design as the "logical strategy of a study" which "deals with the rationale by which a *specific set of procedures,* including both data collection and analysis are expected to meet the particular requirements of a study" (Kahn, 1960). Weiss points out that the classic design for evaluation has been ". . . in exhortation, if less often in practice . . . the experimental model" (Weiss, 1972, p. 60). In experimental design, the hypothesis is explicitly stated at the operational level, conceptually clear, uses empirical referents, and implies a cause-effect relationship. Close, scholarly, scientific scrutiny of the research procedures is a prerequisite to acceptability or rejectibility of the findings (Kahn, 1960, p. 80).

RESEARCH DESIGN AND METHODOLOGY OF THE STUDIES

The designs of the studies selected by Fischer, must meet the demands of experimental design. These demands include:

a) *the formulation of a refutable hypothesis;*

---

† Fischer implied that his conclusions concerning casework effectiveness were based on social work research findings which exemplified the rigorous use of scientific method. His insistence upon evaluation of casework effectiveness through an analysis of experimentally designed social work research, the most rigorous of research designs, led to a look at the rules of scientific method and the application of those rules to the analysis of each study.

b) *the precise specifications, in reliable and valid terms, of the independent variable (the treatment or input) and the dependent variable (means of measuring changes or output);* and

c) *the development of an experimental design that will reduce the likelihood of interpretive error.* (Stuart, 1971, p. 1108)

When using an experimental design, the aim or purpose of the research is to test a hypothesis of a causal relationship between variables, for the purpose of producing empirical generalizations (verified hypotheses). An experimental design attempts to establish cause-effect relationships by minimizing the influence of variables, other than the independent variable, through the use of random assignment of subjects to experimental and control groups (Tripodi *et al.*, 1969, p. 22; Kahn, 1960, p. 55). What is the evidence in the ten studies reviewed?

Brown (1968)* did a comparative study between two treatment models to improve family functioning; Webb and Riley (1970) attempted to improve life adjustment. Both dealt with hypotheses regarding the effects of casework treatment (input) using specific instruments to indicate the effects (output).

Five of the studies have hypotheses dealing implicitly or explicitly with prevention of delinquency. Berleman and Steinburn (1967) were attempting to tighten up experimental research procedures, and define more rigorously the population at risk. They *continuously cautioned* that their project did not represent a test of service effectiveness. Craig and Furst (1965) successfully demonstrated the validity of the Glueck scale for prediction of delinquency. Although the Glueck scale shows delinquency to be a function of the lack of family cohesion, the researchers designed a secondary hypothesis which dealt with the prevention of delinquency through casework and intervention treating only the child, ignoring the family dynamics. Meyer, Borgatta and Jones (1965) have an implicit hypothesis that social work treatment can *prevent*

---

* References to the specific studies are available in the list of references at the end of Part I.

girls identified as potential delinquents from getting into trouble. Miller (1962) hypothesized that a reduction in delinquent behavior was possible *through a total community delinquency control* program effecting community, family and gang. Powers and Witmer (1951) hypothesized that "by wise and friendly counsel, supplemented by social casework techniques . . . young children might be encouraged to make the most of their potential assets and become useful law-abiding citizens."

Two studies, Geismar and Krisberg (1967), and Mullen, Chazen and Feldstein (1972), use a treatment intervention to *prevent* either delinquency or further family disruption. Casework treatment effectiveness was measured as the prevention of future delinquency or of future family dependency. The hypotheses explicitly stated that the interventions were specifically to prevent delinquency and dependency, so it would be possible for a family to show "improvement," but for the treatment to still be adjudged "ineffective" if there were delinquency or dependency in the future.

The final study, Blenkner *et al.* (1971) developed an initial hypothesis stating that casework would lead to less disordered behavior in aged persons who require protective services. There was confusion in the design because of its dual purpose. As a *demonstration of the need for services* and the *effectiveness of casework interventions,* the design did not logically take both into account. In addition, the authors seem to have been moved by their initial findings of a higher death rate among certain "treated" clients to add a follow-up study onto the original demonstration/evaluation project, making three studies in one.

SPECIFICATION OF INPUT AND OUTPUT VARIABLES

On examination of the treatment variables, in three of the studies, the dominant intervention was group work, not casework. This is not serious except that Fischer never talks about the ineffectiveness of group work (Berleman and Steinburn, 1967, p. 417; Meyer, Borgatta and Jones, 1965, p. 96; Powers and Witmer, 1951, pp. 3-4). In the Powers and Witmer study, professional caseworkers were not universally used. Most of the services were provided by untrained workers or other disciplines.

In five of the studies, casework was the dominant intervention (Craig and Furst, 1965, p. 167; Blenkner *et al.*, 1971, p. 489-490; Brown, 1968, p. 28; Mullen, Chazin and Feldstein, 1972, p. ii; Webb and Riley, 1970, p. 567). In two others, casework was one of a variety of interventions (Miller, 1962, p. 188; Geismar and Krisberg, 1967, p. 335).

REDUCTION OF LIKELIHOOD OF INTERPRETIVE ERROR

The experimental design is chosen for its *rigor and inflexibility*. It does not permit changes of the independent variable after the research has been initiated. It requires the use of randomization procedures in selection of the sample (if possible), and random assignment of subjects to experimental and to control groups. Sample size must be stipulated in order to assure within a given degree of certainty that the sample findings do not differ by more than a specified amount from the total population. All important variables are assumed to be known and rigorously controlled.

Some of the studies invalidated their own conclusions by changing the independent variable (treatment) in the middle of the study (Blenkner *et al.*, 1971; Meyer, Borgatta and Jones, 1965). Others biased their results in the sampling process by introducing biased samples through such actions as introducing extraneous subjects into the sample (Berleman and Steinburn, 1967); or nonrandom assignment to groups (Miller, 1962; Powers and Witmer, 1951; Berleman and Steinburn, 1967). Due to the fact that none of the studies have been replicated, the reliability of the findings is also to be held as problematic.

Since all of the studies spoke to specific populations with a definite skewing on the side of young children, generalizability of results beyond specific populations addressed is restricted at best, and dubious, to say the least. The failure of most researchers to define concisely the treatment variable, makes it almost impossible to ascribe any outcome to the treatment, thereby invalidating any conclusions about a causal relationship between input and outcome.

All the above not withstanding, the research analyzed above makes a contribution to the field. The research serves to remind us of the need to clarify the theoretical bases and shortcomings in the field, and to sharpen our ability to conceptualize the research tasks ahead. It also shows the willingness of the profession of social work to hold itself accountable for what it does.

RESEARCH DESIGN AND METHODOLOGY USED BY FISCHER IN ANALYZING STUDIES

Fischer purports to have set up a review of research findings in such a way as to generate reliable conclusions which can be scrutinized and tested by independent investigation. Our analysis indicates that there is reason to question the validity of the conclusions drawn by the present research. In the absence of valid data, it is difficult to see how Fischer could make a valid statement regarding the effectiveness of social casework. Having accepted what might be considered conclusions of questionable validity, Fischer presents them as justification for his generalization that casework is ineffective. Such a generalization is not justified.

SUMMARY

Fischer's conclusions regarding the ineffectiveness of casework based on "scientific analysis" has created a great deal of controversy within the field of social work, as evidenced in the *Letters to the Editor* in the issues of *Social Work* following the printing of his article (Fischer, 1973). The contribution of Fischer's work can perhaps be best measured by the degree to which it makes apparent to the profession the limitations of our practice and knowledge base, but also causes us to be skeptical and to commit ourselves to question results given in the name of scientific analysis. It may be that greater familiarity with the scientific method, its logic and its limitations will allow us to be critical of sweeping generalizations based on data of limited validity. More importantly, it may point up the need for the profession of social work to involve itself with greater concern as to the definition and limitations of casework practice, so that we no longer find acceptable a statement that social casework practice is whatever an M.S.W. social worker does. One can neither describe nor evaluate a variable which is so broad and ill-defined even when cloaked with the guise of scientific methodology.

I end this brief chapter by quoting Fischer's beginning, "The entire thrust of science is a movement toward freedom from misconception" (Ullmann & Krasner, 1969).

REFERENCES

Briar, S. and Miller, H. *Problems and Issues in Social Casework.* New York: Columbia, 1971.

Briar, S. "Effective Social Work Intervention in Direct Practice: Implications for Education," Briar, S. *et al.* (eds.), *Facing the Challenge.* New York: CS-WE, 1973, pp. 17-30.

Campbell, D. T. and Stanley, J. C. *Experimental and Quasi-Experimental Designs for Research.* Chicago: Rand-McNally and Co., 1969.

Fischer, J. "Is Casework Effective? A Review." *Social Work,* Vol. 18, 1973, pp. 5-20.

Kahn, A. J. "The Design of Research," Polansky, N. (ed.), *Social Work Research.* Chicago: University of Chicago Press, 1960, pp. 48-73.

Stuart, R. D. "Research in Social Work: Social Casework and Social Group Work," Morris, R. (ed.), *Encyclopedia of Social Work,* Vol. 2, 16th Issue, New York: N.A.S.W., 1971, pp. 1106-1122.

Tripodi, T. P. *et al. Assessment of Social Research.* Itasca, Ill.: F. E. Peacock, 1969.

Ullmann, L. P. and Krasner, L. *A Psychological Approach to Abnormal Behavior.* Englewood Cliffs, N.J.: Prentice-Hall, 1969.

Weiss, C. (ed.) *Evaluating Action Programs.* Boston: Allyn and Bacon, 1972.

CHAPTER 9 THE EFFECTIVENESS OF EFFECTIVENESS RESEARCH

HARVEY L. GOCHROS

Professor, School of Social Work
University of Hawaii
Honolulu, Hawaii

DEAR JOEL:

I was pleased that you chose to ask me to react to your ideas and your collation of research on casework effectiveness. Yet, I probably share some of the reactions of many of those who have challenged the value of your efforts. Briefly, I question if the presentation and sensationalization of alleged evidence that casework does not "work" really helps our field or does it justice, and more important, in the long run, does it improve the quality of the services we deliver?

I am aware of your belief that such a point of view is a product of the defensiveness of the old guard preserving the sanctity of the status quo. I don't think that is true. As both a practitioner and educator, I am well aware of the limitations of casework both as it is conceptualized in general, and, in varying degrees, as currently practiced by individuals. Much of what we do can and should be improved upon, and I am as impatient as you that seemingly useful approaches and technologies are sometimes agonizingly slow to filter down into social work education and practice, while outmoded myths about human behavior and ineffective casework procedures seem resistant to extinction. I doubt, however, whether a book such as this is an effective vehicle to bring about these changes.

Now I also know that no one likes bad news, and as a consequence, no one likes the bearer of bad news. And this book is full of bad news. My objection is not to your *right* to report this bad news, or even to your perception of your *responsibility* to report the bad news. I have two objections: one, the many research studies you review fail to prove what you imply, that most casework services do no good; and two, I challenge your assumption that the presentation of such conclusions, presented in simplistic terms of "either its effective or it isn't" serves to accomplish what I *think* you want to accomplish, that is, moving the field to the delivery of more effective social work services. It is because I would be contributing to that possible destructive impact that I hesitated to contribute to your book. It is because I wanted to raise this objection that I decided to do it.

The validity of the various research efforts you review will doubtlessly be challenged by other contributors to this volume far more versed than I in research methodology. However, in reviewing the research on effectiveness of professional casework included in this volume, I was particularly bothered by four areas which I think you have not adequately handled:

1. I was struck by your looseness in accepting the researchers' definition of the outcome variables, that is, what it is that would "prove" to researchers that interventions had been effective. Very few of us live a totally problemless existence, and many of the clients covered in the research projects you reported live in exceedingly difficult situations. If the only acceptable goal of casework is eradication of complex dysfunctional behaviors such as avoiding recidivism for a prisoner, eliminating poverty for persons with low income and living forevermore in a blissful marriage relationship as opposed to obtaining a divorce for those with marital conflict then I suppose that any type of intervention would prove far from effective. No profession ever has or likely will achieve complete mastery over the problems it is concerned with. Physicians have not overcome illness and death, lawyers and police have not overcome crime, and politicians have not overcome just about anything—and they've all been at it much longer than caseworkers. But there are desirable outcomes far different from those ideal cures or so-

lutions. We can still reduce suffering, and help people get more power over their environment and even over themselves. Often just helping people through the process of understanding themselves and the behavior of those around them *is* a worthwhile end in itself. Yes, Joel, some people do value such amorphous outcomes as self-awareness and enhancement of problem-solving capacity. These outcomes can generate a whole constellation of improvements in social functioning long after the caseworker and researcher have gone home. True, many of these outcomes are exceedingly difficult to measure. They are often diffuse and the "benefits" not always predictable. It is quite possible that your research shows less than effective outcomes because we have not reached the point of research methodology—and we may never reach it—where we can quantify many of the outcomes that social workers work toward achieving, whether it is reduction of anxiety, making rational decisions, reducing inappropriate guilt, or even liking oneself and others better. While measurements for such outcomes are slowly evolving, they were not yet available or for other reasons not used in many of the studies you included.

2. Many of the outcomes which were considered desirable in the eyes of the researcher were in effect the successful application of social control, for example, keeping delinquents from committing crimes, getting people off welfare and so on. While these might be legitimate goals in the eyes of the researcher, they may not be what either the social worker or the client had in mind. There are indeed behaviors which may be contrary to socially expected behaviors but are functional for particular individuals living in particular situations. We, as social workers, have moved beyond making *conformity* our overriding goal. Therefore, the effective test of outcome is the achieving of goals determined by the worker and the client, not the researcher.

3. I would raise some question about whether the "casework" being evaluated in some of the studies was indeed casework performed by professionally trained social workers. Many

of the evaluated intervention efforts were not "casework" activities *per se,* but involved group approaches, advocacy, and a variety of other social work activities. As long as the activities referred to loosely as "casework" were so poorly defined, and whether or not these were professional caseworkers engaging in group methods and other activities (as most appeared to be), or professional group workers also providing individual services, much of the research cannot be considered an accurate test of the effectiveness of "casework," *per se.*

4. I would recognize, as anyone would, that there are more and less effective social workers. The fact that there are ineffective social workers and even some who are destructive does not in any way change the fact that there also *are* highly effective social workers. However, when the outcomes are averaged, the scores of the ineffective workers will inevitably pull down the scores of the effective social workers, giving a more pallid impression of the outcomes of *all* social workers. It would be far more useful to have studies that show differential results of social workers using different types of skills with different types of problems in different types of situations.

However, even if the measures and outcomes of the studies are acceptable, I question the effectiveness of such research, and reviews of such research, to bring about desired changes. Social work is first and foremost a change profession. Therefore, I expect the research done within social work to have as its goal helping to change those phenomena that are being studied and in the final analysis to produce more effective practice. I doubt whether your efforts indeed serve the cause of improving casework effectiveness.

Research into "whether or not" casework works raises some very pragmatic issues. First and foremost, has this research and your approach to reporting this research really moved the profession? As a practice instructor I am concerned not with pure research alone but with research that guides social work practice. Therefore, I doubt whether your efforts have helped a greater number of social workers to perform with greater competence with a greater variety of clients.

There is a clear precedent for your work in the field of psychotherapy. Hans Eysenck, a generation ago pointed out the questionable outcome of a large number of therapeutic interventions resulting from more or less traditional psychotherapeutic practice. While it was shocking and well publicized, I am not sure that Eysenck, through his work, can lay claim to the advances made in many areas of psychotherapy. In fact, many of the types of psychotherapies Eysenck criticized are still very much in vogue and still attract a great many customers. Rather than having research which simply points out whether or not casework helps— a basically black and white orientation to complex interpersonal and social behavior—wouldn't it be far more constructive to study what does work, when, with whom, under what conditions? Certainly, there is no shortage of such studies in other fields. The work of Truax and Carkhuff* shows that certain relationship skills of clinicians are positively correlated with successful outcomes in a wide variety of cases. Many behaviorists have well based studies showing that certain behavioral techniques are highly effective in changing specific behavior. Even the research that you yourself report shows that there *are* situations in which *certain* types of interventions worked under *certain* conditions with *certain* populations having *certain* problems because of *certain* reasons. How much more useful it would be to have a book entitled "What Works with Whom, When?" than a book that has the rather nihilistic tone of this book, implying—but not proving—that nothing seems to work with anybody, ever.

Furthermore, if we are to assume that social workers, collectively, are people, then they must respond to the same laws of behavior that apply to other people. As you know, the best way to strengthen a response is to reinforce it when it occurs, rather than punish the person when it does *not* occur. Thus, caseworkers are more likely to respond and change their behavior according to positive reinforcement or modeling by individuals who are engag-

---

* Truax, C. and Carkhuff, R. *Toward Effective Counseling & Psychotherapy.* Chicago, Aldine, 1967.

ing in effective practice and being reinforced for it, than they are to respond to punishment for dysfunctional ("noneffective") behavior alone. In other words, if your *real* goal is to improve the performance of social work practitioners, you would be far more effective in providing data on what kinds of behaviors caseworkers could engage in which are likely to bring them positive reinforcement, i.e. effective outcomes of intervention. The nihilistic approach of this book serves neither the needs of the profession nor its consumers.

Finally, as noted earlier, a great proportion of the problems that social workers deal with do not lend themselves to neat behavioral parcels (such as committing antisocial acts, wetting one's bed or smoking too many "joints"). Much of the behavior that social workers deal with is complex and diffuse. If this were not the case, then almost all the problems social workers deal with could be handled through behavior modification, which is undeniably extremely effective in changing certain specific dysfunctional behaviors. The thrust of your approach seems to suggest that if we all start using behavior modification or similar "scientifically-based" procedures, we would all be successful. *People just are not built that way.* You seem to be operating on a premise that very much concerns me: Anything that has any meaning can be counted or measured. If it can't be counted or measured (the "test-tube syndrome") then it either doesn't exist or isn't worth considering. Certainly there are many problems that caseworkers encounter that lend themselves to counting and measuring. These may be approached through behavior modification approaches which provide useful and effective procedures.

But there are also a wide range of problems experienced by many of the people we serve which do not lend themselves to counting or measuring. I believe it is for these kinds of problems that available research has so far proven of little use. Empirical research generally requires categorization—putting "similar" events, behaviors and even interventive outcomes into neat little boxes. I know, Joel, that you abhor this categorization of people. We both teach the core conditions of interpersonal effectiveness— empathy, warmth and genuineness—which suggest the need to individualize each client, to see them as a unique totality, not just as examples of another variable to be counted. There is much we do as social workers that deals with vague problems in the areas of self actualization, self-understanding, decision making, assertiveness and the quest for meaning and joy in life. It is, perhaps, significant that a behaviorist, Arnold Lazarus, in a study entitled, "Where Do Behavior Therapists Take Their Troubles?" (*Psychological Reports*, 1971, Vol. 28, pp. 349-350), reported that many behavior therapists chose psychoanalytically-oriented therapy or some other form of self-awareness therapy when they themselves experienced social or emotional problems. Apparently, pure behavior change isn't always enough.

So, please, Joel, stop telling us that we are not doing any good. We know better and you know better. Instead, how about turning your considerable talents to showing how individual social workers using specific procedures with particular people having particular problems under particular circumstances are likely to be of most help. If you do that—if we all do that—perhaps we can get somewhere.

Aloha,
Harv

CHAPTER 10 SPECIAL PROBLEMS IN THE ASSESSMENT OF GROWTH AND DETERIORATION*

WALTER W. HUDSON

Associate Professor
George Warren Brown School of Social Work
Washington University
St. Louis, Missouri

T HROUGHOUT THE FIRST part of this volume Fischer has claimed that the benefits of casework are only putative, and he has attempted to marshal support for that thesis. More importantly, he has placed special emphasis on the moral obligation of the practitioner and the profession at large to make best use of our available scientific tools to evaluate the effectiveness of casework services. Obviously, this involves an assessment of client change with a view to demonstrating that casework services will produce positive change or growth in one or several criterion variables. Clearly, earlier optimism concerning such a demonstration has been challenged and many cases have been cited that suggest a more appropriate stance to be one of considerable skepticism regarding the benefits of casework treatment. Nonetheless, the task of demonstrating that deterioration is a function of treatment is as large as that of showing that growth in a specific problem area is also caused by treatment.

It is the thesis of this chapter that Fischer has not established many clear-cut cases to support the demise of "mighty casework." On the other hand, caseworkers may insure their own demise if

* I would like to thank Professors Martin Bloom and William Butterfield for their assistance in preparing this paper. (W. Hudson)

197

they ignore his message. Sins of research and sins of treatment have been committed in both Fischerian and non-Fischerian camps, and the remainder of this chapter points to some of the special problems that must be accounted for or dealt with in future efforts to assess or evaluate casework services.

Before turning to our major task it is necessary to set the stage for what follows. A significant portion of this chapter will consist of a reply to Fischer in the sense of taking issue with a number of his assertions about and interpretations of that portion of the research literature he has reviewed. In the first part of this text Fischer criticizes many if not all of the studies that he reviews, and appears to question their adequacy, from a scientific point of view, to demonstrate whether casework is or is not effective. Then, he appears to take the position that many of these same studies actually show that casework either does not work or that it causes client deterioration. It is simply our thesis that if a study is not scientifically adequate to show that client growth is due to treatment then it is not adequate to show that treatment has failed or that it has caused client deterioration. On the other hand, we find considerable agreement with Fischer with respect to many of the criticisms of the reviewed studies. In this regard we go beyond Fischer and claim they are simply not adequate to either support or attack casework treatment. However, in order to do that we focus, not on the particular studies in question, but the special problems that give rise to the inadequacies Fischer has noted. In other words, the predominant focus of this chapter will be upon special issues and problems related to evaluative research in general, but we shall refer occasionally to the first part of the text to make our discussion relevant to the specific studies and issues therein. In order to do this we shall look carefully at a number of the trees rather than the whole forest, and while the reader is presented with what may appear to be a set of loosely connected discussions we shall attempt to integrate them in a final summary.

CONTROL AND QUANTIFICATION

Control and quantification are without a doubt the cornerstones of modern science, and a careful reading of the first part of this text reveals that our major failures in assessing casework services lie precisely in these two areas. In this context it is important to understand that control is not equated with control groups. Rather, control means the ability to precisely define and manipulate a treatment variable in order to then examine its effect upon some outcome variable. To paraphrase Sidman (1960) we can say that control is characterized in terms of the variables that are manipulated and the consequences that follow upon such manipulation.

Perhaps the single most pernicious problem that is encountered repeatedly in experimental assessments of casework effectiveness is failure to properly define our treatment variables. If we cannot define them we certainly cannot quantify or manipulate them. When we ask, "Does casework work?" we are posing an essentially unanswerable and silly question. That is very much like asking whether medicine, religion, science, architecture, civil engineering, education, thunderstorms, magic, etc. "works." As Fischer reports in the first chapter, casework is so broadly defined that it can comfortably encompass anything the profession's gatekeepers will allow.

The simple truth is that "casework treatment" cannot be manipulated because we cannot, and probably dare not, define it in operationally specific terms as a variable. We are deceiving ourselves when we suggest that our independent variable can be manipulated by giving "casework" to some and withholding it from others. Given the definitions of casework provided in this text, such a statement means that we are doing *something* to one group of clients, withholding it from others, and then asking which one is better! Casework, as a treatment variable, has no scientifically meaningful definition and therefore cannot be used as a variable in research that is built upon scientific methods.

However desirable it may be to define casework so broadly, for nonscience purposes, such definitions cannot and have not served our efforts to utilize the tools of science in the evaluation of services provided to our clients by professional social workers. We have learned all too harshly that it is no longer adequate (it never was) to define the independent variable of an experiment as consisting of intensive versus regular casework services, professional versus nonprofessional services, casework treatment versus no case-work treatment, Rogerian versus Freudian psychotherapy, ego development versus behavior modification therapy, etc. Neither is it sufficient to use such statements as "we provided counseling services designed to help the client confront and integrate the competing motivational forces giving rise to conflict in order that he could better cope with crisis situations." Attempts to evaluate "casework" treatment, when so broadly defined, have proven to be a waste of manpower and research resources. Even if we find a study that proves "casework works" we will have learned virtually nothing that will aid in the development of our knowledge base or our treatment skills. Indeed, a review of the studies discussed by Fischer in the previous chapters of this book shows that each of them is largely based on such extremely broad definitions of the independent variable. That alone may account for the overwhelming majority of the failures to show significant gains that could be attributed to treatment.

By focusing on "casework" as an independent variable we are setting up a straw man and then tearing him down, because casework as such is not measurable or manipulable. An the other hand, we can measure and manipulate the *behaviors* of caseworkers and ask whether variations in those behaviors have measurable consequences in terms of client outcome variables. For example, we can videotape a series of treatment sessions and then count the number of times that a worker demonstrates genuine, nonpossessive empathy. We can count the number of times a worker confronts a depressive client with his or her attempts to wallow in self-pity. We can count the number of times that a worker calls employment agencies to help get a job for a welfare client. We can count the number of times that a worker gives direct advice to a client with respect to a given problem. In short, "anything that occurs, occurs with some frequency and can therefore be counted" (Gottman & Leiblum, 1974), and therein lies enormous untapped potential for the definition and quantification of treatment variables. But we must remember that "casework" does not treat clients—caseworkers treat clients, and it is ultimately their treatment behaviors that constitute the independent variables of interest. If we adopt this approach to the assessment of services we may begin to learn which behaviors of caseworkers are or are not effective in helping what types of clients with what kinds of problems in what magnitudes.

Thus far we have been discussing issues of control and quantification as they apply to the independent variables in an experiment, but an equally serious problem arises with respect to the dependent variables in social work research designed to evaluate services. Many of the studies reported in this volume define a very broad array of social problems within a single treatment population and then attempt to measure all of them as a single dependent variable. Others measure many different problems but retain each as a separate variable. Thus, the treatment problems may consist of excessive use of drugs, excessive use of alcohol, absenteeism from school, disruptive behavior in the classroom, failure to complete homework assignments, out-of-wedlock pregnancy, depression, lowered self-esteem, hostility toward superiors, fighting with peers, burglary, etc. The problem with such an approach is that it is sheer folly to presume that a single treatment method will effectively modify such a wide array of problems within a single treatment population wherein each problem is represented *in various magnitudes among the separate members*.

As with the independent variable we have tended too often to define dependent variables in broad general terms that really cannot have much scientific utility. For example, a very large number of studies have been designed to show that casework treatment can and will reduce or prevent "delinquency." Delinquency is a very big word for which there is no accepted definition and which, therefore, cannot be treated as a proper dependent variable. Of course, we can and should measure and count a huge array of individual behaviors and events, and under proper circumstances these can be used as dependent variables. However, it is a meaningless and unproductive exercise to lump them all together as a measure of "delinquency." When this happens we can hold out little hope of manipulating one or several specific and measurable independent variables and thereby control "delinquency." The same holds for other such variables as "social functioning," "illegitimacy," "mental illness," "acting out behavior," etc. At various times in our lives all of us have behaved in ways that others would regard as delinquent, illegitimate, acting-out, and mentally ill.

One of the very great weaknesses of our past research efforts consists of an almost universal failure to define *homogeneous problem populations*. In other words, we rarely if ever define a treatment population in terms of a single dependent variable, but that is precisely what we must do if we are to have any substantial success in determining which worker behaviors (treatment variables) are successful with respect to specific personal, social, and economic problems. If we define a problem population in terms of a single dependent variable (or at best a very small number of them) we can then hope to learn which of several intervention techniques does a better job of alleviating the specific problem or problems that define the population. In these terms, a homogeneous problem population is not one whose members all have the same personal, social, and economic characteristics but one whose members have *the same problems in essentially the same magnitudes* (or rates, frequencies, etc.).

Suppose, for example, that we test a pool of 100 clients using a depression scale* which has a clinical cutting score† of 30 and whose scores range from 0 to 100. Suppose further that we find their scores to be normally distributed with a mean of 22 and a standard deviation of four points where a high score indicates greater depression and a low score shows the client to be free of depression. Obviously, there is little merit in giving treatment to such a group, and even if we did we could expect very little change. Suppose, however, that we test another pool of 100 clients and find their scores to be normally distributed with a mean of 50 and a standard deviation of four points. Perhaps we can

---

* In concert with our previous discussion of multiple dependent measures we must recognize that a single scale purporting to measure a construct such as depression may itself be multidimensional, and if so the scale must be treated with analytic tools that are appropriate for such data.

† Regardless of the score range for a given instrument, a clinical cutting score represents the point on the scale above or below which the client or patient is seen as having no need for treatment.

now offer treatment for depression and determine which of several treatment methods does a better job of reducing the magnitude of depression for the group. The essential point here is that the magnitude of the problem is large enough to both warrant treatment and expect positive gains as a result of it. Moreover, the dispersion of the problem is small enough within this population that we can define it as a homogeneous one. This is a very important issue that can be further examined using a somewhat different example.

Suppose we test a third pool of clients and find their depression scores to be normally distributed with a mean of 50, but they have a standard deviation of 20 points. We no longer have a homogeneous population with respect to the dependent variable, and the analysis of data becomes much more complicated. First, a table of areas of the normal curve tells us that 28.4 percent of our clients have scores equal to or less than 20 and should not be given any treatment at all! Even if we make the mistake of including them in treatment they will probably show little or no gain. If our clinical cutting point is a score of 30 then 32.9 percent should not get treatment and would probably show little if any gain. In short, nearly one third of our experimental subjects are persons who not only should not be treated, but will tend to mask the effect of treatment.

The foregoing examples clearly do not represent the typical case in social work experiments designed to evaluate casework services. In those experiments we are more likely to find multidimensional measures that are treated as if they are unidimensional. One might, for example, develop a fifty-item scale wherein each item could measure an entirely different domain. If one then cumulates all of these ratings into a total score called, say, "social adjustment" and treats this as the dependent variable in an experiment designed to evaluate services the result will nearly always be an ambiguous one. The reasons for this are subtle and easily overlooked.

If such a summary scale really does measure, perhaps, fifteen to fifty different problem domains it is extremely unlikely that each subject in a treatment population will have all of these problems in similar magnitudes. Instead, it is likely that a given client will have one, two or at best a very few of the problems represented by the scale while another client will also have a very few but different problems. Stated differently, most of the clients will be problem free on most of the dimensions and each will have a somewhat different problem profile. Susan might have a problem with respect to items 4, 9, and 17, but Jack may be problematic with respect to items 7, 16, and 32. Now, if we use a treatment technique that really deals effectively with only problems represented by items 9, 15, and 24 only Susan will be helped and then with respect to only one problem (this interpretation might not hold if that problem is causally related to others). What is worse, there will likely be so much noise in the data that we cannot even detect the gains that Susan made in one problem area. Moreover, by analyzing the change in total score we will not even know where Susan was helped.

Surely, some will say that we can easily overcome these difficulties by analyzing each domain or performance area separately. Yes, we can do that, but it is very likely that most of the clients will not even have a problem in many of the domains and their failure to show gain (they did not need treatment for the problems) will mask entirely the real gains that were made by the very small proportion of the subjects who did need treatment. Unfortunately, in most social work research designed to separately test the effects of treatment with respect to several dependent variables a t-test or analysis of variance model (or other analytic tools) is employed that is appropriate if and only if each of the dependent variables is statistically independent of one another. They rarely are, and such methods are then not valid. If we wish to measure a group of clients with respect to several problem domains and then determine whether the treatment was effective we must use an appropriate statistical model such as the multivariate generalization of the t-test or analysis of variance. If we use multivariate measures and analyze them using univariate statistical procedures it is quite possible to find no statistically significant differences with respect to any of measures at the .05 level whereas a multivariate test could reveal that our groups were in fact statistically different at even the .0001 level (Tatsuoka, 1971).

In concluding this section we should note how the foregoing relates to the review task that Fischer has undertaken. In the first chapter of the text he defined social casework as the services provided by professional caseworkers and indicated that such a definition provides a clear basis for including any and all studies involving professional caseworkers. However, he has included primarily those studies that define the independent variable (s) in so broad terms that outcome is doomed to either failure or ambiguity. By adhering to an older tradition of defining independent variables he has failed to include any studies which treat the *behaviors* of caseworkers as the proper independent variables that ultimately define the "treatment" variables. In addition, while he correctly points out that "change processes tend to be divergent and multifactorial," he does not include a single study that properly uses multivariate methods to examine multivariate change processes—they all use univariate methods to examine sometimes huge numbers of dependent variables.

DESIGN ISSUES

In this section we discuss a few design issues that are not often taken into account. Many have written about design components that are intended to control extraneous effects and to untangle experimental effects, and Fischer has dealt with those problems rather extensively. Consequently, we shall focus attention on a single design that has considerable appeal among social work scholars and then examine some of its deficiencies. Most, if not all, of the deficiencies noted here apply equally to the more elaborate versions of the classical experimental paradigm.

A common procedure in designing an experiment aimed at evaluating effectiveness of casework services is to define a social or personal problem to be solved and then to measure its frequency or magnitude among a pool of subjects or clients. Next, each client is randomly assigned to a control group or one of several experimental groups. After these assignments have been made treatment is begun and allowed to continue for some specified period of time. The magnitude of the problem is again measured and the experiment is then terminated. We now have a set of pretest and posttest data and are ready to proceed to the analysis and conclusions. No doubt, we have all used, or are familiar with, this elementary but elegant research paradigm, and our research behavior testifies to the implicit faith we have in it.

One of the greatest shortcomings of the classical experimental design, when used in evaluative casework research, is its inability to provide feedback to the worker. In a typical experiment one collects pretest data, runs the experiment, collects posttest data and then terminates the research. By the time the data are analyzed and reported the treatment has been terminated and the worker has been deprived of the very information that might assist him in providing better treatment. Of course, the data may be useful in guiding very important administrative, planning and economic decision processes within an agency, community, or governmental system. However, if that is the major reason for conducting evaluative studies it is little wonder that caseworkers and researchers do not get along very well. On the other hand, if the purpose of evaluation is to assess, monitor and *guide* treatment for the benefit of the client and the worker the traditional experiment is particularly ill-suited to the task. If we can create research designs and procedures that aim first to help the client and the worker we will then have taken a major step toward better science and better treatment. Moreover, we can still thereby provide information for planning and administration and do a better job of it as well. More often than not, however, the results of our research have little more utility than to provide either a pat on the back or a slap in the face for the worker.

Part of the foregoing problem arises from the fact that simple prepost experiments depend solely on point estimates of the magnitude of a problem to detect change whereas the worker conducting treatment needs to monitor treatment on a continuous basis. Thus, this limitation can be partially overcome by incorporating repeated measures of our dependent variables into the experimental design. Often, however, the measures of interest to the researcher are not of interest to the worker, and if that is the case neither the client nor the worker is well served by the research. Even when the two agree on the importance of the measures taken the researcher often hoards the data and allows the worker to see it only at the end of the experiment.

Clearly, not one single study reviewed by Fischer was designed explicitly to monitor and *guide* treatment. One then wonders who the real clients were in these studies. Without speaking directly to the point Fischer; Mullen and Dumpson (1972); Eysenck (1966) and others have provided an enormous service by reviewing studies and discussing the essentially negative outcomes. By so doing they have called attention to the need for a different kind of work. While it is necessary to call attention to specific errors that they* or we have committed the larger task is one of incorporating rather than denying or refuting the major findings. We believe that a major limitation of most evaluative research is seen in its failure to assist and benefit the primary client and the worker who attempts to aid him. That failure has led us to adhere to designs and procedures that are of little benefit to the client, the worker or the profession.

Another issue in the classical design that is not well understood is the use of the control group. What do we really mean by "control group"? What is it that we are controlling? The term "control" as used in "control group" is nearly always a misnomer. In scientific research we set about to describe the relationship between two or more variables while controlling† the impact of extraneous forces that have little or no direct interest and which might distort the relationships under investigation.

Kerlinger (1967) makes the point that there is and can be no science without variance and formal comparisons, and this can be illustrated with an example. Suppose we conduct an experiment to detect and measure the effect of alcohol on the ability to

---

* Bergin's (1971) reanalysis of Eysenck's review calls attention rather forcefully to the way in which reviewer bias can and does color both the treatment and interpretation of data.

† Kerlinger (1967) identifies a number of techniques for doing this but none of them rely on control groups, e.g. using control variables that are built into an analysis of variance design, analysis of covariance, matching, control through elimination, etc.

read and understand "light novel" literature. First, we have a pool of subjects read, say, ten pages of a novel and then take a reading comprehension test about the material. Then, we randomly determine that some of our subjects will get (A) no alcohol, (B) one ounce of alcohol, (C) two ounces of alcohol. . . . and (F) five ounces of alcohol. We then ask groups B through F to "chug-a-lug" their alcohol dosage, wait twenty-five minutes and ask them to read new material. We then give them a new reading comprehension test and examine the results.

Many will surely regard group A as the control group in such a study, but what is being controlled? Nothing! Each group in this experiment merely represents a crude effort to quantify the independent variable,* and Group A simply represents the zero point on this scale. Given these six groups we have met the two basic requirements of science—the independent variable "varies" and we have provided the basis for formal comparisons. The magnitude of the independent variable *varies* from zero to five ounces of alcohol, and because there are six groups we can conduct fifteen different formal comparisons as well as examine the trend between reading comprehension and alcohol consumption. The point here is that we have *comparison* groups and not control groups.

The same holds for casework treatment experiments. If we are going to describe the relationship between a problem variable and a treatment variable we must insure that the treatment variable varies. However, most of the treatment variables discussed in this volume are dichotomous rather than continuous. Thus, we might provide fight training to a group of clients seeking help with their marriage and provide no fight training to another group. The second group is not a control group but a comparison group, and it represents a crude attempt on our part to establish a zero point on our dimension of fight training. In other studies we might choose not to use a "no treatment" group and instead a "standard treatment" as a baseline for comparison with an "ex-

---

* This discussion relates more directly to our earlier comments regarding control and quantification but was placed here because "control" groups are most often discussed in relation to types of research designs.

perimental" treatment. The only difference is that we choose not to establish a zero point on the scale of the independent variable.

In spite of all this we shall no doubt continue to refer to certain types of comparison groups as control groups, and we should not get bogged down with quibbling over words. However, we should understand that a minimum of two groups is needed in order to create a comparison, and if we have only one treatment group there is no variance in the independent variable of an experiment. We may indeed be able to show that patients in a single group do improve, and that may be important. However, such a finding says virtually nothing about the *relationship* between the problem and the independent variable. While there may be variance in the problem there is no variance in the treatment, and if there is no variance in the treatment there is and can be no science.

Fischer quite often bemoans the fact that many of the evaluation studies he reviewed did not have adequate comparison groups, and rightly so. Even if we have a "no treatment" group we cannot rest. When using such a group it is usually our intention to deprive a group of clients of any and all treatment while letting them be equal in all other respects to the group of subjects who receive the experimental treatment. If we know that two groups had the same mean and variance with respect to the criterion variable at the beginning of an experiment and that, as groups, they were identical except that one got treatment and one did not we should be able to conclude that any changes or differences between the groups at the end of the experiment can be attributed to the effect of treatment. Such is the neat and almost unassailable logic of the classical experiment, but we must not forget that such logic represents only a *model*.

A central question we must never overlook is one concerning the extent to which we conduct experiments that fit such a model. When we place subjects in a "no treatment" comparison group and thereby deny them the services they sought from us what is to prevent them from taking a bus ride to another agency to get the help they wanted? If a social worker will not help them perhaps a priest, minister, rabbi, friend, lover, spouse or another professional will. Then, if we do not know about the outside help we will observe, perhaps, a result which we discount as "spontaneous remission" (Bergin, 1971). In an educational experiment with young children it was learned that a number of mothers enrolled their "no treatment" children in other preschool training programs when deprived of the one offered by the experiment (Hudson, 1971). Many people simply refuse to stand still with their problems, and the longer an experiment runs over time the more likely is it that "control" groups will become treatment groups.

One of the reasons that we have been so enamoured of the classical experimental design is that it provides a scheme for systematically collecting objective information to be used in making formal comparisons in the study of growth and deterioration in treatment. It also provides a means of controlling or holding constant extraneous variables that might distort the relationships we seek to investigate, and this is done largely through random assignment of subjects to the comparison groups. Potent as these features are, they are not the most important reasons for use of the classical experimental design. The most important reason for using this design rests upon the fact that social and psychological measures usually are subject to considerable error. By using many subjects rather than one (or a very few) a great deal of the statistical noise in our measures can be averaged out. Assuming that the arithmetic mean represents a better estimate of the true magnitude of a problem than does the score from a single individual we adopt the procedure of comparing mean scores and mean changes for two or more experimental groups. Moreover, we have all too often claimed that the study of the single case is not adequate as it is nothing more than a special instance of the "one-shot case study" wherein we do not have a basis for formal comparison (Kerlinger, 1967).

Actually, we have available to us only two basic strategems for the assessment of change in client functioning. We can evaluate change using a single subject or a group of subjects. Although this is an obvious distinction it is also an important one. When we are working with *a* client to solve *a* single major problem (or several of them) we would like very much to know whether we are helping *that* client. Since casework is nearly always based on work with people on a case-by-case basis one wonders why we have been so engulfed in group research methods. In this regard we have done a generally feeble job of teaching clinical workers methods that will enable them to monitor their own progress with single clients. Instead, we teach them group research procedures knowing full well that the overwhelming majority of those workers will never utilize such knowledge or skill within the context of their practice and its evaluation. In short, we have not shown our students that research is relevant to practice, and that may be a very large reason for the usually dismal outcomes obtained in typical experiments designed to evaluate casework treatment. That is, the research methodology employed in such studies may simply not be relevant to the problem at hand.

Recently however, an abundant and growing literature has become available to test an altogether different approach to the study of treatment and its outcomes. That approach is variously referred to as intensive research (Thorsen & Anton, 1974), N = 1 or single subject designs (Dukes, 1965; Sidman, 1960; Tharp & Wetzel, 1969; Gottman, 1972, 1973; Gottman & Leiblum, 1974; Howe, 1974) and regression-discontinuity designs (Campbell, 1970). There are clearly very serious design problems and issues that must be accounted for in working with single subjects to validate the effects of treatment. However, we have seen earlier that the classical group design is by no means free of the very same problems, and it has its own to deal with. Actually, a number of social workers are successfully using N = 1 designs and have done so for quite some time (Butterfield, 1973, 1974a, 1974b; Frankel & Glasser, 1974; Jehu, 1967; Rose, 1969, 1974; Staats & Butterfield, 1969; Thomas & Carter, 1971). We would do well to examine this work carefully and learn from it, and Howe (1974) has made this point rather forcefully in his paper. When we contrast the types of research reported in this volume with that reported in the behavior modification literature it strikes us that learning theorists and behavior modification therapists have been able to achieve rather astounding results (by comparison) through the use of three important "innovations": behaviorally specific dependent variables, behaviorally specific independent variables, and the time-series analysis of data. Although Campbell (1970), Gottman (1973), Glass *et al.* (1974), and others caution us to use appropriate statistics in time-series data there are many clear-cut cases where simple graphic techniques obviate the need for any statistical analysis as we generally use the term.

ANALYZING CHANGE SCORE DATA

As I indicated in an earlier review, it may be possible to demonstrate, with a well designed and carefully controlled study, that casework does in fact harm clients (Hudson, 1974). However, we must employ the same standards of rigor in assessing deterioration as we do in assessing growth. One of the commonest fallacies of group research data arises when we attempt to interpret an individual positive change score as gain and a negative change score as deterioration. In Chapter 4 Fischer appears to do this frequently when discussing instances wherein more of the experimental group subjects were worse off or failed to gain as much as did the members of the "no treatment" comparison groups. This becomes a valid statement only when there is a statistically significant relationship between the dependent and independent variables. Moreover, it does little good for Fischer to point out that nearly three quarters of the reviewed studies show deterioration among the experimental groups. After all, he selected them on a purely *post hoc* basis! Thus, his figure of three-fourths deterioration due to treatment is an *observed* frequency based on a sample of studies *he* gathered together. What would be the results if we examined *all* published studies of casework intervention? Moreover, in Chapters 2 and 3 Fischer renders a number of criticisms that raise serious question as to whether the studies are capable of showing any effect to be due to treatment —positive or negative. In light of this it seems scientifically inconsistent to use the same studies to show that they produce deterioration. Following Fischer's own logic we might say that given the enormous number of variables that were measured in all these studies by so many different workers involved with so many

different clients under tremendously varying conditions the piti-
fully few pieces of evidence pointing to deterioration must
surely make it apparent that we could attribute them to chance.

In order to understand and properly interpret change score
data it is useful to recall that most of our statistical analyses
with continuous dependent measures are based on normal curve
theory. In this regard we should note that only three parameters
are needed to completely determine a normal distribution; the
size of the sample, the arithmetic mean, and the variance or
standard deviation. Sample size markedly affects the sensitivity of
an experiment, the mean is a location parameter, and the standard deviation is a measure of the dispersion of scores or values
around the mean. The effect of differences in sample size has
been widely discussed and is not a critical issue in the study of
change scores, however, the mean and variance *are* important.

The mean is a crucially important device for determining
whether an experimental group *as a whole* showed a gain or loss
when compared with a different treatment group or a "no treatment" group. In an earlier paper (Hudson, 1974) we pointed
out that there are only thirteen possible outcomes for a simple
two-group, before-after design. Five of those outcomes support
the conclusion that the experimental group did better than the
"control" group and they are shown in Figure 10-1. In each of
these cases the *observed* mean change suggests that the experimental group actually did better than the "control" group or that the
experiment had the effect of retarding deterioration (we assume
in all of these cases both random assignment of subjects to
groups and equality of pretest means).

However, these are only *observed* changes, and we must use
some formal test to rule out the effect of chance as an alternate
or competing hypothesis. The simplest way to do that is to com-
pute a change score for each person and conduct a t-test of the
differences between the means provided that the cases represent
independent observations. If we find that the difference between
the two means is significant we can reject the hypothesis that
mere chance fluctuations accounted for the observed differences.

Figure 10-2 shows three experimental outcomes for the same

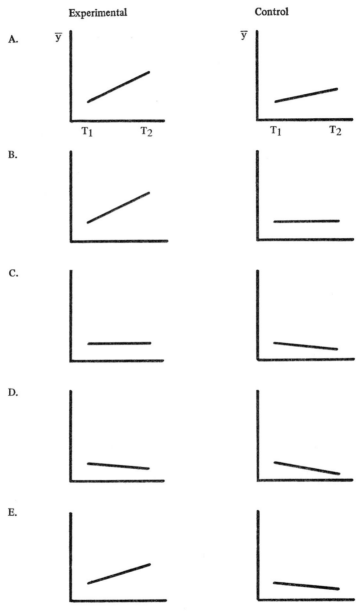

Figure 10-1.

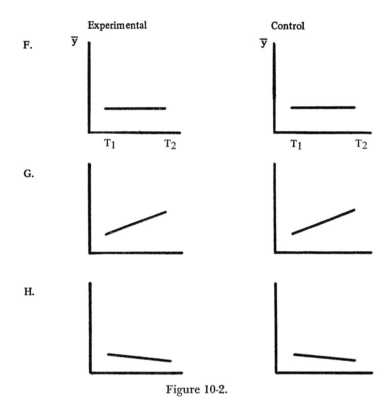

Figure 10-2.

design that suggest the "control" and the experimental groups did equally well. In one case it appears that both groups improved, in another both groups got worse, and in the third neither group showed any change. In Figure 10-3 we see five outcomes that suggest the experimental group caused deterioration, and each one is merely the converse of the outcomes shown in Figure 10-1. If we find, using the same t-test, that any of the outcomes shown in Figure 10-3 are statistically significant we then have evidence that casework may have produced deterioration.

It is extremely important to remember that all of the foregoing pertains only to the means or mean changes and not to individual change. In other words, the classical design enables us to test hypotheses about the group as a whole, but it is ill-suited to

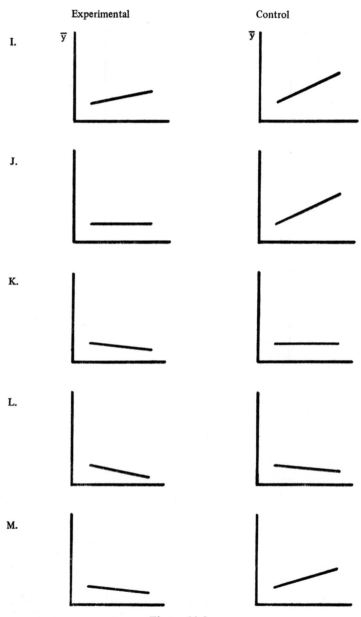

Figure 10-3.

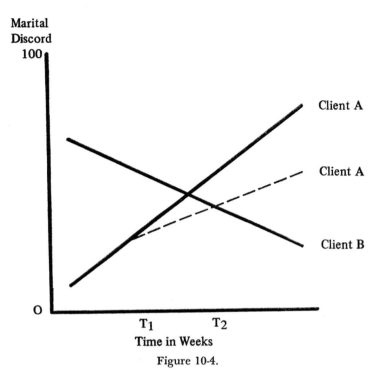

Figure 10-4.

provide us with tests about single individuals and the way they have been helped or harmed. Perhaps we can illustrate this with examples. Suppose that a client comes to us at a point where he is beginning to experience difficulty in his marriage. Assume that if he does not get help the difficulty will increase, but that treatment is given and it is effective. This outcome is shown as client A in Figure 10-4 where we see that a pretest measure taken at time, T1, and a posttest measure taken at time, T2, would indicate that treatment "harmed" the client.

A second client may come to us for help but only after he has experienced considerable difficulty. Suppose that this client, shown as client B in Figure 10-4, has actually begun to resolve his problems, that if left alone he would resolve them completely, and that our treatment efforts were wholly ineffectual. If we take a pretest measure at T1 and a posttest measure at T2 we would likely conclude that treatment has helped this person when in fact it has done neither good nor harm. The major point we must keep in mind is that without such trend data for each subject we cannot be sure of the meaning of either a positive or negative change score for single subjects. The power of the group design that uses many subjects is that the kinds of trend effects shown in Figure 10-4 get averaged out, but the weakness of this design is that it permits us to test hypotheses only about average changes.

Trend effects of the kind noted in Figure 10-4 are also responsible for what Fischer has referred to as regression artifacts, and therein lies another reason for caution in interpreting change scores for individuals when such data are obtained from multi-person group experiments using point estimates of problem magnitudes. In other words, those with higher scores at pretest will tend to have somewhat lower scores at posttest while those with extremely low scores at pretest will tend to have higher ones at posttest. This is a function of both real changes experienced by each individual over time and the imperfect reliabilities of our measuring devices. However, such regression artifacts can occur even if we have perfectly reliable measurements.

The foregoing discussion has focused primarily on the arithmetic mean and its role in both describing the experimental outcome and in testing hypotheses about differences among means. In such hypothesis testing the variance and standard deviation also play crucial roles. In the usual t-test or F-test used in an analysis of variance it is assumed that the within-cell variances are equal within the limits of sampling variation. If they are not, that fact alone establishes that the two groups are significantly different from one another *regardless of the value of their means*. In other words, two groups can differ in their means, their variances or both.

What can we say when we find that the experimental and "control" group variances differ in an experiment designed to assess casework effectiveness? Some have pointed out that in experimental evaluations of therapy there is a tendency for the experimental group variance to get larger from pretest to posttest as compared to the "control" group and that this provides direct evidence of deterioration by some patients within the experimental group (Bergin, 1971). This is decidedly not true, and we must examine that issue carefully.

Suppose we test a pool of 100 clients on a marital satisfaction scale whose score range is 0 to 100 with a clinical cutting point of 30 and find their mean score to be 65 with a standard deviation of four points. Assume that high scores represent greater problems in the marriage and low scores indicate few marital problems. Next, we randomly assign fifty people to each of two groups—one treatment group and one "no treatment" group. After four months of treatment we test them again and find the results as reported in Table 10-I.

Obviously, this table shows that the experimental group standard deviation suffered a four-fold increase and might suggest that some people who got treatment got better and others got worse. Not so! All we need for such an outcome is that twenty-five people in the experimental group remain the same and the other twenty-five drop to a mean score of 32. Here then is a case where half of the people were helped and half were not (but none were harmed). The results are shown in a slightly different form in Table 10-II to better illustrate how a variance in the experimental group can get larger without indicating that group members are deteriorating.

This example is both fictitious and unrealistic but it very well shows that we must be careful about the way we interpret heterogeneous variances. Rarely can they be taken at face value. Nonetheless, properly handled they are important aids in the

TABLE 10-I

	Experimental			Control		
	N	$\overline{X}$	σ	N	$\overline{X}$	σ
Pretest	50	65.00	4.00	50	65.00	4.00
Posttest	50	48.50	16.98	50	65.00	4.00

TABLE 10-II

	Experimental			Control		
	N	$\overline{X}$	σ	N	$\overline{X}$	σ
	25	65.00	4.00			
Pretest				50	65.00	4.00
	25	65.00	4.00			
	25	65.00	4.00			
Posttest				50	65.00	4.00
	25	32.00	4.00			

evaluation of treatment services. At the very least one should have a frequency distribution of the pre-post scores for each group as an aid to interpretation.

Earlier we discussed some of the problems that arise when using markedly heterogeneous problem populations or groups, and we should note that within-cell variances can thereby be affected. Suppose we have 100 subjects assigned to a treatment and a no-treatment group with pretest means of 50 and standard deviations of 20 in both groups on a depression scale. We already pointed out that it is unlikely for one third of the experimental group to show any important changes simply because they did not need treatment. If treatment really is effective in helping to reduce depression the variance in the experimental group will *decrease* at posttest. Of course, one third of the no-treatment group will also likely show little change but two thirds of the no-treatment group might get help from friends, colleagues and others. Thus, they too might show growth "spontaneously" and if that occurs their variance will also diminish at posttest. The question then arises as to whether the treatment or no-treatment group had the larger mean and variance decrease.

Unfortunately, treatment might very well do some harm—we cannot ignore that possibility as Fischer has strongly urged. If the treatment actually brought about deterioration among the one-third who did not even need treatment, then the experimental group variance would again diminish at posttest provided that those above the cutting score of 30 did not change. In such a case we would see both a rise in the experimental group mean and a decrease in that group variance at posttest. As we can see, life is made much simpler when experiments have equal subclass numbers and equal within-cell variances. We can largely control the numbers of persons in our study groups but the means and variances are in the hands of the clients and the workers. When they provide us with unequal means and unequal variances we must take both into account in order to properly interpret the outcome as representing either growth or deterioration.

Summary and Concluding Comments

In this chapter we have taken issue with some of Fischer's interpretations, conclusions and points of view with respect to the studies he has reviewed in this volume. We have done that believing that he has pushed the data to certain conclusions that are not warranted. Throughout the first part of this text his stance appears to be one of claiming that casework does not work and that in some instances casework has actually harmed clients by producing deterioration. In Chapter 4 he reviews certain studies wherein there does appear clear evidence of deterioration, and that cannot be ignored. However, most of the studies in that chapter do not provide statistically significant results to support the claim that either growth or deterioration is a function of casework. In that chapter he refers to one study wherein "20 percent of the treated group scored more negatively at posttest than on pretest" and underplays the fact that 80 percent apparently showed some gain. Such selective reporting both weakens his own case and provides a disservice to the reader.

One of the major points we tried to make in this chapter is the fact that "casework" is an undefined independent variable in virtually all of the studies reviewed by Fischer. Worse yet, "casework" has been so broadly defined that it cannot even be regarded as a variable from a scientific point of view. Instead, it is an unspecified conglomerate of activities carried out by individual workers in relation to an equally unspecified conglomerate of personal, social and economic problems. When either we or Fischer claim that casework works or casework does not work we are making essentially meaningless statements. Similarly, when strong evidence of deterioration arises we have only the evidence of deterioration and do not know to what that should be attributed. It is meaningless to attribute it to casework.

When a patient dies in surgery do we then have evidence that "medicine" has failed, that "medicine" killed him, or the "medicine" was unable to solve the problem? Such questions are nonsense questions. On the other hand, we cannot pretend that we do not harm our clients, and we probably do so much more often than we care to admit. The problem, however, is that our sciencing is so crude and our scientifically validated knowledge base is so thin that we really do not know much about which of our treatment behaviors help our clients and which of them is hurtful.

In spite of our disagreements with Fischer we find considerable agreement with some of his major points. It will do us no good to continue research evaluations of social work services that do not identify and evaluate the specific behaviors of therapists that function as the independent variables intended to cause client growth with respect to equally specific client behaviors that are defined as personal and social problems. Moreover, it is our view that the greatest progress will be made in the short run by adopting a wholly different research strategy. Therein we should seriously consider and begin to test on a very wide front the use of single-case studies of movement over time.

There are several major advantages to this strategy. First, the process of assessment and evaluation becomes an integral part of treatment. Second, the time-series design for a single case is without a doubt the best tool available to the worker in helping him to do the job given him. In this context the primary role of evaluation becomes one of helping the worker *guide* treatment to a successful conclusion. When the worker sees little progress over a reasonable period of time he then has evidence (feedback) that the treatment technique is not helping the client and that he must begin to think about, develop and use an alternate strategy. Multiperson classical designs can be powerful aids to our knowledge building, but they are also complex and costly. Unfortunately, they are not useful in aiding the individual efforts of workers who are charged with the task of assisting individual clients and their families, and that is the primary business to which we should turn our attention. A predictable outcome is better treatment, better research, and a richly expanded knowledge base for the profession.

REFERENCES

Bergin, A. E. "The Evaluation of Therapeutic Outcomes," Bergin, A. E. and Garfield, S. L. (eds.), *Handbook of Psychotherapy and Behavior Change: An Empirical Analysis*. New York: John Wiley and Sons, Inc., 1971.

Butterfield, W. H. and Parson, R. "Modeling and Shaping by Parents to Develop Chewing Behavior in Their Retarded Child," *Journal of Behavior Therapy and Experimental Psychiatry*, Vol. 4, 1973.

Butterfield, W. H. "Behavior Modification: Counterconditioning Techniques," *Update International; World Wide Family Medicine*, Vol. 1, 1974.

Butterfield, W. H. "Behavior Modification: Changing Behavior by Modifying Its Consequences," *Update International; World Wide Family Medicine*, Vol. 1, 1974.

Campbell, Donald T. "Legal Reforms as Experiments." *Journal of Legal Education*, Vol. 23, 1970, pp. 217-239.

Dukes, William F. "N = 1." *Psychological Bulletin*, Vol. 64, 1, 1965, pp. 74-79.

Eysenck, H. J. *The Effects of Psychotherapy*. New York: International Science Press, 1966.

Frankel, A. and Glasser, P. "Behavioral Approaches to Group Therapy," *Social Work*, Vol. 2, 1974.

Glass, G. V., Willson, V. L. and Gottman, J. M. *Design and Analysis of Time Series Experiments*. Boulder, Colo.: Laboratory of Educational Research Press, 1973.

Gottman, J. M., McFall, R. M. and Burnett, J. T. "Design and Analysis of Research Using Time Series," *Psychological Bulletin*, Vol. 72, 1969, pp. 299-306.

Gottman, J. M. "N-of-One and N-of-Two Research in Psychotherapy," *Psychological Bulletin*, Vol. 80, 1973, pp. 93-105.

Gottman, J. and Leiblum, S. *How to Do Psychotherapy and How to Evaluate It: A Manual for Beginners*. New York: Holt, Rinehart and Winston, Inc., 1974.

Howe, Michael W. "Casework Self-Evaluation: A Single Subject Approach," *Social Service Review*, Vol. 48, 1974, pp. 1-23.

Hudson, W. W. "An Autotelic Teaching Experiment with Ancillary Casework Services," *American Educational Research Journal*, Vol. 8, 1971.

Hudson, W. W. "Casework as a Causative Agent in Client Deterioration: A

Research Note on the Fischer Assessment," *Social Service Review,* Vol. 48, 1974.

Jehu, E. *Learning Theory and Social Casework.* London: Routledge Kegan Paul Publishing, 1967.

Kerlinger, F. N. *Foundations of Behavioral Research.* New York: Holt, Rinehart and Winston, 1967.

Mullen, E. J. and Dumpson, J. R. (eds.). *Evaluation of Social Intervention.* San Francisco: Jossey-Bass, 1972.

Rose, S. "A Behavioral Approach to the Group Treatment of Parents," *Social Work,* Vol. 14, 1969.

Rose, S. "Group Training of Parents as Behavior Modifiers," *Social Work,* Vol. 2, 1974.

Sidman, M. *Tactics of Scientific Research.* New York: Basic Books, 1960.

Staats, A. W. and Butterfield, W. H. "Treatment of Nonreading in a Culturally Deprived Juvenile Delinquent: An Application of Reinforcement Principles," *Child Development,* Vol. 5, 1965.

Tatsuoka, M. *Multivariate Analysis.* New York: John Wiley and Sons, Inc., 1971.

Tharp, R. G. and Wetzel, R. J. *Behavior Modification in the Natural Environment.* New York: Academic Press, 1969.

Thomas, E. and Carter, R. D. "Instigative Modification with a Multi-problem Family," *Social Casework,* Vol. 52, 1971.

Thomas, E., Abrams, K. S. and Johnson, J. B. "Self Monitoring and Reciprocal Inhibition in the Modification of Multiple Tics of Gilles de la Tourette's Syndrome," *Journal of Behavior Therapy and Experimental Psychiatry,* Vol. 2, 1971.

Thorsen, C. E. and Anton, J. "Intensive Experimental Research in Counseling," *Journal of Counseling Psychology,* 1974 (in press).

CHAPTER 11 SPECIFYING CASEWORK EFFECTS

EDWARD J. MULLEN

Professor
Graduate School of Social Service
Fordham University
New York, New York

CONSENSUS APPEARS to be developing among social work researchers and theorists that after a decade of experimentation the effectiveness of social work programs has not yet been clearly established (Fischer, 1973; Mullen, Dumpson and Associates, 1972). "What these assessments have said as a group is that the interventions studied failed to make major differences in the lives of the people experiencing the services, that is, differences that could be documented by the research" (Mullen, 1973, p. 41). The observation that controlled evaluative research, to date, has been unable to clearly support the position that social work programs *in general* do achieve the expectations set for such programs, no longer appears to be seriously debated (Meyer, 1972; Perlman, 1972).

Fischer asks a more specific and qualitatively different type of question when he asks "Are the services of professional caseworkers more effective than either no services at all, or haphazardly received or informal services?" (Chapter 2) or "services provided by nonprofessional workers?" (Chapter 3). Fischer's question probes the effects of the program variable, professional casework service and, therefore, moves considerably beyond the more general issue of the observable impact of total, undifferentiated social agency programs, which do include professional social work services as elements.

From the perspective of evaluative research the design requirements necessary to answer these two qualitatively different questions vary considerably. Considering the more general question,
it may be sufficient to treat the program being evaluated in an undifferentiated fashion, even to treat it as an unknown "black
box." In such cases it would not be necessary to specify the consequences of particular program elements. To understand the
nature of such programs such designs would need to allow for
a description of the program and its elements. However, the nature of the question would not require specification of the consequences of these program elements. In a sense in such cases the
total program is treated as a single quality or variable. Evaluation
studies directed by such general total program impact questions
do not require a controlled examination of the process criterion
(Suchman, 1967), that is, specification of cause and effect relationships by program variables. Such studies obviously have little
potential for adding to scientific knowledge or theory. Such designs have been used for research evaluations of demonstration
programs conducted by social agencies in which the agency's objective has been to provide evidence that the desired consequences
followed from their demonstration program. In such evaluations
the accent was neither on increasing understanding in the scientific or theoretical sense about why such programs did or did not
achieve the expected results, nor was the accent on specifying
what program elements were followed by specific consequences.

Fischer's question places greater burdens on the designs of
evaluative research. Questions about the effectiveness of casework
require research designs that are powerful enough to isolate and
control the elements of social agency programs that are "casework" and to identify the consequences of the casework elements
as contrasted with the consequences of other program qualities.
An examination of the process criterion is required (Suchman,
1967). Such designs would need to be powerful enough to examine the main effects of the casework, that is the consequences directly attributable to the casework, as well as the interaction effects, that is the consequences of the casework in combination

with other elements of the program. Such evaluations would need to rest on a rather thorough understanding not only of casework but of social agencies and the dynamics of their programs. A high degree of control over the relevant program elements including the casework would also be essential.

Investigators seeking to answer the question of casework effectiveness and who proceed to answer this question by employing research designs not permitting variable specification (not employing the process criterion) must explicitly or implicitly assume that the casework (the acts of the individual caseworkers taken collectively) is *the* program and that these caseworker acts are relatively uneffected by the social agency and the larger service delivery system.

On the other hand, if casework is viewed as an element in a larger service delivery system or social agency program which both potentially influences and is influenced by the larger service system, then clearly variable specification is required to answer in any scientific way the question of casework effectiveness.

It does, in fact, appear that recent formulations of casework do emphasize this second, social system, view of casework (Hartman, 1974; Meyer, 1970; Pincus & Minahan, 1973). Within the system's frame of reference emphasis is placed not on the caseworker as a solo practitioner, equipped with a powerful armamentarium of methods and techniques who alone would confront the situation of the client, but rather accent is given to the caseworker as part of a system of intervention who is often seeking to influence other elements in the service delivery system as well as to influence the client system. From this point of view then, casework would not properly be viewed as a "program" but rather as a set of interventions occurring in interaction with other interventions as part of complex programs of social agencies.

Viewing casework from a systems frame of reference leads to the conclusion that to answer the question of casework effectiveness research evaluations would need to be available that have adequately specified the consequences of casework intervention as distinct from the effects of other program variables, in particular organizational, bureaucratic, and political influences (Rossi & Williams, 1972).

The research evaluations of social work effectiveness which have used experimental or quasiexperimental designs and which have been seriously reviewed by the profession (Fischer, 1973; Mullen, Dumpson & Associates, 1972) provide little scientific evidence concerning the question of social casework impact as distinct from the overall impact of programs. For the most part these evaluations have not had as a major purpose contribution to theoretical knowledge but rather have more or less resembled demonstration projects in which social agencies set about to implement new programs and included research evaluations so that the overall effects of the programs could be objectively verified. Such evaluations were for the most part conducted within the context of justification rather than a context of knowledge discovery or knowledge verification. As such, these evaluations were not designed to specify the consequences of specific program elements such as casework. Some of the experimental evaluations reviewed elsewhere (Mullen, Dumpson & Associates, 1972) did concern themselves directly with variable specification and some were concerned primarily with the development of social work theory (Blenker *et al.*, 1964; Reid & Shyne, 1969; and Schwartz & Sample, 1970); however, none of these are included in Fischer's review since they do not fall within the criteria established for that review.

In answer then to the question: Are the services of professional caseworkers more effective than no services at all, or haphazardly received services, or informal services, or services provided by nonprofessional workers? It seems that the scientific community would have to conclude that the question has not been adequately researched and that as a consequence the information required to answer the question is not available.

NEGATIVE EFFECTS

Fischer has observed that in nearly three fourths of the studies reviewed clients receiving services from professional caseworkers were shown to deteriorate over the course of treatment. He notes that the primary issue is: Did the casework produce the deterioration? He observes that in nine of the twelve studies where deterioration occurred control group procedures "make it appear likely that the deterioration in the experimental group could be attributed to some aspect of the casework program." He concludes that, "It seems not only that professional casework, on the whole, is not helpful, but that clients are often actually harmed by casework services."

These are indeed arresting observations. It does appear that in a relatively large number of instances unintended negative outcomes do occur among some clients participating in the reported evaluations. The issue of causation, however, is complex. There are several limitations that inhibit such cause and effect inferences. First, deterioration or negative effects were not anticipated or hypothesized but observed after the fact. While such unanticipated findings are noteworthy and deserving of further attention, cause and effect inferences are not, scientifically speaking, able to be made with any reasonable degree of confidence. This is especially the case with the studies reviewed by Fischer since alternative explanations for these negative findings were not adequately controlled or for that matter extensively considered.

A second limitation restricting such cause and effect inferences, related to the previous limitation but yet somewhat distinct, concerns the absence of any theoretical rationale that would suggest why negative consequences would be a result of casework. Without some antecedent theoretical explanation for negative consequences it is most difficult to generalize beyond the particular experiences of these specific evaluations.

Finally, and perhaps the most restricting of the limitations, is the lack of variable specification in most of the studies reported. It does appear that unintended negative consequences did occur in the majority of evaluations reviewed by Fischer. However, given the nature of the designs it is impossible to attribute these consequences to specific program variables such as the casework. It could just as well be that the negative results were a consequence of the policies of the social agencies, or the structure of the overall service system, or other qualities of the service program.

In summary then, it does appear that deterioration did occur among some of the clients in a large proportion of the evaluations reviewed by Fischer; however, these outcomes were not anticipated nor are they theoretically meaningful. Further, the evaluation designs do not permit inferences that these consequences are attributable to the programs, or to specific program elements such as the casework.

CASEWORK EFFECTIVENESS

While it is not possible on the basis of available evidence to conclude that casework has been demonstrated to be ineffective, neither is it possible to conclude that casework's effectiveness has been demonstrated and scientifically established. This may be an arresting observation after nearly two decades of evaluative research activity in social work. However, a review of the available research suggests that relatively little research has been addressed to the question of casework effectiveness. The research to date has for the most part assessed general effects of social agency programs without specifying casework effects. As such the burden of proof does still weigh heavily on the casework community to demonstrate the effectiveness of casework activities.

Hopefully, the next generation of social work evaluations will not equate any particular social work method or technique with social agency programs but rather will begin with a view of program as a system of intervention and will develop designs capable of specifying the effects of program elements including social work methods and techniques. Hopefully, too, such evaluations will directly anticipate negative as well as positive consequences and so conceptualize and design their evaluations so as to specify such effects.

I would concur with the hope that a moratorium be called on the diffuse total program evaluations that have characterized the past two decades of social work research. And I would urge that in addition to the case study methods currently being advocated (Fischer, Chapter 6; Howe, 1974) additional resources be invested in even more rigorous experimental evaluations of social work impact capable of specifying cause and effect relationships between specific variables. Only through such controlled experimentation and variable analysis will the effects of professional intervention be scientifically established.

REFERENCES

Blenkner, M., Jahn, J. and Wasser, E. *Serving the Aging: An Experiment in Social Work and Public Health Nursing.* New York: Community Service Society of New York, 1964.

Editorial, *Social Service Review,* Vol. 46, 1972.

Editorial, *Social Work,* Vol. 18, 1973, p. 1.

Fischer, J. "Is Casework Effective?" *Social Work,* Vol. 18, January, 1973, pp. 5-20.

Hartman, A. "The Generic Stance and the Family Agency," *Social Casework,* Vol. 55, 4, April, 1974, pp. 199-208.

Howe, M. "Casework Self-Evaluation: A Single-Subject Approach," *Social Service Review,* Vol. 48, 1, March, 1974, pp. 1-23.

Meyer, C. "Practice on Microsystem Level," Mullen, E., Dumpson, J. and Associates (eds.), *Evaluation of Social Intervention.* San Francisco: Jossey-Bass, 1972, pp. 158-190.

Meyer, C. *Social Work Practice: A Response to the Urban Crisis.* Free Press, 1970.

Mullen, E., Dumpson, J. and Associates. *Evaluation of Social Intervention.* San Francisco: Jossey-Bass, 1972.

Mullen, E. "Evaluative Research in Social Work," Jackson, R. and Morton, J. (eds.), *Evaluation of Social Work Services in Community Health and Medical Care Programs.* Program in Public Health Social Work, University of California, Berkeley, 1973, pp. 37-54.

Perlman, H. "Once More, With Feeling," in Mullen, E., Dumpson, J. and Associates (eds.), *Evaluation of Social Intervention.* San Francisco: Jossey-Bass, 1972, pp. 191-209.

Pincus, A. and Minahan, A. *Social Work Practice: Models and Methods.* Itasca, Ill.: Peacock Publishers, 1973.

Reid, W. and Shyne, A. *Brief and Extended Casework.* New York: Columbia University Press, 1969.

Rossi, P. and Williams, W. (eds.). *Evaluating Social Programs.* New York: Seminar Press, 1972.

Schwartz, E. and Sample, W. *Organization and Utilization of Public Assistance Personnel: The Midway Office Field Experiment.* Chicago: The School of Social Service Administration, University of Chicago, 1970.

Suchman, E. *Evaluative Research.* New York: Russell Sage Foundation, 1967.

CHAPTER 12 IS THE CASE CLOSED?

BERNICE POLEMIS

Professor
School of Social Work
University of Hawaii
Honolulu, Hawaii

S OCIAL WORKERS are idealistic, naive and foolhardy.* They are a marvelous people, who wish to help even when there is little chance of success. What other profession would risk extinction by attempting to show by research that it is effective? Would we be better off without architects, lawyers, or even doctors? Which of these professions would have any intention of putting itself on trial, as Dr. Fischer has done in this book with social casework? The evidence appears to be enormous and unassailable. In fact, this book might be compared to the brief of an adept and skillful prosecuting attorney. Social casework has been put on trial and judged guilty of ineffectiveness. Perhaps other professions will take the cue.

What are the implications of this verdict? Some people (caseworkers) have obviously been under the impression that they were helping when in fact they were not at all; other people (clients) were perhaps under the impression that they were being helped, when in fact they were not. Still other people (teachers in schools of social work) have been under the impression that they are teaching students to be helpers, when this is not the case. And a fourth group (you and I) have been paying for all of this, through taxes and contributions to philanthropic organiza-

---

* Dr. Polemis is not a social worker; however, some of her best friends are social workers. (J. Fischer)

tions, when in fact these organizations are giving ineffective service insofar as they are employing social caseworkers (it is not clear whether they are effective if they employ psychologists, psychiatrists, or simply nonprofessional people with warmth, empathy and genuineness).

This is a very serious situation. As Dr. Fischer says: "How could this incredible situation have come about?" Most of us are deceived at least part of the time, so the possibility of this enormous deception is certainly worthy of consideration. Illusion breaking is highly desirable. No one could argue that workers should be protected from the illusion of having helped, that students should be protected from the illusion of having learned, clients from the illusion of having been helped, and researchers from the illusion of having contributed to knowledge.

In reviewing this book, I had the distinct impression of being prepared for the birth of an elephant, and having a mouse appear instead. As I read Dr. Fischer's apparently well-documented and authoritative book, showing so clearly that social casework is ineffective, I expected him to recommend that schools of social work be closed, that social casework agencies shut their doors, that social work be permitted to die a natural death, and certainly that no more money be spent on it, either through taxes or philanthropy. Instead, I find such minor recommendations as "the use of structure," involving "planning, control of variables involved in the problem, introducing certainty into the client's situation, commitment to action on the part of the worker, use of direct influence, and above all else, being systematic," "use of behavior modification," and giving attention to the core conditions of warmth, empathy and genuineness.

The judgment is "guilty," but the verdict is "reform." Dr. Fischer explains this apparently anomalous situation by indicating that the value system on which the profession of social casework is based (such aspects as regard for the individual, opposition to the dehumanizing influences of industrialization, etc.) ought to be retained, and therefore, if social caseworkers will only follow this advice, all may not be lost.

The verdict has been given. However, are there sufficient grounds for an appeal? Is a reexamination of the evidence in order? Dr. Fischer uses as his evidence seventeen studies. He has prepared an abstract of each of the studies, and has then reviewed each study in the light of his own framework for study evaluation. Although no study, regardless of the nature of its results, is spared his critical eye, studies with positive results are negatived and studies with negative results are sustained. In reexamining this evidence, we might ask several questions: (1) What is the nature of the evidence, its quality and quantity? (2) What is the nature of the defendant or defendants? (3) Is the method of examining the evidence an appropriate one?

The Nature of the Evidence

First, let us consider the nature of the studies and the research model used in these studies. After a careful consideration of the original reports on the seventeen studies, I have concluded that these studies are of two types: The first type is a study of ongoing agency practice, with the usual agency workers, and the customary clients. The second type includes a series of evaluations of new programs or projects, one group with the usual agency workers, a second with workers hired especially to carry out the project; a third group are special projects quite independent of a single established agency.

In the case of the studies of on-going agency practice, one would expect the evaluation to read predominantly positive. If this is not the case, there is either irresponsible practice or irresponsible research or both. It would seem to an outsider that an established agency, in its collective experience in practice, should have become quite aware of the kinds of cases which will yield to the particular type of treatment provided by that agency and the kinds that will not. While it may make mistakes in its intake operation, and also it may as a policy not exclude types of cases which have a smaller chance of success, the major portion of its cases should belong to the category of probable success. Perhaps this view is contrary to the position of the top echelons in social work and also contrary to present trends in social work education (in which it appears that any student should be trained to do everything); however, I do not believe that social work is an exception to the principle of the economics of specialization, and that while the idea of the generalist seems most appealing, this idea is contrary to any cost-benefit concept.

What about the studies of established agency practice? There are three such studies among the seventeen. The first two are studies of child guidance clinics and the third is a study of the practice of a single marriage counselor.

The first of these studies is a one-year follow-up of cases seen in the Jewish Board of Guardians child guidance clinic (Lehrman *et al.,* 1949).* The method of treatment here is called transference psychotherapy. This study not only shows an overall difference in outcome in favor of the treatment group over the defector control group, but this difference appears to exist for nearly all subgroups (boys and girls, different age groups, different diagnostic groups, different home situations). Differences between treatment and control vary considerably for the different categories. In only one instance (one of the diagnostic categories) is the treatment group less successful than the control. Where the child has two adequate parents, the treatment group has a success rate of 77 percent while the control one of 31 percent. Success rate varies by age, with greater success among the older children, but for each category, the treatment group is from 15 to 27 percentage points higher towards success than the control group. Where there are psychiatric disorders in one or both parents, the treatment group does very little better than the control. In addition this study shows a considerable change in success with length of treatment up to two years. Dr. Fischer criticizes the data analysis in this study, since the category "partially improved" was considered separately from the category "improved." However, he fails to note that the category "partially improved" does not mean "a little bit improved." In accordance with the explicit operational definitions included in the study, partially improved means improved in some areas and not in others (Lehrman *et al.,* 1949,

---

* References to the specific studies are available in the list of references at the end of Part I.

p. 31).* While it is Dr. Fischer's personal preference that the analysis be based on "improved" versus "unimproved," I am puzzled by the assumption that a chi-square based on a 3 by 2 table ignores half the data, any more than a chi-square based on a 2 by 2 table does.

The second study is a five-year follow-up of children who were seen or whose parents were seen at the Illinois Institute for Juvenile Research (Levitt *et al.*, 1959). This study is very surprising. The Illinois Institute for Juvenile Research is a highly respected agency within the State of Illinois, as well as elsewhere. This follow-up study indicates that outcome of its treatment cases differed hardly at all from the defector controls with respect to a large number of variables. The implication of this research is that on the average, these families would have been as well off if they had not bothered. (No description of treatment is included.) The authors explain this strange result as due to the fact that half the cases were treated by workers with less than one year of experience, and that the agency is a training institution, as though a training institution is permitted to be worse, rather than better, than other institutions. However, there are major sources of variation within this study, on which no outcome data are included in the published report—differences within the client groups (boys vs. girls, older vs. younger children), differences in terms of who was treated (child only, parent only, both child and parent), differences in who gave the treatment (psychologists, psychiatrists, social workers, social work students). Is work by students of the same quality as that of psychiatrists? Are social workers injuring their cases while psychologists are producing improve-

---

* "The two clinical ratings, the first covering the objective aspects of the child's behavior and the second covering the subjective aspects, were then translated into a final clinical rating of "improved," "partially improved" or "unimproved" in accordance with the following formula. If either the original problems or symptoms or both were favorably modified and the subjective pressures which were associated with them were also favorably modified, the condition of the child at the point of closing was considered "improved." If neither the problems nor the symptoms were favorably modified, the condition of the child was called "unimproved." If either the problems or the symptoms were favorably modified, without concomitant favorable modification in the subjective discomfort, the condition of the child was called "partially improved."

ment? Or is everyone ineffective? Or was the research so poor and so irrelevant and this is well known within the agency, that no attention need be paid to it?

Two factors should be noted here. The first is the contrast in data analysis to the Jewish Board of Guardians study mentioned above. In the latter study the data showed specific sources of variation in outcome, and yet these same sources of variation were ignored in the I.J.R. study, although the authors were familiar with the earlier study. Why? Secondly, the statement that half the cases were treated by inexperienced workers carries the implication that experienced workers are better than inexperienced (an implication which is intuitively appealing to most people other than social workers). Why were the cases not examined on the basis of experience of the worker? (If such a data analysis was done, and it was found that experience, or other factors, was not relevant, then this information would certainly be of tremendous importance to the field.) Whatever the nature of the answers to these questions, someone ought to be quite concerned about the factors underlying such strange results from a well-respected agency.

The third study concerned the clients of a single marriage counsellor (Most, 1964). At first, I was inclined to dismiss this study as not worthy of research consideration, since it has only one worker. However, this one worker went to considerable lengths to evaluate her practice, and since I think that evaluation of practice by individual workers should be encouraged, I should like to give recognition to this attempt. This worker developed an instrument, gave it to clients at the beginning of treatment and at the close, and had the results analyzed by two other people besides herself. She selected a control group, which she afterwards realized was not the ideal control, since the initial scores on her instrument were much higher for the control than for her treatment group. However, she did find within the control group a subgroup with scores at the same level as her clients, and found that her clients improved far more than this subgroup. This study is one of the few that might be said to have some specific relationship to practice. The only thing that is missing is a description of the treatment given, i.e. it is not quite clear what is being evaluated (as it is not quite clear in many of the studies). While such studies as this one do not show effectiveness in the research sense, they are much to be encouraged as a beginning of a scientific examination of practice. Just as instructors find out what they thought they were teaching when they construct examinations, so caseworkers may discover their actual objectives when they construct instruments to measure change in their clients. They may also find out what their clients think about their practice.* Since Dr. Fischer is quite interested in a scientific approach to practice, this study should have interested him.

The remaining studies cluster into three types of special projects. The first type is the treatment of a new clientele in a regularly established agency.

Meyer *et al.,* 1965 (Girls at Vocational High)

Craig & Furst, 1965 (Treatment of predelinquent first-grade boys)

Webb & Riley, 1970 (Treatment of girls on probation)

Mullen *et al.,* 1972 (Services to the newly dependent)

The second type includes special projects attached to an established agency, but with workers specially hired for this purpose.

Berleman *et al.,* 1972 (Seattle Atlantic Street Project—treatment of delinquent boys)

Cohen & Krause, 1971 (Wives of Alcoholics)

McCabe, 1967 (Pursuit of Promise)

Blenkner *et al.,* 1971 (Services to the Aged)

Brown, 1968 (Chemung County Study)

A third set of projects are completely divorced from established on-going agencies.

Powers & Witmer, 1951 (Cambridge-Somerville Delinquency Prevention Project)

Geismar & Krisberg, 1967 (Multiproblem Families)

Miller, 1962 (Boston Midcity Delinquency Control Project)

What is the importance of separating the projects into these

---

* A publication describing what clients say about their workers may be of some interest here (see Mayer & Timms, 1970) .

several types? No importance at all, if one is willing to make the following assumptions: (1) Any social worker, regardless of training or experience can use any treatment modality in dealing with any client population. (2) A social worker with years of experience in child welfare deals equally well with the aged as someone who has years of experience in geriatrics. (3) A social worker whose entire training is in one-to-one counseling can organize and lead groups equally as well as someone trained in group work. (4) A group worker can do one-to-one counseling equally as well as a caseworker. (5) A worker from a psychiatrically oriented family agency will be equally as effective with public assistance clients, as will workers, trained or untrained, who have years of experience with public assistance clients. If these assumptions are correct, then social workers are a most remarkable group of people, quite unlike ordinary mortals. I believe, however, that these are untenable assumptions.

Social work has great need for a research and development model. Innovation is greatly valued in this field, which is individually and collectively very dissatisfied with its practice, much more so than other professions which perhaps have as much reason to be. However, the model that has been adopted is an experimental model from the physical and biological sciences, rather than a developmental model. The result has been testing before development. System feedback has rarely been used. The model of the research has produced results that are not useful for practice, whether they are positive or negative. That some thought is being given to the models of evaluation (although not yet to the models of development) is indicated in a recent article by Weiss (1974). In the absence of such developmental models, the large scale study has been mounted, with little thought of how the results could be interpreted. And then everyone is surprised and disappointed at the results. Why should we imagine that the development and testing of treatment modalities or of new ways of delivering service should be simpler than the development of computer programs or of engineering models? Why doesn't something work? Mostly, it is the "little things" (or sometimes the big things) that one did not know, did not think of, or thought were much less important than they actually were. Examples of some of these little things follow:

1. *The nature of the environmental situation.* In Craig and Furst (1965), for example, which was devoted to the treatment of first grade predelinquent boys, it is clearly indicated that the mothers were totally uncooperative. (This is to some extent true of most of the delinquency studies, where young children were involved.) Surely no caseworker believes that children as young as this can be treated when the family situation is destructive and the mothers uncooperative. Or do they?

2. *Very low treatment contact.* This was true of the famous Girls at Vocational High (Meyer *et al.,* 1965), where the treatment contact was less than once a month. It is also true of the equally famous Chemung County Study (as well as to other studies in the group) where the treatment contact was about twice a month (Brown, 1968). It seems to an observer that there must be many other things more important in the lives of these people than such infrequent contact with a therapist. Note also that a large portion (half or close to half) of the group studied had less contact than the average.

3. *Worker reaction to the consistently difficult caseloads.* Most of these studies deal with the most severe of society's problems—delinquency, poverty, the multiproblem family, alcoholism. Workers are not machines. They are human beings and however well trained they may be and however warm, empathetic and genuine they are, have limits to their endurance. Worker reactions are indicated in several studies. In Cohen and Krause, 1971 (Wives of Alcoholics), there is considerable evidence of worker reaction to the nature of the cases, to the unexpectedly high caseloads (because reapplications from the treatment group had to be accepted by treatment workers), uncertainty about general acceptance of this treatment method, all of which culminated in the departure of three of the four treatment workers within the first eight months of the project. In Geismar and Krisberg (1967) there is evidence of worker reaction to the lives of the multiprob-

lem families, eventuating in considerable worker turnover. In Meyer *et al.*, 1965 (Vocational High), there is evidence of the difficulty the workers had of knowing what to do with girls who had no conscious problems and were seeking no help. In Brown, 1968 (Chemung County), it is to be noted that, although there is no indication of the reactions of the workers, of the two workers who were first hired, one left the project. In the Atlantic Street Delinquency Control Project (Berleman *et al.*, 1972), one of the first three workers resigned. While one expects turnover in any group of people, and all of these may be due to personal situations, they may also be evidence of the difficulty of the project, since the importance of the personal situation may well be weighed differently depending on the work situation.

Dr. Fischer regards all of these trials of new programs as failures. Were they all complete failures? To some degree, I believe that it is improper to regard the trial of a new program as a success or failure, but rather to look at it from a developmental point of view. What information can this program give us that will be useful for development of new programs, or for the practice of an on-going agency? Looked at from this point of view, these projects, even with the meager data analysis that some of them have, have some potentialities. I shall summarize this rather briefly, not to evaluate the success of casework, but to perhaps intrigue the reader into reading the original documents on these studies.

Webb and Riley, 1970 (Girls on Probation). Involuntary clients *were* involved in treatment, with a distribution of treatment interviews at least comparable to the ordinary client. The treatment group improved on the variables measured more than the control group, and on some variables (the reduction of anxiety, for example) the difference appears to be large, although without the variances, it is not possible to determine whether the differences are statistically significant. Reduction in recidivism appears to be nearly significant.

Geismar and Krisberg (1967). Advocacy for the multiproblem family in the area of medical care was quite successful, perhaps more successful than anything else.

Berleman et al. (1972). On a follow-up interview, the boys and their families apparently perceived the program as helpful, would participate again in a similar program and generally perceived their behavior as either positively changed or not problematic.

Miller (1962). Gang type activities yielded to legitimate group activities and access to adult institutions was made available to these youths. These two major projects are discussed in more detail later in this chapter.

In *McCabe (1967)*, the Puerto Rican treatment group improved more than the controls.

In *Brown (1968)*, the treatment group improved more, though not significantly more than the control group.

In other words, many of the studies offer interesting food for thought, if one looks at them from a developmental point of view.

Negative Effects

Now, what about the possibility that social casework might actually harm someone instead of helping him, a possibility which horrifies Dr. Fischer. Perhaps to some people, the verdict of "ineffectiveness" may be preferable to accepting the condition that some casework (in fact, some treatment of any kind) may harm some people while it helps others. Do some social workers, as well as some forms of social treatment hurt some clients? The answer is undoubtedly in the affirmative just as some doctors, some forms of medical treatment, some lawyers, architects, etc. do harm rather than good (whatever their intentions). A recent analysis of prescriptive glasses indicates that a substantial portion of the glasses were incorrectly prescribed, to give just one instance of deficiency in the practice of another profession.*

---

* An article in a local paper in Honolulu on October 13, 1974 *(Star-Bulletin* and *Advertiser)* cited two studies: the first by the Optometric Center of New York (a nonprofit institution affiliated with the State University of New York) found that 35 percent of all glasses studied had lenses ground incorrectly or set incorrectly into the frames. A check on the accuracy of prescriptions by optometrists and physicians yielded an error of 15 to 20 percent. Another study conducted by The National Medical Center, Washington, D.C. found that nearly three quarters of the children studied were wearing glasses not corrected appropriately or adequately.

The only possible way to avoid the chance of a negative result is to take no action whatever, to do nothing, or else to take such peripheral or unimportant actions that they can have little effect for good or for evil. The moment one takes a serious action, intervenes massively in the situation, one is taking the chance that such intervention will injure some people and will benefit others. Only those who do not act at all take no chance of making mistakes. This seems quite obvious in ordinary life, and certainly it is a fact of professional life. The giving of service itself implies the acceptance of responsibility for errors of omission and commission, of doing something one should not have done, or of not doing something one should have done. It also implies a responsibility for taking such action as will reduce the errors of commission to a reasonable level, without greatly increasing the errors of omission.

In two of the reports, the definite possibility of negative results were recognized. First in Powers and Witmer (1951):

To suggest that social work activities may be actually harmful may seem rather shocking, so accustomed are we to thinking that well-intentioned actions in the field of human relations can at worst be only ineffectual. Such a point of view, of course, is not maintained in the field of medical or psychological therapy, where it is well recognized that under certain circumstances a specified form of treatment may make matters worse. In social work, however, where friendly counseling and the provision of various forms of concrete assistance are the services afforded, it is seldom thought that damage can be done. Nevertheless, if it can happen, it is very important that practitioners know what kinds of actions may be harmful and by what signs social treatment is contraindicated.

In a more recent study, Blenkner *et al.* (1971) had theorized in her original project proposal on services to the aged that because hopelessness could kill, and because institutionalization generated feelings of hopelessness, whichever group, demonstration or control, had the higher placement rate would also have the higher death rate. To quote: "Every service, every program, every helping act that is strong enough to have a real effect on the course of events may also be strong enough to be stressful, noxious, or even lethal to some, no matter how beneficient the intent" (Blenkner, 1971, p. 494). She goes on to indicate that medicine learned this long ago, and that social work, as it matures and moves towards a scientifically based status, must also adopt it.

Do the studies furnish us with any hints about the types of actions which are negative? Such indications are to be found in three studies.

1. Negative effects due to lack of training of the worker. In Powers and Witmer (1951) there is a warning against the development of close relationships with seriously maladjusted individuals, unless the worker is thoroughly trained in the handling of such relationships. This warning emerged from analysis of the casework in those cases in which there was serious recidivism or negative change in behavior. "An untrained worker always runs the risk of breaking trust with a neurotic boy whose sensitivities he does not understand, or of increasing his anxiety and guilt. It would seem better that untrained counselors should be helped to recognize individuals such as these and thereby avoid the close involvement that may follow upon discussions of personal problems" (Powers & Witmer, 1951, p. 509).

2. Use of massive environmental changes. Involuntary institutionalization of the elderly or of a delinquent child may differentially benefit some and injure others. In the case of the elderly person, one might hypothesize that the intervention will harm more of the clients than it will benefit. In the case of the delinquent child there has been little evidence of who is benefited and who is harmed, although there is certainly a body of opinion that children sent to reform schools are more likely to be adult criminals. Note that in both of the instances discussed here, the individual involved is to some degree dependent, and is in some way a cause of concern to the general community (not just to the social worker). The delinquent in his antisocial acts, and the mentally impaired elderly person without close family

or friends able and willing to care for him both creates a pressure on neighbors and other community resources (professional and nonprofessional). Thus in these cases there is a third party in the situation.

3. Pressure towards a change of life situation. An illustration of this is to be found in the study of wives of alcoholics. More of the treatment group than of either of the controls separated from their husbands. Did the nature of the treatment create a pressure or influence towards separation? And was this desirable? Did some of those who separated feel better, or did they feel worse? What about the costs to the children? Was the separation better for them? Little information is contained in the report on the consequences of this type of treatment intervention on the lives of the individuals involved.

The Research Model

As I indicated earlier, the research model which has been adopted in these evaluation studies is a peculiar adaptation of the experimental model which originated in agricultural research and has been used in the field of psychology and medicine. I should like to quote Helen Witmer's description of this research model (Powers & Witmer, 1951, p. 343).

> In planning the study, Dr. Cabot was apparently using a medical analogy. He seemed to be assuming that the disorder in question was like a medical disorder, in that it transcended the differences in the subjects in which it appeared, and that the treatment method to be employed was also (like a drug or other medical remedy) sufficiently uniform that variation in its application from case to case could be disregarded. . . .

However, she goes on to say that delinquency as well as other social problems are not analogous to diseases, and that social services do not have the unitary character of a specific medical remedy. And rather humorously she compared the Cambridge-Somerville study to a medical experiment in which different kinds of medicine are given to patients suffering from different kinds of disorders by doctors who hold different theories as to the causes of illnesses. And, as Dr. Fischer so cogently points out, even if these studies showed positive results, such results would be no more explainable than are negative results. In other words, the large-scale experiment is the last stage, rather than the first stage in a developmental model.

These studies are replete with averages and comparisons of averages. However, with only two or three exceptions, they do not take into consideration the three major sources of variation in the effects of treatment:

1. Variation among individuals in the groups as to type of problem (diagnosis), degree of motivation for treatment, capacity (intellectual and emotional) and in his environment (both physical environment and people-environment). For some illustrations of the effects of these variables see Ripple *et al.* (1964) and Deykin (1972).

2. Variation within the groups treated as to the extent of involvement, both intensively and extensively. The Jewish Board of Guardians study seems to indicate that length of contact is related to success rate, although the relationship does not appear to be linear, but changes little for shorter periods of contact, and builds up to a maximum at two years.

3. Variation among the social workers in length of experience, and the type of experience as related to the type of clients treated and to the methods used.

In most of the studies, there is great concern with the comparability of the treatment group and the control group. Tests of significance are run on as many variables as possible. Why this great concern? Why should it be important to have the same proportion of boys in the treatment and control groups, for example, or to have the same proportion of younger boys in treatment and control? The only reason that I can imagine is that it is anticipated that the treatment will have a differential effect on boys and girls, or on younger versus older boys. If this is so, and everyone anticipates that it will be so, then what would be the meaning of results from these studies? Overall results are meaningless. The only meaningful results would be those that were analyzed by the subgroups in the study. And yet, most of these studies have no subgroup analysis at all, even when the sample size is sufficiently large, and the data are available for both treatment and control groups.

The meaning of differential outcomes may be illustrated by the following examples:

Suppose that, in a particular client group, there are three diagnostic categories: A, B, and C. For category A, the best treatment is intrapsychic, for category B, the best treatment is peer group activity, and for category C, there is no known treatment. Now, suppose that the overall treatment is intrapsychic. Then those in category A may respond positively, those in category B may actually respond negatively to the treatment and become worse, and those in category C may respond in no way to the treatment (or may remain uninvolved). Meanwhile, many other events and conditions are affecting the lives of all these individuals, and these events may in some way be related to the diagnostic categories. Then the outcome of the experiment will depend on what proportion of the group is in each of the three categories. If category C predominates, the outcome may be "no change" on the average. If category B predominates, the overall result may be negative, if category A predominates, the overall result will be positive. Note, however, that whether the result is "no change," positive, or negative, it is meaningless.

A second example—suppose that both boys and girls are in a particular study. The treatment given is equally good for either. However, the boys in this study happen to have very much worse home conditions than the girls, so that the probability of the treatment overcoming the negative effects of the home situation is very low. The average effect of the treatment, then, may be affected by the proportion of boys in the study, not because there is a differential effect of the treatment on boys and girls, but because of a differential association of sex with another negative factor. These are the simplest possible examples of differential effectiveness.

There may be two major reasons why this analysis by subgroup or according to the sources of variability was not done, or if done, was not published:

1. Simple weariness with the data. After all, the study has been done, and why should one bother with the details. That this may be the case is indicated in the following quotation from Lehrman *et al.* (1949, p. 87):

> It is interesting to note that the design of this study suffered from one complication which is often present in social research undertakings. An attempt was made to gather too much information with the hopeful idea of answering a multitude of questions; the supposition being evidently that while you are about it you might as well gather as much information as possible. The result was that literally hundreds of tables were prepared in the first instance, supplying data not only about the pertinent areas covered in this report, but also about such related and extraneous factors as number of psychiatric appointments, length of experience of the therapist, utilization of group therapy, Big Brothers, and summer camps, etc. It then became necessary to strip away from the tabulations quite a lot of complicated information before the pertinent facts could be examined.

   This quotation probably illustrates one of the differences in point of view between the researcher and the practitioner. To the practitioner it is the details that are important. To the traditional researcher, it is the big picture, regardless of the fact that this big picture may be irrelevant in producing data useful for practice. Since I held this same point of view prior to my encounter with the question of the usefulness of research for social work practice, I understand it well.

2. Lack of understanding of the variables and failure to distinguish types of treatment. There is some evidence of this in one of the reports, and of course it may exist elsewhere. The bias here may be based upon previous experience and other research. For example, the following conclusions from Levitt *et al.* (1959, p. 346):

> Certainly, our results should not be generalized to clinics which are staffed with experienced, well-trained therapists, nor to the fully trained private practitioner.

In conclusion, it should be pointed out that a recent survey . . . of thirty-seven investigations of the efficacy of psychotherapy with children, indicates that absence of difference between treated children and defector controls is widespread. It is significant that most of the 8,000 child patients involved in the survey were treated in clinics.

This point of view may go back to the medical model of research. Without the knowledge of sources of variation in outcome of treatment, one is not likely to analyze the results.

Who Is the Defendant?

Sometimes in an investigation, a verdict is brought in that the crime was committed by person or persons unknown. In this case I must confess that I had a little difficulty in keeping the defendant identified properly. Dr. Fischer identifies casework as that which caseworkers do. But in these studies many things are done by many people with different backgrounds. It is not at all clear to me whether it is the things they do that are on trial, i.e. if they did different things, then everything would be all right. Or is it the caseworkers themselves, i.e. by virtue of having a degree from a school of social work, are they automatically ineffective? If so, is it all the caseworkers in these studies who are ineffective, or are they being regarded as a sample of all caseworkers? If we are looking at a sample of caseworkers, we should have the individual work of each worker, rather than the average work of two, three, four . . . workers. This is a little confusing to an observer, since some of the workers were not caseworkers, and much of what they did was not one-to-one counseling, but included group work, community organization, and outreach gang work. To illustrate the variation, I present below the types of treatment modalities in eight of the studies.

Miller   —Outreach work with gangs to involve the boys in
(1962)   legitimate group activities, using counseling, advocacy
           with employers and schools, modeling, teaching, etc.
           (workers with casework, group work degrees or both).
           (Intervention into the adolescent system)

Berleman —Work with boys and significant others (client fam-
et al. ily system, but not peer group), individually and in
(1972) randomly selected groups of project boys, and some
family groups (3 of the 4 workers had experience
with adolescents and their families). (Intervention
into the family system)

Powers —Friendly service; provide needy boys with adult
& Witmer friends who would try to discover the reasons for the
(1951) boys' maladjustment and provide the needed service—
not intended to be casework oriented.

Cohen & —In-office interviews based upon Jellinke's disease
Krause concept of alcoholism, involved round-the-clock avail-
(1971) ability to the client, use of literature on alcoholism
as a disease, emphatic statement of competence.
(Original workers left project, new workers hired
from outside the agency)

Lehrman —Use of "transference psychotherapy," with psychi-
et al. atric social workers actually conducting the interviews,
(1949) but with the treatment team—supervisor, psychiatrist,
and social worker—determining treatment plans, alter-
ing, confirming expanding them. (Treatment of children; not clear whether parents were included in any
cases)

Geismar —Objective was to serve the hardcore multiproblem
& Krisberg family as counselors, advocates, facilitators with oth-
(1967) er agencies (included both professional and nonprofessional workers).

Levitt —No description of treatment, but the therapists in-
et al. cluded social workers, psychiatrists and psychologists.
(1959) In 46 percent of the cases both parents and child
were seen, in 44 percent parents only, and in 10 percent child only.

McCabe —Children's activity groups, led by trained group
(1967) leaders (not otherwise identified) man for the boys,
woman for the girls.
Parents groups led by one social caseworker.

In other words, there is among the various studies such a wide range of approaches that to imagine that a single "unitary" concept is being evaluated is sheer nonsense.

Nature and Size of the Sample

The above discussion leads into the question of the nature and size of the sample in these studies. Is the appropriate sample the number of clients who were served by these various agencies and by these various projects? If so, the number is substantial, although the number in specific projects may be quite small. Or is the sample one of *caseworkers,* in which case the sample is much smaller. Or is the sample one of casework done by caseworkers, group work done by caseworkers, group work done by group workers, casework done by group workers, in which case, the size of the sample is indeterminate.

If the studies are regarded as samples of all activities done by caseworkers, then the sample consists of the caseworkers, rather than the clients. Treatment is given by individuals. As we have observed above under the discussion of the research model, the individual caseworkers are not all alike, dealing out some stan-

TABLE 12-I

NUMBER OF CASEWORKERS IN EFFECTIVENESS STUDIES

Study	Number and Type of Workers at One Time	Total Number of Project Workers
Brown	2 professional caseworkers	3
Tait and Hodges	2	—
Berleman *et al.*	3	4
McCabe	1 social caseworker 3-4 "experienced group leaders"	—
Blenkner *et al.*	4	—
Miller	7 (some caseworkers, some group workers, some both)	—
Powers and Witmer	10	19 (includes 8 professional social workers, 6 had completed part of requirements, 2 experienced boys' workers, 2 psychologists, 1 nurse)
Cohen and Krause	4	7

dard medicine. Therefore, in order to have a sample of casework, one needs a sample of caseworkers. The larger the number
of clients served by a particular caseworker, the more reliable a
sample one has of the casework dealt out by that particular caseworker, but not by others.

How many caseworkers are there? This is very difficult to determine in several of the studies. In fact, in most of those studies which deal with the workers in a regular ongoing agency, the
information is not given. In eight of the seventeen studies I
found it possible to determine the number of workers (see Table
12.I). In some of the studies, as is apparent from the Table, the
number of workers is quite small. Where these workers are also
unfamiliar with the particular client population (someone from a
psychiatrically oriented family agency dealing with public assistance clients, for example, or someone with years of child welfare
experience dealing with the mentally impaired elderly), the appropriateness of the sample as well as its size might be seriously
questioned, at least by an outside observer.

The Delinquency Studies

A complete treatment of the delinquency prevention and treatment studies would be a book in itself. Many of these studies
have almost no statistical analysis, little description of treatment,
and treatment with low intensity and length of time. Two of
them, however, had high treatment intensity on the average over
some period of time, and apparently had little difficulty in involving at least a large part of the client group in treatment.
Both were innovative in the sense that systematic long term work
of this kind with substantial client groups had not been undertaken previously. The two projects were alike in their objectives,
but quite different in their approach to the objective. They were
also alike in the fact that neither of them showed any apparent
statistical effect on delinquency. One of the projects was located
in a predominantly black ghetto in Seattle and the other in an
area of high gang activity in Boston.

Berleman et al. (1972). This study had as its objective work with
delinquency prone boys as well as their families in a black ghetto,

primarily to enable the boys and their families to "adjust." (Treatment has been described earlier.) The statistical measures of outcome are sophisticated and complex, involving concepts of seriousness of offense and of at-risk days for both school and police offenses. On the basis of these scales, four groups of boys were identified: two small groups, one with none or minor offenses, both police and school, the other with moderate or severe on both police and school. The two large groups, however, are moderate or high in one area (police or school) but not in both. At a minimum, the two large groups of boys should have been looked at, to determine whether there were any differential effects.

This study also contains some peculiar and contradictory data. While it was apparently found that the treatment and control groups did not differ on offenses, when a follow-up interview was conducted, the treatment boys and their parents nearly unanimously said that they would participate in this type of study again, and, further, over half the boys perceived decreases in violative behavior in school and over two-thirds perceived reductions in police violative behavior. Their parents also perceived reductions in school violative behavior (43%) and in police violative behavior (47%).

These are puzzling results. The boys and their parents apparently perceived the service as helpful, would participate again in a similar program, and generally perceived behavior as positively changed or as not problematic. What are some possible explanations?

1. The parents and boys told the follow-up interviewers what they thought the interviewers wanted to hear.

2. The parents and boys did not perceive the situation correctly, i.e. they thought the service was good and they had been helped, but this was not true, i.e. they really did not know what was going on.

3. This kind of service (high involvement with the total family group) may have high possibilities for positive results or for negative results depending on the type of family and the affective relationship of the boys to the family. Perhaps also the randomly selected treatment groups were not

all of equal effectiveness or equally desirable for boys of different personalities and different family situations.

Miller (1962). In this case the treatment was outreach work with indigenous gangs. The intensity of service to the groups was high, involving three contacts a week, with five to six hours per contact on the average. This of course was contact with the group, so that actual contact with individuals may have been much less. While there was no difference between treatment and control groups with respect to delinquency, apparently there were considerable changes in nonviolative behavior. Group relations were changed from the street gang to the club or athletic team, group members were involved in organized, rule-governed activities, including athletic contests, dances, fund-raising dinners. Athletic teams moved from cellar to championships; one group grossed close to a thousand dollars at a fund raising dance; gang members and community adults served together on joint committees working in the area of community improvement (one such committee obtained an allocation of $60,000 from the city administration for the improvement of a local ball field). Gang members gained access to legitimate adult institutions and organization. Something was accomplished in this project, although it apparently was not a reduction in delinquency. However, one piece of information in the project report is puzzling. To quote: "Was there a significant reduction in the relative frequency of disapproved actions during the period of worker contact? . . . No." On the same page the author states: "Of the fourteen behavior areas, only one (school-oriented behavior) showed a statistically significant reduction in disapproved actions, one no change, and two . . . showed increases. Of the seven analysis groups, only one (white, male, younger, high social status) showed a statistically significant reduction. Of the remaining six, five showed decreases in disapproved actions, one no change, and one . . . an increase." To restate this finding: there was no change, except that out of fourteen behavior areas, eleven showed a positive change. And out of seven groups, six showed reductions. Other important questions are not answered: Was there a reduction in gang wars? Did the nature of the violations change? Who were the violators?

Did those who were the central figures in the legitimate groups also commit the more serious crimes? Or was it those who lost their leadership position as the group changed from the informal street corner to a more formal legitimate activity? Or did the group workers have more success than the caseworkers in this project?

Thus in these two very interesting projects, even with the very summary type of data analysis that is presented, it appears that there are many unexplained results. Why were they not pursued, or if they were, why not published? Undoubtedly a great deal of money was invested in these projects, and yet little in the way of new knowledge has emerged.

A further note on the treatment of delinquency may be appropriate here. One hypothesis that should have been considered by all of these projects is that where the environment is very negative, one or both parents are inadequate, or have some psychiatric disorder, there may be little that a social worker or anyone else can do without the removal of the child from the home (Montreal *Educateur* or Tennessee Reeducation model). It may well be that delinquency is really delinquencies (as some sociologists maintain), and that a unitary approach to delinquency is self-deceit.

Other Studies

It is impossible to comment on all the studies in this brief chapter. However, two of them deserve a little more than passing attention. First, the study of services to the newly dependent (Mullen *et al.*, 1972). The authors comment on the fact that there is little information of public assistance recipients. Some research which is in process between the University of Hawaii School of Social Work and the Hawaii Department of Social Services and Housing has indicated that most public assistance recipients, in this state at least, do not perceive themselves as in need of services of any kind. Approximately 25 percent felt a need for help in the areas of child rearing or interpersonal relations (particularly dealing with boy friends or ex-husbands). Only a small proportion needed help with housing or budgeting. It appears that the Boston experiment might better have been postponed until a descriptive study had provided enough information to make an experiment meaningful. Secondly, the study of services to the aged (Blenkner et al., 1971). On an overall basis, this appears to be a very unfortunate study. However, the objective was good—apparently to keep the experimental group from being institutionalized, by providing all sorts or services in their own homes. Why did it work out otherwise? Too much attention from workers who were not familiar with the elderly? Or did the "community others" on whom the burden of caring for these people, of making their lives possible outside of an institution, create some pressure for institutionalization? One should note here that the general public believes that the mentally impaired elderly person belongs in an institution. How do those not institutionalized get along? An investigation along this line might have added much to our knowledge. Further, there is a hint in the report that the men, rather than the women, tended to be institutionalized. It seems difficult to understand why data were not presented separately for men and women.

The Framework

Dr. Fischer presents a detailed and well-organized framework for the evaluation of research studies (one not dissimilar from those that have been used by teachers of research in schools of social work for a number of years). This framework is to be used to determine how well the study fulfills all necessary conditions. There are specific aspects of this framework that might be questioned. However, I should like to question the usefulness of the critical approach to research in general. This may seem like a strange point of view for a researcher and teacher of research, but perhaps my point of view will become clearer with some explanation.

The critical point of view may be likened to giving each study a grade (A, B, . . . F) on the basis of how well it has run the gamut of evaluation. However, it is not quite clear what happens after the grade has been given. Does one discard the study if it has a low grade? Does one believe its conclusions if it has a high grade? What is the pay-off for the reader in this method?

On an overall evaluation, how many studies will have a grade of A or even B+? There are few studies that have no problems, no errors, unwarranted assumptions, accidents, uncontrolled operations, unknown conditions, confusing data. That these are not more frequently reported in research studies is perhaps due to the defensiveness created by the critical evaluation approach to research. "Let's not give them the ammunition to mow us down" is something I have frequently heard among researchers. And yet, the more competent the researcher, the more aware he is of the problems in his research.

What is the effect of the critical approach? On researchers, I think it produces defensiveness and concealment. There may be a tendency to report only the clear parts of the research, to conceal the problems and the confusions. On students and practitioners this approach has a clearly negative effect. It is much fun to tear a study to pieces, but very quickly, the student gets the idea that there are no studies that do not have something wrong with them, and how important that something is considered to be may depend to a large extent on the biases of the reader. A short time ago a student in one of my classes said: "Why read research, anyway? I thought I had a study that might be important for my practice, and then I found out that Dr. ——— doesn't think that it is a good study." Thus, to the student and the practitioner, the critical approach results in a negative attitude, to the avoidance of research.

A second question that one might ask with respect to the analysis of a study which supports the null hypothesis under this critical framework is: What is the payoff for the reader in this case? There is none. Even if the study is a poor one, with perhaps a grade of D—, the reader is still left with the null hypothesis. Thus the application of the framework is only to see whether positive results can be eliminated.

A third question might be asked: Does this framework really enable one to glean from the study something new to think about which relates to practice in a particular area, or to theory? The framework directs one to the statistical and research considerations, but it gives one little knowledge about the content.

The critical approach to research makes research a game for the researchers, greatly decreases student and practitioner interest in research, and may possibly have led to the decreasing interest in research in many schools of social work. There is simply too little pay-off for the reader in this approach, given the investment of time and intellectual energy in this approach. Again, the approach requires a considerable knowledge of statistical methodology which may not be available to the student and practitioner.

What is the alternative? Certainly we cannot just accept all studies at face value. Some have poor designs and are badly carried out. But may I suggest a somewhat different approach, which gets one out of the game of critiquing, and into the search game? This approach nearly always has a pay-off for the reader. Instead of asking the question: What is wrong with this picture? It asks: What useful information is there in this study? Instead of asking for broad generalizations, it asks for the specific facts of the study. It asks for something useful to think about, instead of a broad judgment. It looks at research in the light of theory and practice.

The various components of this approach, which I shall not attempt to develop in any detail in this paper are:

- A differential approach to research depending on one's knowledge of the topic,
- An approach which asks of a research study a contribution to ways of thinking about the topic rather than broad results,
- An approach which recognizes that any research study, regardless of its size, is only a specific study, under specific circumstances, specific people, specific conditions,
- Conclusions and generalizations in the study are looked upon as unimportant,
- The findings (data) are first examined. If there are no findings, the study is abandoned.
- More than one study on a particular topic needs to be examined, preferably done by more than one researcher. It is recognized that where only one study is available, not too much is known anyway.
- The questions—why did the researchers do what they did, could they have done better—are considered.

- It is recognized that all research studies have elements of uncertainty.

An approach such as the above may give social work a more realistic and more useful approach to the reading of research.

I should state here that one point on which I can agree with Dr. Fischer quite thoroughly is that the large scale experimental project should be abandoned, and a beginning of the scientific approach to the analysis of case studies needs to be made.

Implications of the Research

We have here seventeen studies, some of which must have been very expensive. Is there anything to be learned from these studies as a whole? I believe that there is much that a social work practitioner could obtain from these studies, but I shall here summarize what I see in them:

1. In general much more attention needs to be given to casework theory, as well as the theories in the content field, before undertaking research.
2. Very little that is useful for practice can be gleaned from the type of data analysis in most of these studies.
3. That there may be an "ideal model" of treatment, with very little concept of the cost in terms of time and money of this ideal model of treatment.
4. That severe and destructive environmental situations require much more expensive treatment than has been existent in any of these projects.
5. And finally, what is society's charge to social work? Is it to work with the worst cases, or is it work with the cases which will most readily yield to treatment?

Was the Appeal Successful?

This analysis was begun to review the evidence on which casework was convicted of ineffectiveness. In reviewing this evidence, we have found that only three studies refer to the practice of established agencies with the usual workers and usual clientele, that all other studies are field experiments in innovation either with clients unusual to the agency, new workers, or are special projects with no established agency. We have also seen that the definition of casework is untenable in view of the variety of activities, and the variety of training of the workers, and that the research model is inappropriate to the situation. In addition, the sample size of the caseworkers is generally small. The only possible conclusion is that the case should be thrown out of court, and the prosecutor should turn his attention to more useful activities.

Summary

This series of studies raises a serious question in my mind about the worth of that which is published under the name of evaluation. A consideration of Dr. Fischer's book also points up the tremendous responsibility that researchers who engage in evaluation studies must carry. Evaluation is the new game, and the apparent custom is that anyone can evaluate anything regardless of his specific knowledge of what he is evaluating, or his general research competence.

What are the possible audiences for this book? Four main ones, probably: faculties and students in schools of social work, social work practitioners, funding agencies, and the general concerned public. Perhaps Dr. Fischer intends to direct his treatise towards the first two of these audiences, particularly towards reform in the teaching of methods or practice in schools of social work, and towards the reform of that practice in the field. It is clear that he has an intense dislike for the ego psychology approach to human behavior, and this dislike may have influenced the particular orientation of this book, the definition of casework, and his failure to distinguish among the studies.

However, regardless of his intended audience, the book will be read and quoted or misquoted by others. References to his earlier article on this subject have begun. There is a group of concerned citizenry who have always known that the proper treatment of delinquents is a good stiff prison sentence, and that all social programs are merely mollycoddling the lazy and the criminal. To this group, this book will be a boon and it will be used to its fullest, appropriately and inappropriately. Certainly university administrations will be wondering about their graduate and undergraduate programs in social work.

But, one might well say, if this is the effect of the truth, so be it. Let us not conceal truth, even if the effect of telling the truth is not exactly what we had in mind. Agreed. But before we tell it, let us make very sure that it is the truth, for the effect of an error here may be felt for generations.

The reader may then ask: Will this book do harm? The answer is—YES. And is it the truth? The answer is—NO.

REFERENCES

Deykin, E. "Life Functioning in Families of Delinquent Boys: An Assessment Model," *Social Service Review,* Vol. 46, 1972, pp. 90-102.

Mayer, J. E. and Timms, H. *The Client Speaks.* Chicago: Adline, 1970.

Ripple, L., Alexander, E. and Polemis, B. *Motivation, Capacity and Opportunity as Related to the Use of Casework Services.* University of Chicago Monograph, 1964.

Weiss, C. "Alternative Models of Program Evaluation," *Social Work,* Vol. 19, 1974, pp. 675-681.

CHAPTER 13 NEEDED: A NEW SCIENCE FOR CLINICAL SOCIAL WORK

WILLIAM J. REID

George Herbert Jones Professor
School of Social Service Administration
University of Chicago
Chicago, Illinois

Aɴʏ ʜᴇʟᴘɪɴɢ ᴘʀᴏꜰᴇꜱꜱɪᴏɴ has an obligation to provide evidence that its technology achieves desired objectives and to make continual efforts to improve that technology. Following the example of medicine, clinical social work has turned to scientific methods as a way of meeting both parts of that obligation.

A STRATEGY THAT FAILED

The application of scientific methods to the testing and improvement of the methods of clinical social work has followed an implicit strategy during the past two decades. The activities of the social worker designated as "helpful" or "therapeutic" have been taken as methods to be tested. The precise nature of these activities has not been at all clear, and given their diversity and often vague conception, it has proved impossible to describe them accurately. Nevertheless, they have been assumed to constitute an "effective" means of helping clients achieve a variety of ends, ranging from feeling more content to staying out of trouble with the police.

Basically, research and development strategy has followed a fairly standard paradigm for evaluative studies of social programs. Researchers have been given the task of determining whether or not complex *programs* of social work intervention were effective under varying conditions. A strict division of labor has been the rule in the studies that have resulted: The practitioners (and their chiefs) have conceived and carried out the treatment programs; researchers have been cast largely in technical roles. They have been responsible for framing the programs with research designs, for collecting, analyzing and reporting ensuing data. One design in particular—the field experiment—has emerged as the form for conducting definitive tests of the social workers' methods. As we have seen, this strategy has called for tests of the activities of professional social workers against lesser forms of intervention or against what clients might accomplish on their own initiative. It was expected that "scientific proof" of the efficacy of the efforts of professional social workers could be obtained. Further, it was thought that programs found to be particularly effective could be "disseminated," and their ingredients analyzed to isolate the factors contributing to their success.

Fischer has ably laid before us the fruits of that strategy. They are certainly not what had been hoped for.

What went wrong? It is possible, as Fischer argues so persuasively, to put the blame on the inadequacies of the treatment programs, on the assumption that the research methods used to test them were essentially sound. Or it is possible to point an accusing finger at the crudeness of the research methods and to claim that they did not give the treatment programs a fair test. In my judgment, the proper target for criticism is the research and development strategy as a whole, a product of the joint efforts of researchers and practitioners.

In effect, this strategy has produced a series of studies in which few traces of the impact of the experimental variables could be found in the outcome measures. This could have resulted from weak inputs or insensitive measurement or, as seems most likely, from some combination of the two. Whatever the social workers were doing, it was apparently not powerful or enduring enough to register on the rather gross measures provided by the researchers. In short, the whole treatment-research paradigm has failed to pay off. It has not produced the reassuring "proof" of the effectiveness that practitioners and administrators have sought.

More important, it has not isolated clearly effective programs and, hence, has not been able to proceed to the next logical step —factoring out the active ingredients of effective treatment approaches. Thus its results have provided little guidance for the improvement of practice.

This strategy has failed because, in large part, it was unwittingly designed to produce flawed experiments. Experimental variables, derived from complex and poorly articulated practitioner efforts, were not specified. The implementation of these variables, left entirely in the hands of practitioners, was badly controlled. Hypothesized effects were derived from diffuse, diverse and, probably, unrealistic hope of "what casework could do." Yet these posited effects were used as the basis for developing outcome measures, spread tissue-thin in order to cover all possible outcome contingencies. Since experimental variables, according to prevailing notions, had to operate over extended periods of time (months, if not years), the treatment phases of the experiments were of long duration.

If an experiment is well controlled, its duration may not necessarily be a weakness, as long-term experiments with laboratory animals have demonstrated. But extended durations serve to compound the flaws of the kind of poorly controlled investigation we have had in social work: control and specification of experimental variables become even more difficult; problems of mortality or "drop-outs" become more serious; various sources of extraneous variance have more of a chance to operate and outcome measures in effect are driven further away from possible points of impact.

To be sure, many of these designs should evoke praise, if not awe, for the amount of control they were able to achieve under the circumstances, but none, in my judgment, achieved a level of rigor adequate to the purposes. Given the overall strategy that spawned them, they could not.

It would be wrong to say that the resulting studies have produced nothing of value. They have cast legitimate doubt on the unwarranted claims of various programs of intervention, in particular, claims that unspecified methods of casework could significantly alter the course of delinquency or economic dependency. They have made practitioners and program developers more open to innovation. They have enabled researchers to test and perfect measures of input and outcome.

Perhaps the whole phase was inevitable in the development of a scientific base of the profession. But enough is enough, we need to learn from our mistakes and move on.

A NEW DIRECTION

I would like to devote the remainder of this chapter to setting forth and illustrating a rather different and, hopefully, more fruitful approach for the use of the scientific method to assess and improve practice. In general this strategy calls for the development and testing of practice modules or units that are built from clearly explicated, controllable techniques and that are aimed at achieving highly specific short-term effects amenable to relatively precise measurement. This strategy flows from certain premises: I assume that the controlled experiment, despite its poor showing in the studies reviewed earlier, is still one of our most potent means of increasing the effectiveness of our practice technology. But in order to use this tool to optimal advantage, we must concentrate its application to variables we can clearly specify and control and whose effects can be promptly and rigorously assessed. This may mean ruling out treatment operations that do not meet these criteria or developing forms of them that do. Experimental science should not be expected to have a role in the testing and developing of everything practitioners do—one of the lessons that should have been learned from the studies reviewed in the first portion of this volume.

Moreover, the operations and outcomes of variables may be best studied over part of the life of a case or in respect to some aspect of the case. It is not necessary to use the complete case as a unit of attention. In fact, specific effects may often be lost in global or aggregated measures of case outcome.

The implementers of this strategy should ideally be expert in methods of both research and treatment—clinical scientists—to use Briar's (1974) phrase. Or, close working teams of research-oriented practitioners and practice-knowledgeable researchers might suffice. The usual arrangement of the practitioner "doing his thing" with the researcher looking over his shoulder, would not do at all.

The elements of this strategy are outlined below. What follows is by no means an original program but, rather, an attempt to synthesize recent developments in the applications of the scientific method to the study of improvement of clinical practice.

1. *Identification and Explication of Treatment Modules*

A treatment module is a specific method or configuration of practice methods designed to produce a specific effect. In order to qualify, the methods must be operationalized in terms of measurable practitioner behavior. The expected effects are closely and clearly linked to the methods. For example, a module might consist of techniques for helping clients rehearse certain behaviors with the expected effect that clients would be able to carry out those behaviors in given situations. Or the method might be the communication of accurate empathy, as defined by the Truax (1967) scale, with the expected effect that clients would report "feeling understood" by their caseworkers.

2. *Input Control*

In experimental research it is important that the treatment method be carried out with a reasonable degree of fidelity to its formal description. Otherwise what is actually tested may turn out to be something quite different from what the experiment was designed to test. Practitioners must be trained in the method. Their work must be monitored through tape recordings, conferences or other means, in order to identify and correct systematic deviations in the application of the method. This task can be satisfactorily accomplished only if prescribed practitioner activities have been spelled out clearly in the first place.

3. *Measurement of Input*

The experimental variables *actually* tested can only be determined by careful measurement of what the practitioners actually did, not by what they said they would do. Practitioner recordings of their experimental operations may be an adequate source of data if their accuracy can be checked against tape recordings or direct observations of practice.

4. *Measurement of Effects*

Measurement is concentrated on determining outcomes of the particular methods tested. Measurement of other types of outcome serve primarily to add to understanding of the effects of these methods. For example, there may be interest in determining if other changes (either positive or negative) have occurred that may be related to experimental effects. Focusing on a delimited range of possible effects enables the researcher to take more detailed and sensitive measurements. Measures of behavior change based on direct observation are obtained when applicable and feasible. Otherwise an effort is made to obtain multiple measures which can be checked against one another—for example, a youngster's account of change in his classroom behavior and teachers' reports of that behavior.

5. *Duration of Treatment and Timing of Measurement*

A rather short lease is kept on treatment variables. Duration of treatment methods prior to assessment of effects is measured in days, or perhaps weeks, not months or years. Experimental treatments may be continued for longer periods in "time series" designs in which repeated measures of change are taken between intervals of treatment. Measures to test the *duration* of effects may be taken at varying periods following termination of the experimental treatment.

6. *Design Possibilities*

A radical reduction in the scope and duration of experiments opens up new design possibilities. Ethical and practical problems are minimized when methods of treatment are withheld or manipulated over brief periods of time with ample opportunity for practitioners to treat without restriction before or after experimental phases. Thus treatment can be withheld for a week or so for a control group while an intervention is being tested in an experimental group. Or it becomes possible to introduce a particular experimental intervention in one group of cases, withhold it from another, while both groups of cases are being given some general form of treatment; or contrasting interventions may be introduced simultaneously in each to test the relative efficacy of different methods. A "cross-over" design may be used. Treatment may be suspended for one client group for a brief period, while an experimental intervention is introduced in a comparable group. The format is then switched: Treatment is suspended in the first group and begun in the second; following the cross-over, treatment can be continued as long as needed for both groups.

Other examples can be readily imagined. Designs of this kind may offer special promise for experimental research with clients who seek help on their own initiative—a group scarcely dealt with in the studies reviewed by Fischer. Reluctance to withhold treatment from such clients or the inability to hold them on waiting lists for extended periods of time have discouraged use of "no-treatment" control group. The withholding of treatment for brief periods or the withholding of limited techniques should be quite possible for clients of this kind.

7. *Development Strategy*

Obviously, any one experiment of the kind described is going to yield a rather limited amount of information, at least in comparison to amounts *hoped for* in the large scale experiments reviewed by Fischer. But because it focuses on immediate effects of specific methods and uses more exacting measurements, the micro-experiment is more likely to yield "positive findings," that is, evidence that the methods tested do, in fact, achieve certain effects.

Such experimentation should generate knowledge about what *does* work, knowledge for use in the development of practice theory and methods. Modules found to be effective can be combined into full scale treatment models. This building would take place incrementally with tests conducted at each stage of construction. One would not proceed with the building process until the effects of what had already been put together could be demonstrated. In this way, full scale models of probable effectiveness could be gradually constructed.

Tested treatment modules need not necessarily be combined. They could be used as units within the context of eclectic practice that may draw upon a variety of methods, both tested and untested. In fact, the practice of clinical social work seems to be becoming increasingly eclectic. As it does, the case for experimental tests of whatever may be called "casework" or "clinical social work" becomes even less defensible. Perhaps our most feasible research and development strategy will be to test and improve the separate elements that comprise eclectic practice—to provide practitioners with effective techniques to choose among. Evaluations of programs of social work intervention (in which different combinations of these elements would be used) will still be needed for purposes of administrative accountability but these evaluations should not be expected to carry the burden of testing and improving particular forms of intervention. Also, overall program evaluations would probably be more useful if they concentrated less on establishing the effectiveness of basic treatment methods and more on determining whether or not methods of known effectiveness were being properly carried out.

An Example

An illustration of this strategy will be drawn from a research and development program on task-centered treatment being conducted at the School of Social Service Administration, the University of Chicago (Reid & Epstein, 1972). A part of this program has been concerned with the construction and testing of a sequence of interventions designed to help clients carry out very specific behavioral tasks or problem-solving actions during the week following the interview in which the interventions were used. The sequence of techniques, which was referred to as the Task Implementation Sequence (T.I.S.), would approximate my earlier description of a treatment module, although the T.I.S. was more complex and less well specified than the ideal module should be.

A test of the T.I.S. was conducted along lines suggested by the research and development paradigm outlined earlier. The techniques comprising the modules were explicated in the form of written guidelines specifying the behaviors practitioners were to use in carrying them out. For example, practitioners were informed on how to specify the task, how to analyze obstacles to task accomplishment with the clients, how to use modeling and rehearsal to help the client learn task behaviors. These techniques, organized in a step-wise sequence, were designed to enable clients to carry out such tasks as arriving at school on time, keeping quiet while other children recited, trying out a certain job, or joining an organization.

Practitioners selected to test the T.I.S. (16 students in the school's task-centered program) were trained in the use of the module. Their application of it was monitored through practitioner recordings, conferences and tape recordings of their interviews. Corrective feedback was given to individual practitioners and to the group as a whole. Practitioner and tape recordings were used as a basis for more formal analysis of inputs.

An experimental design was used for the test. Briefly, each practitioner was assigned two research cases, randomly allocated to experimental and control conditions. The cases (n = 32) were drawn from school and mental health settings. In the experimental case, practitioners applied the T.I.S. to work on a given task in approximately the fourth interview. In the control case, practitioners developed a comparable task with the client at about the same point in treatment, but made no effort to help the client carry it out. Although the selection of experimental and control tasks was left up to the practitioners, we could detect no systematic differences between the two sets of tasks in respect to a wide range of variables, including the client's commitment to the task or the difficulty of the task.

In effect the experiment was restricted to only one interview in the case. The remainder of the case was treated in accordance with the task-centered model as a whole but no additional experimental variables were introduced.

Task progress was reviewed with the client by the practitioner the week following the application or withholding of the experimental treatment. The same kind of review was used with experimental and control cases. Tape recordings of these reviews were listened to by two judges who did not know which case was experimental and which control. The judges independently rated task progress (with a high degree of reliability). Whenever possible, ratings were checked against other sources of evidence, including direct observation of task behavior by the practitioner or reports of parents and teachers. This additional evidence generally accorded with the judges' ratings.

The findings will be briefly summarized. Since each worker had a pair of cases, one experimental and one control, data were analyzed in terms of the resulting sixteen pairs. In eleven of these pairs, the task progress ratings for the experimental cases exceeded ratings for the control cases; in three pairs, ratings were tied, and in two, the control cases did better. These differences significantly favored the experimental cases ($p < .05$, sign test). When the magnitudes of differences in the ratings were taken into account, the gap between the experimental and control cases became even greater ($p < .005$, Wilcoxon Signed Ranks Test). That is, the larger numerical differences in the ratings occurred in pairs in which the experimental case did better.

After considering a variety of plausible alternative explanations, we concluded that the caseworkers' input was largely responsible for the greater progress on the experimental tasks. We are still in the process, however, of determining what that input was exactly, since its scope and complexity far exceeded our prior descriptions of it.

The Task Implementation Sequence will be revised on the basis of that analysis. In our next experiment, the efficacy of the revised T.I.S. will be tested as cases as a whole, using a variation of that kind of cross-over design described earlier. Meanwhile, the T.I.S. will be accepted as provisionally "effective" and will be incorporated into the task-centered model.

Its imperfections notwithstanding, the experiment illustrates the kind of reduction in the scope of social work treatment that may be necessary at this stage of the art in order to achieve "positive findings." On the one hand, it is encouraging to be able to show that caseworkers can be *effective* in a scientifically demonstrable sense, particularly against the background provided by the studies in Fischer's review. On the other, we are sobered by the limited accomplishments of the interventions tested.

Conclusion

Perhaps the central idea in the research and development strategy I have advocated is this: scientifically-based models of practice must be built from the ground up, brick by brick. The implementation of this strategy will be laborious and time-consuming and we can expect few dramatic "breakthroughs." But the results will eventually justify the effort.

This strategy is but one variant of a more general paradigm that is guiding a considerable amount of research and development effort throughout the helping professions. Application of learning theory and single-subject designs to the study and modification of behavior offer a wide range of examples. We need, however, to develop forms of this paradigm suited to the special needs and problems of social work.

How much experimental science can contribute to the building of practice methods is an open question. If we wish to take full advantage of the power of science to advance technology, then we must develop methods that are amenable to rigorous testing. Many current practice approaches do not, in my judgment, lend themselves to testing of this kind. The typical technology examined in large scale "tests of casework" do not, nor does the kind of long-term, psychoanalytically-oriented treatment often used with voluntary clients. This is not to say we should abandon those forms of intervention; it is rather to say we should not look to experimental science as a means of improving them or as a means of justifying their existence.

REFERENCES

Briar, S. "Clinical Scientists in Social Work: Where Are They?" Paper read at the School of Social Service Administration Alumni Conference, May 4, 1974, at the School of Social Service Administration, the University of Chicago, Chicago, Illinois.

Reid, W. J. and Epstein, L. *Task-Centered Casework*. New York: Columbia University Press, 1972.

Truax, C. B. "A Scale for the Rating of Accurate Empathy," Rogers, C. *et al.* (eds.), *The Therapeutic Relationship and Its Impact*. Madison: University of Wisconsin Press, 1967, pp. 555-568.

CHAPTER 14 IS THE PSYCHOANALYTIC MODEL OBSOLETE?

HERBERT S. STREAN

Professor
Graduate School of Social Work
Rutgers University
New Brunswick, New Jersey

S EVERAL TIMES while studying Professor Fischer's research, I was reminded of Ibsen's play, "The Enemy of the People." In this play, the leading character who is a physician exposed the fact that the water in the city in which he lived and worked was contaminated by bacteria. Unfortunately, most of the residents of the city made a living directly or indirectly from the water supply inasmuch as the water was utilized for therapeutic baths. Therefore, many people from surrounding towns constantly visited the city to enhance their "psychosocial functioning."

Rather than carefully listening to the physician's report and studying the implications of his research, his colleagues, friends, and even members of his family blasted him. They told the good doctor that he was really making unnecessary waves, that his research methodology was faulty, his attitude was arrogant, his training was poor and that in effect, he was a heretic who did not know what he was talking about. How dare he interfere with the status quo? It harmed the city's prestige, interfered with people's livelihoods, and activated distrust in the city's potential clientele.

Unlike the physician in Ibsen's play, I am hopeful that Dr. Fischer will not be ostracized by his colleagues. When a researcher painstakingly reviews and evaluates dozens of research studies,

273

we tend to overlook his efforts and the implications of his find-ings if the results of the research disappoint or displease us. Rather than condemning Fischer for his findings, I believe we have an obligation to our clients, students, the profession and our communities to seriously ponder Professor Fischer's findings, conclusions, and his stated implications.

Professor David Fanshel of Columbia University's School of Social Work has commented that one of the sources of strain be-tween researchers and practitioners is that after the researcher has thoughtfully and rigorously designed a study, worked ardu-ously on it, and then presents his conclusions, the practitioner is often prone to respond "I knew it all the time!" (Fanshel, 1967). With mixed feelings and apologies, I must say to Dr. Fischer, "I knew it all the time!"

Although I have no quarrel with Dr. Fischer's study, research design, or conclusions, I am in disagreement with him on some of the implications of his study. The one implication that I wish to discuss in some detail is whether or not one can really conclude that because the "psychodynamic model" was used extensively by most of the caseworkers whose activities were studied in this book, it is the use of the psychodynamic model that makes the casework ineffective.

As a psychoanalyst as well as a caseworker, one of my convic-tions (which remains to be formally researched) is that psycho-dynamic theory is poorly and fragmentally utilized, abused and misapplied by many if not most caseworkers in their practices (Strean, 1972). Like many other psychotherapists, many case-workers fail to fully comprehend the complex metapsychology and therapeutic implications of the work of people like Freud, Hartmann, Erikson, Anna Freud and others. Notions like **psycho-**social and psychosexual development, transference, resistance, the corrective emotional experience, etc., in my opinion are half un-derstood and incorrectly used by the modal **caseworker.**

For example, I have seen many economically poor and de-pressed clients gratified and indulged, i.e. patronized in the man-ner of the friendly visitor of Mary Richmond's day, when a full grasp of the client's psychodynamics would have prompted the caseworker to work with the client's resistances against the expression of aggression toward all whom he distrusts and hates including his social worker and the profession of social work. If just this one facet of psychodynamic theory were utilized more planfully, some clients would feel less tension, ego functioning would be enhanced, and then the services that Professor Fischer would like them to receive could be received by these clients profitably. However, gratifying people who have such hatred and self-hatred in them only induces them to throw up what the worker has delivered and can lead to deterioration and no change in functioning.

Because so many of our colleagues who practice casework so frequently desire to have "love and be loved" relationships with their clients, they can not provide our angry, depressed and impoverished clients what they frequently need—an experience wherein the client can blast the caseworker who often represents in the transference everything or most things that the client thinks are evil. So many of our welfare clients have done better with self-initiated Welfare Rights groups because the social worker's "kindness" or "helpfulness" was not there to inhibit and frustrate their assertiveness and wish for action.

A better understanding and mastery of the psychodynamic model by caseworkers would enable the latter to help those clients who distrust, to verbalize their distrust to and at the caseworker (Erickson, 1950; Strean, 1974). It would also assist the caseworker to recognize that many individuals who are full of self-doubt and lack a sufficient feeling of autonomy and self-worth (Erickson, 1950) need an experience where their demands are not gratified immediately, but where their requests are studied with the caseworker and often frustrated. All too often a caseworker, not utilizing dynamic understanding appropriately, gratifies when he should frustrate and acts for the client when instead he should examine with the client why the latter cannot act for himself.

All too often I have observed, and I am sure others have made the same observation, that marital and family counselling by caseworkers frequently involves many subjective counter-transference reactions on their part. Too frequently seemingly well intended caseworkers support one spouse against the other and/ or champion and reinforce romantic fantasies rather than introduce the reality principle. In my supervision of and consultation with caseworkers over the years in what I think are prestigious and well established agencies, I have found it the rule rather than the exception, that caseworkers avoid many of the dimensions of their clients' real conflicts and instead tend to act out their own wishes, anxieties, and fears under the guise of "support," "gratification," "the positive relationship" and "the corrective emotional experience."

In child guidance clinics and family agencies I have, all too often, observed workers overidentify with children and subtly criticize parents to the detriment of both. With delinquents, I have seen too many caseworkers either subtly or overtly champion the youngster's acting-out—or else—become too punitive. Too frequently, under the guise of advocacy and social brokerage I have seen too many clients made to feel more helpless and resourceless than in fact they were to begin with.

I could give many other examples of how psychodynamic knowledge is misapplied, misused and abused by many caseworkers and by other psychotherapists and psychoanalysts as well. What Dr. Fischer has inspired me to think about is how to demonstrate in the future, with the use of rigorous research designs that he advocates, that with a well formulated psychosocial diagnosis, with careful thought given to therapeutic procedures and with the work well supervised, by one well versed in psychodynamic practice theory, casework based on psychodynamic principles can be effective!

As I have stated elsewhere and demonstrated through dozens of case examples, casework that as thoroughly as possible understands the client-in-his situation, that understands and relates to the client's presses and stresses, that notes and helps the client with his maturational tasks, and that provides a carefully controlled treatment relationship with full respect given to the client's resistances, fixations, regressions, and transference responses, can and does enrich psychosocial functioning (Strean, 1974). However, the presentation of case examples is insufficient research evidence to prove a hypothesis.

Many social work critics of psychodynamic principles (e.g. Briar & Miller, 1971; Werner, 1970; Stuart, 1970) have, in my opinion, missed the boat. Rather than recognize what Dr. Fischer has noted, that many if not most caseworkers intuitively practice their art and therefore misapply, misuse, and abuse psychodynamic principles of diagnosis and treatment, these critics have insisted that the theory is at fault. To use Dr. Fischer's baseball analogy to which he has referred elsewhere (Fischer, 1973), if every time I get up to bat, I strike out, it does not necessarily follow that there is something wrong with my bat. It could be that my stance, swing, timing, etc. are incorrect.

In addition to my impression that many caseworkers relate to their clients in a haphazard, intuitive, subjective manner, there are other forces at work which may account in part for the conclusion that casework is ineffective. Unlike other helping professions, we social workers take flight from our clients in many ways. We reward our good practitioners by removing them from practice and elevate them to supervisory and administrative positions. We, in casework, tend to place our least trained workers in places where clients hurt the most, e.g. welfare, probation, hospitals, etc. and put our better skilled social workers where the needs of clients are not so profound (Strean, 1972)! While Dr. Fischer has demonstrated that holding an M.S.W. degree does not guarantee success in casework, I would still hypothesize that in most agencies, the more disturbed and least resourceful clients are assigned to the least resourceful caseworkers, whether they have an M.S.W. or not! How accurate this hypothesis is, of course, has to be researched.

Schools of social work also subtly demean practice. More and more of the faculty members in a school of social work are either Doctors of Social Work who have had limited practice experience or are teachers who were great practitioners in their day but have not seen a client in years! Both are undesirable mentors and role models for students, and certainly interfere with the student's learning how to do effective casework.

In conclusion, I think Dr. Fischer's work is a valuable stimulant to the profession. While I disagree with some of the implications of his study, I am grateful to him for inspiring me and

I am sure many others, to think through more carefully and re-search more rigorously our hypotheses and biases. I applaud Dr. Fischer's efforts and to quote Ibsen's conclusion in "The Enemy of the People," which may offer some solace, "The strongest man is he who stands most alone!"

REFERENCES

Briar, S. and Miller, H. *Problems and Issues in Social Casework.* New York: Columbia University Press, 1971.

Erikson, E. *Childhood and Society.* New York: Norton, 1950.

Fanshel, D. "Sources of Strain in Practice-Oriented Research," *Social Casework,* Vol. 47, no. 6, 1967, pp. 357-362.

Fischer, J. "Has Mighty Casework Struck Out?" *Social Work,* Vol. 18, 1973, pp. 107-110.

Strean, H. *The Social Worker as Psychotherapist.* Metuchen, New Jersey: Scarecrow Press, 1974.

———. "Whither Casework?" *Psychotherapy and Social Science Review,* Vol. 6, no. 1, January 1972, pp. 19-23.

Stuart, R. B. *Trick or Treatment: How and When Psychotherapy Fails.* Champaign, Illinois: Research Press, 1970.

Werner, H. *New Understandings of Human Behavior.* New York: Association Press, 1970.

CHAPTER 15 SOME BRIEF COMMENTS ON THE MATTER OF EVALUATION OF CASEWORK EFFECTIVENESS

EUGENE TALSMA

Executive Director
Family Service Agency of Genesee County
Flint, Michigan

THE REVIEW OF THE RESEARCH in Part I of this book can serve as an implicit suggestion that a change of research direction should be seriously considered, initiated and expanded as rapidly as possible. Not only is the current evaluative research effort producing inconclusive results, the light generated is dim at best. Current evaluative research provides few clues or much in the way of empirically based guidelines that are useful for planning and developing service programs better or more demonstrably effective than those currently existing. In addition, most of the evaluative research into casework effectiveness, so far as I can see, has not been particularly helpful to the social caseworker in daily practice.

Much of the evaluative research into casework effectiveness has been far too global to produce reasonable and generally agreeable conclusiveness. Research efforts directed toward whole service programs or using large numbers of subjects and "control" groups is a potentially valuable endeavor, but it is also especially fraught with technical problems in respect to reliability, validity and specificity. And research into whole programs or using large sample/control groups for comparison purposes might sometimes provide general inferential information regarding case-work generally, but certainly leaves something to be desired in terms of evaluating various, more specific casework methods and procedures or casework as individually practiced.

In contrast to the gross evaluative research reviewed in this book, a change of research directions and a change of research attention has been explicitly suggested by various writers. Fischer, in his section "Implications for Research" (Chapter 6) properly calls for a moratorium on gross evaluative research and goes on to present several alternatives, one of which is the use of single case studies. Polansky, in the 1971 *Encyclopedia of Social Work,* makes a similar suggestion regarding single case studies: " . . . insightful analyses of the single case—whether it be a person, a group, or a community—will regain respectability as an occasional venture for the research worker." It might be added that Polansky, in the same breath and perhaps unintentionally, makes the use of single case "research" somewhat more palatable to caseworkers themselves by suggesting that, ". . . the present enchantment with statistics will decline. . . ."

The use of a single case study approach does not require sophisticated statistical or mathematical knowledge and skills. In effect and in its most elementary form, the single case study requires no greater mathematical/statistical knowledge than that possessed by the average seventh grader who can count, add and subtract simple numbers. Of course, this is not to say nor imply that more sophisticated and complex statistical and mathematical procedures are without value and cannot be applied to the single case study. They are valuable and useful and should be used whenever such expertise is practically available. Furthermore, for the general field of social casework, more rigorous research procedures will be necessary in order to satisfy scientific requirements, e.g. for reliability, validity, significance and generalizations across various situations.

In view of the high probability that more rigorous research procedures are certain to be advocated and used by the *research community,* it may be more appropriate here to advocate the single case study as available and appropriate for use by the casework *practitioner.* In a most elementary but compelling form, single case studies should be of interest to the practitioner since single cases are the daily affair of all caseworkers. In a most fundamental way, each case comes to the caseworker with a request for help in changing something, and if the caseworker accepts the case there is at least an implied agreement that the caseworker will help or try to help change something. The single case study, simply stated, addresses itself to the question, did something change during the time of casework attention? Slightly more precisely, and addressing the question crucial to the matter of casework effectiveness, did the change occur as a result of or in response to casework? Other similar and related questions may also be raised and addressed via the single case study. For example, assuming that change did occur, one should be interested in the direction and amount of the change. Does the change correspond to the client request and the help agreed to be provided by the caseworker?

Two variations in single case study designs may be used to address the effectiveness question. The first and most frequently seen in some psychology literature, e.g. the *Journal of Applied Behavior Analysis,* is the A,B,A,B, procedure which, in effect, measures the change target before, during and after the treatment has been used, and then runs through the same procedure once again. The letters A and B refer to two time spans during which the selected and specified client difficulties are measured, usually by simple counts as to how frequently the problem occurs (due considerations, cautions, and procedures for obtaining the count are taken into account in order to gain reliability and validity, etc.). The first time period, designated by the first "A," contains the measure of the problem in its natural, pretreatment environment; the second time period, designated by the first "B," contains the frequency count of the problem during treatment; the third time span, designated by the second "A," contains the count of the problem during the period when the treatment (implemented during the first "B" period) is stopped and the situation returns as nearly as possible to the normal conditions of the first "A" period; and in the second "B" period, the treatment is reinstated and the frequency count for that time period is reflected in the second "B" time span. Assuming there is a change in the problem and these changes are indicated by the frequency counting which is maintained consistently throughout the four time spans, a functional relationship between problem change and treatment is presumed to exist.

Plotting the problem counts on graph paper, a fairly easy task in most cases, and keeping track of the A,B,A,B time spans on the same graph almost always provides a clear summary of the data and provides an excellent vehicle to compare the various time spans. The graph in Figure 15-1 illustrates the situation quite clearly. In the illustration, five specified problems were included and carried through each time phase. The changes are clearly reflected in the graphic display and the rates during the four time spans (A,B,A,B) are easily compared showing evident differences between treatment/nontreatment time periods.

The second single case study design uses a "multiple-baseline" procedure. In this situation, several problems are identified as change targets in a single case. Each of the specified problems is measured (by frequency count as in the A,B,A,B design) over a time period so that the baseline (pretreatment) rate is established. Treatment of one of the problems is undertaken, during which data collection on all previously selected problems continues. After a period of effort and time has been expended on the one problem, the treatment focused on that problem ceases and is refocused on another of the problems. Additional shifts in treatment focus can follow. Data collection continues consistently throughout the time the procedures are employed and as in the A,B,A,B design, and problem rate changes coincidental with the treatment times is taken to indicate a functional relationship between problem change and treatment.

As was stated earlier, the main statistical/mathematical skill needed for these procedures, both A,B,A,B and multiple-baseline designs as briefly described above, is a simple count of the occurrence of selected problems. As also mentioned previously, more sophisticated research procedures may be applied to the data produced in either research effort. Analysis-of-variance (ANOVA) is an

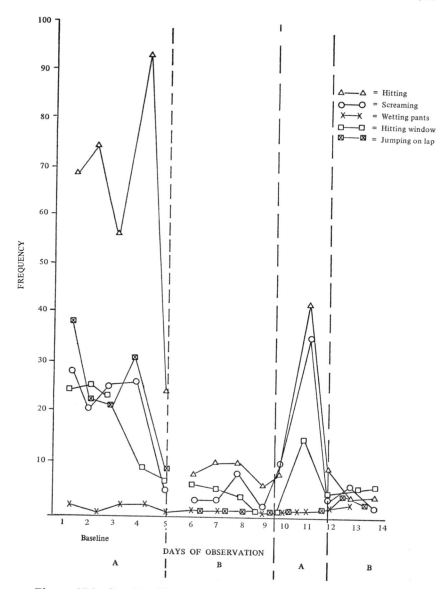

Figure 15-1. Graphic illustration of A,B,A,B design with five problems of a ten-year-old retarded boy under concurrent attention. (J. D. Smith, Family Service Agency, Flint, Michigan, 1970)

example of the application of a statistical procedure which may be applied for purposes of ascertaining the statistical significance of the changes (Gentile *et al.*, 1972). Other statistical/mathematical procedures are also available for use with single case studies. Discussion of these, as well as additional and more extensive discussions of the single case study, may be found in several of the resources listed in the bibliography. Especially helpful are the articles by Risley (1969) and Stuart (1971).

At this point and at this time, perhaps some brief commentary about selected single case study factors may be appropriate. To begin, it may have become patently obvious that specificity of problems is highly desirable, and perhaps essential, in making single case study research meaningful. Measurement is a key ingredient in effectiveness research and in the single case approaches described, the case problems are counted throughout the period of investigation of effectiveness. Counting the occurrence (frequency) of problems requires that they be identified and described in a manner which allows for counting. Obviously some client problems fit that requirement much more readily that do others. However, on the basis of somewhat casual daily observation as well as periodic sampled intake information from one fairly typical casework agency (Family Service, Flint, Michigan), at least two thirds of all intake cases immediately offer countable problems adequate to single case study. Clients requesting help appear to have an uncanny ability to state their requests and describe their problems in practical, straightforward language. And those problems, in at least 50 to 75 percent of the cases, are problems which at most require only minor refinement in order that they are measureable and, in that respect, acceptable for single case study. Assuming that casework should be responsive to clients' requests, and since those requests reflect practical, daily living problems, most caseworkers have an ample supply of single case subjects from which they can suitably select one or a few for single case studies of casework effectiveness.

Another factor which might be briefly considered is the matter of variations in casework—differing conceptualizations and theoretical bases, various methodologies, techniques, application strategies and styles, etc. Assuming that all casework is intended to be responsive to client "needs," and assuming that clients frequently state fairly clearly what their problems are and what they expect from "help," then, for effectiveness evaluation, it would seem that it makes little difference what brand or style of casework is used. The client states what is wrong, the client states what he/she/they want, the caseworker is the "expert" sought after as the one who is going to help attain the desired goal. In many, if not most instances, the client is primarily interested in results; methodology might also be of interest to the client (as it should be for the caseworker) in respect to ethics, legalities, morality and the like. However, assuming appropriate consideration for those issues, the client's concern is for results. Parents are interested in results regarding enuresis, encopresis, hyperactivity, noncompliance and the like; parents and teachers are interested in results of efforts directed at underachievement, school attendance, homework performances, when their teenagers come home; husbands and wives are interested in changing unsatisfactory sexual and other interpersonal relations. And they look to casework for results in areas such as those illustrated. For purposes of single case studies of effectiveness, variations of casework treatment for the moment and as a beginning may be considered of little consequence. Differing casework approaches, methods, techniques, etc., may rapidly become significant issues once effectiveness evaluation provides greater clarity and more conclusive results. But then, more effective helping approaches are highly desired and more clear, potentially more conclusive effectiveness evaluation procedures should be welcomed and encouraged regardless of their impact on current concepts, theories, techniques and the like. Caseworkers as well as researchers have opportunity to participate in evaluation of their own work, and practical, fairly easily applied techniques for such evaluation are available. It remains for caseworkers themselves to make the most of these opportunities which have much promise of improving skills and advancing casework knowledge.

REFERENCES

Allyon, T. and Skuban, W. "Accountability in Psychotherapy: A Test Case," *Journal of Behavior Therapy and Experimental Psychiatry,* Vol. 4, 1973, pp. 19-30.

Davidson, P. O., Clark, F. W. and Hamerlynck, L. A. (eds.) *Evaluation of Behavioral Programs—in Community, Residential and School Settings,* Champaign: Research Press, 1974.

Gentile, J. R., Roden, A. H. and Klein, R. D. "An Analysis-of-Variance Model for the Intrasubject Replication Design," *Journal of Applied Behavior Analysis,* Vol. 5, 1972, pp. 193-198.

Mullen, E. J., Dumpson, J. R., and Associates (eds.) *Evaluation of Social Intervention.* San Francisco: Jossey-Boss, 1972.

Polansky, N. A. "Research in Social Work," Morris, R. (ed.) *Encyclopedia of Social Work,* Vol. 2, 16th issue. New York: N.A.S.W., 1971, pp. 1098-1106.

Risley, T. R. "Behavior Modification: An Experimental-Therapeutic Endeavor," Hamerlynck, I. A., Davidson, P. O. and Acker, L. E. (eds.) *Behavior Modification and Ideal Mental Health Service.* Calgary, Canada: University of Calgary, 1969, pp. 101-127.

Skinner, B. F. "A Case History in Scientific Method," and "The Flight from the Laboratory," *In Cumulative Record, A Selection of Papers,* Third Edition. New York: Appleton-Century-Grofts, 1972, pp. 101-124 and pp. 314-330.

Smith, J. D. "Utilization of Behaviorally Trained Homemaker: A Case Example." Unpublished paper. Family Service Agency, Flint, Michigan, 1970.

Stuart, R. B. *Trick or Treatment: How and When Psychotherapy Fails.* Champaign: Research Press, 1970.

Stuart, R. B. "Research in Social Work: Social Casework and Social Group Work," Morris, R. (ed.) *Encyclopedia of Social Work,* Vol. 2, 16th issue. New York: N.A.S.W., 1971, pp. 1106-1122.

CHAPTER 16 THE EFFECTIVENESS OF SOCIAL CASEWORK: SOME COMMENTS

FRANCIS J. TURNER

Acting Vice President: Academic
Wilfred Laurier University
Waterloo, Ontario, Canada

Doctor Joel Fischer has asked a group of colleagues to respond to material in the first seven chapters of this book. He is to be commended for this invitation as it gives the reader an opportunity to see a range of responses to this material without the usual wait for widely scattered reviews. He is also to be commended for bringing together under one cover an examination of projects that cover over thirty years of social work practice. This has obviously required much energy and strong commitment.

I found it difficult to decide how best to organize my thoughts in response to this material. There is much I want to agree with and applaud; but there is much I want to disagree with and to query. Since my preference is to look ahead rather than to look back, I have chosen to stay future-oriented. Thus, I will focus most of my comments on the material from a viewpoint of what we can learn from it, rather than a line-by-line reexamination and critique on it. But before looking ahead, I do want to challenge some aspects of this material since what one concludes from it no doubt will influence future directions and decisions.

My overriding concern with the material is Doctor Fischer's tendency to overstress and overinterpret the outcome of the studies. Thus, for example, the studies here examined do not prove that over the thirty- to forty-year span studied casework has been ineffective. Presuming that the reports of the project are valid summaries, they only support a conclusion that the practice activities of social workers in these studies have not been significantly effective. Over and over again in his remarks, Doctor Fischer tells us that the results of many of the projects are inconclusive. If so, we cannot conclude the intervention studied was ineffective. To do so we should use the author's own ground rules that he carefully and precisely spells out. Thus it would have to be shown that the seventeen projects did examine a common variable, casework, and did represent a sufficiently large random sample of casework over the decades studied. This he has not done. What I particularly found puzzling, was his apparent readiness to accept unvalidated instruments and inconclusive findings as proof of ineffectual intervention and to speculate on these conclusions. Certainly, it is his prerogative to believe that it is unwise to permit social workers to intervene with children or to provide direct services to the poor, but he should not, as a researcher, imply that the data of these studies provide him with an established basis for these assumptions.

A particularly helpful contribution of his material is the eighty-item checklist he has developed. Several times in his own writing it appears he has not followed it. For example, I think he dismisses too readily the question about the clarity of the casework variable. Whether it is the fault of the caseworkers, the nature of the knowledge base, or the inability of the researchers to specify it, surely there has to be serious question about his "specification of variable items" given just the one factor of the time span covered. In the same vein, I think he is too ready to accept that there is sufficient information about the social work input within and between the projects and their respective samples to conclude that a common variable is being considered. He suggests this is the fault of the caseworkers who are diffuse about their activities; it is also the fault of researchers for proceeding with unclear variables yet acting as if they were precisely similar. He apparently forgets his own criteria related to adequacy of conclusions; this is particularly evident in Chapter 4 in which he comments on the possible harmful effects of social work intervention. Over and over again he draws conclusions from the studies, some of which he has declared inconclusive and hence has warned us to be cautious, or he makes use of such terms as "it is likely that," again not appropriate research procedure as he defines it.

Certainly, that casework could be harmful or has been harmful is not a discovery of this project. Any practitioner or teacher knows this is so and has long known it; hence the constant search for greater understanding of the differential impact of methods and procedures. What I think we have not done is to direct sufficient attention and concern to the possible extent and patterning of harmful and ineffective outcomes in both control and experimental groups. As was indicated in some of these studies, particularly around ethnic identity, and has been frequently observed in others, we know that there are patterns of effect. Thus, we must now build on this knowledge. Some essential research is needed to identify the operating variables in these patterns and to experiment with other clusters of intervention. In searching for patterns we should both identify and accept our failures, and profit from them, by striving to abstract as much knowledge from them as we do from our successes.

I would like to identify one further point of criticism. In several places in his discussion of outcomes, Doctor Fischer correctly points out that it is not appropriate to consider a few positive outcomes from a number of measurements as indicators of improvement without testing for the probability of their occurrence. That is, in any set of scores we can expect that by chance some will be in either direction. This is frequently overlooked in some studies as Doctor Fischer mentions. But it is also a mistake to conclude that such outcomes are "statistical artifacts" with no possibility of being related to the variable under consideration. All that can be concluded is that the observed scores may have resulted by chance; they may still be a valid outcome and thus at least can and should be examined for possible relevance.

Summarizing my first observations, I think Doctor Fischer weakened what is an important and well-prepared document by failing to observe the very rigors that he demands of others. He makes some gestures at examining both sides but left me with the impression that he leans towards giving negative interpretations and related inferred conclusions. This is not necessary. I think the case has by now been well made; the available research evidence of casework effectiveness is to date tenuous. To go beyond this conclusion only engages us in ongoing, emotionally charged, unproductive (for the practitioner, although not the journals) debates.

Certainly, we have to be prepared to live with the results of relevant well-designed research, and social work practitioners must address more efforts and resources to evaluation of effect and effectiveness. But so do researchers; the current game seems to be "damn the caseworkers." Perhaps a more objective consideration is to ask, not has casework "struck out," using Fischer's earlier analogy, but has research "struck out." However, rather than pursuing this further: just as practice must improve, so must our research improve.

Anyone who has taught or been engaged in research knows that it is not difficult to fault the design and methodology of most projects published both in our field as well as in related fields of practice. Most of us can look at our own research efforts and do the same. Evaluative research is difficult; we still have much ground to cover in the necessary tooling up for broader based, better designed research.

With Doctor Fischer, I fully agree that we should now cease to reexamine the thirty-five years of research history during which efforts were made to assess the overall impact of intervention. Let us leave each other free to draw his or her own conclusions, since most of these conclusions can only be tentative. Let us also stay away from further overall evaluative studies of social work practice until we are much clearer about what we are attempting to measure. Surely it is the individual pieces and clusters of practice we must first describe, quantify, and then evaluate. Few, if any other, professions attempt to evaluate the effectiveness of entire specialties in one study, having learned that at best such efforts are inconclusive. I believe there are data available that indicate there is no statistical difference in the life span of populations who have access to medical services and those who do not. This does not mean there are no data available that indicate that some components of medical practice can help some presenting situations some of the time. We also know that there are situations where there is no help available, given the present state of knowledge. Our task should be to begin to identify situations more specifically in which we are helpful as well as where we are not.

As we pull in our wings on the extensive nature of our evaluative efforts, let us also become more realistic about our expectations. More acquaintanceship with the history of science would help us here. Thus, in other fields of knowledge, usually hundreds, even thousands, of false starts, experiments and projects were carried out in the search for new facts and processes or in the search to validate deduced correlations or to operationalize concepts. Thus seventeen studies, many of dubious design, carried out over thirty-five years in a field as diverse as ours in an era when research was not our forte, are scarcely cause for concern, except from the viewpoint of their sparcity.

But, as in all research efforts, along with humility we have learned many other things. We have learned how complex a task it is to design and carry out experiments in clinical social work practice. This is one place where I think we researchers have failed our colleagues. Too often I think we have encouraged or let ourselves become involved in projects that were doomed from the start to inconclusiveness. In our commitment to do research and to foster research, we have been party to student and collegial research efforts that were laudable only in their enthusiasm; frequently this results in disappointment that further results in a distrust or turning away from research.

In a related way, I think we have also been remiss as consultants about the cost of research. Too often we have failed colleagues in estimating the full costs of doing well-planned, well-designed and well-implemented research. I would hope that Doctor Fischer would add to his eighty-point checklist an item or items related to adequacy of resources. Most of us have had experiences where we have had to depend on the goodwill of colleagues and students to volunteer extra time to assist in gathering, assessing and preparing data. We have served as our own judges, made compromises on pretests, on interjudge reliability and any number of important factors due to lack of sufficient funds. All of these compromises diminish confidence in our outcomes, be they positive or negative.

This reality of the pragmatics of research should be further stressed in our teaching of research. Having invested so much energy into developing enthusiasm for research among our colleagues in agencies, we now have to help them redirect their interests from all encompassing projects that attempt to demonstrate, for example, that two M.S.W.'s can significantly alter unemployment rates to less dramatic, more precise examination of the interactive influence of specific factors in practice.

As we move to this more focussed kind of evaluative and outcome research, I suggest we give more thought to the dimension of time as a variable, along the lines of recent work on short-term intervention. Several times, in reviewing the material in this book, I noted the value apparently placed on long-term treatment and the implication that length equalled intensity. We know from current practice that long-term can be highly superficial just as short-term intervention can be intensive. There are already clear indicators from practice that there are probably identifiable time points in treatment after which further intervention only results in diminishing returns for some kinds of persons and situations. Thus length, amount and intensity of input and their interrelatedness, should be examined more thoroughly. Fortunately, these are variables that can be more easily specified and controlled than others, such as ego strength, and thus lend themselves to experimental designs.

Related to these former comments, more attention should be given to the terminators or discontinuers in our projects and, of course, in our practice. Perhaps because of our traditional valuing of long-term involvement, we have tended to see discontinuing clients, or terminators as treatment losses or failures. There are growing indications that at least some persons discontinue because they have achieved their own goals. Certainly, this is not always so but clearly we can negatively influence outcome studies if we presume, without evidence, that terminators are failures unless, of course, we have incorrectly set on-going involvement as a criterion of success.

The phenomenon of discontinuers is also important from a methodological viewpoint. As Doctor Fischer points out, anything more than minimal attrition rates in either experimental or control groups renders studies inconclusive. This is a formidable problem in view of the extreme difficulty in locating samples of adequate size in our field, especially as we become more specific about the variables we experience. A noteworthy contribution could be made by some colleague who would assemble available thinking both statistically and methodologically on this question of sample attrition and methods of coping with it.

Throughout his introductory material, Doctor Fischer argues well for the necessity of "no-treatment" control groups in evaluative research. As he points out, without them it is not possible to conclude that "no-treatment" might have been more beneficial than "treatment." I do think, though, he undervalues the use of "other treatment" as a form of control group. This latter strategy is most effective in efforts to isolate the differential impact of selected components of intervention. It is certainly a procedure that aids in learning more about the harmful or less desirable aspects of practice and assists in accumulating data on patterns of effect. Studies employing this design would be of more benefit to us in our present needs than more global ones. Once we have more precise knowledge about the components of practice that are most conducive of change, then we can make better use of nontreatment control groups. For then we can test variables that are much more specific than "what social workers do in their practice."

The above comments are really strategy questions related to the realities of our area of activity. Since it is difficult to locate and protect "no-treatment" control groups, I suggest we should work with "other-treatment" groups as a way of testing for differential effects. If we demonstrate differential effects in this manner, there seems little use in moving to "no-treatment" groups.

A final comment about future research efforts that emerged from a reading of this material relates to the theoretical base of practice. It is, of course, currently fashionable to attribute most of the current difficulties in clinical practice to the evils of our ego-psychological tradition. Doctor Fischer manifests an inclination to do this in this Chapter 6. With this premise, it is then argued that we set it aside in favor of other thought and practice systems. Whatever my clinical convictions may be, as a researcher, I consider this to be an open question. As I become increasingly aware that there are colleagues who claim to be ego-psychologists, or claim other theoretical allegiances, but who demonstrate little knowledge about their chosen system or its applications, I begin to wonder whether frequently our poor treatment results have come from no theory rather than an inappropriate theory.

Thus, I suggest the theoretical base of practice is a rich field for researchers. Several key questions to be examined are: (a) which practitioners do have a discrete theoretical base; (b) what are these bases; (c) to what extent do they effect what is done in practice; and (d) are the differential results in outcomes related to the theoretical base? This would be difficult research but, potentially, we could learn much about similarities or differences in practice between and among colleagues of various orientations and training. Such information would again help us understand the differential effects of practice that, in turn, would help us address the subsequent question of the effectiveness of practice.

The prior comments have been responses to some of the material in Doctor Fischer's chapters. Now, for the final section of this chapter, I would like to offer ten suggestions related to future research efforts in social work clinical practice. I make them from the assumption that the demands on us for direct social work help will continue to increase. I also make them from the assumption that within the vast quantity of good and bad practice that has gone on over the forty years there is a more highly effective cluster of interventive knowledge and skills than has been thus far demonstrated and tested. Our task as researchers, teachers, and practitioners is to continue the struggle to clarify this knowledge through efforts aimed at increased precision, increased objectivity, increased transmutability of knowledge and increased effectiveness. Clearly well-designed research is a part of this task.

Several of the following points only echo some made by Doctor Fischer in his final summary. I repeat them to underscore their importance. My comments on each will be brief as we have been limited in the length of our response and I am approaching my limit.

1. Those of us engaged in the teaching and supervision of students must intensify our insistence that for every case there must be prepared and updated a clear statement of objectives, methods of achieving said objectives, and an evaluation of outcomes.

   This seems obvious, yet over and over again in the work of students and practitioners, are found examples of imprecision and vagueness about who is the client, why he is being seen, what is being attempted, and what is happening.

2. The above should be a part of an on-going effort to instill and positively reinforce a commitment to the values, goals, and roles of the scientist. I think, as a profession, we have let ourselves over-emphasize the differential roles of scientist and practitioner. This permits many of us to become diffuse in our practice, using our alleged human concern and commitment as arguments against precision, measurement, classification and categorization. We must remind ourselves that every process of assessment or diagnosis is in fact the process of formulating a hypothesis based on some view of human behavior. "Because this is so, I will do this" and "expect that this will eventuate." As we become more explicit in this process there is a greater possibility of knowing when our hypotheses are accurate and when it is necessary to alter our theory by addition, deletion, or modification.

3. As researchers, I suggest we need to do a better public relations job with our practicing colleagues. I think there are components of the field who feel themselves betrayed by researchers. For a long time we urged the necessity of more

research and now we seem to have turned the results of research against them. This may occur in two ways: either by disparaging their research efforts as of no value or by using their findings to criticize their practice by suggesting they know little and achieve less.

I am in no way suggesting that we ignore poor research designs or that we blind ourselves to outcomes we do not like. What I do urge is that we be more understanding about the realities of research and more objective about the implications of conclusions and not use the guise of research to push our own untested opinions and viewpoints.

4. Thus, as a fourth point, I suggest we strive to be better research resources to our colleagues in practice by putting more effort into the methodological challenges identified in this project. There is a risk that our skilled researchers could become too divorced from practice and emerge as the critics of clinical research rather than the doers of the same. In my experience, the more we become involved in the practicalities of research, the more tolerant we become of other persons' efforts and procedural compromises. This is not again an argument against objectivity; it is a plea for a more positive helping attitude.

5. My fifth point stems from the latter two points. I strongly urge that we avoid developing a climate in which persons become reluctant to share their evaluative efforts, or even worse, become reluctant to embark upon them or let others do so. If a person begins to expect that whatever he does will be criticized, it is not surprising that there will be less than full enthusiasm about involvement in research projects.

6. In spite of my earlier comments about the use of "other-treated" as controls, I suggest we should expand our use of untreated control groups. There have been a number of reasons why we have avoided extensive use of this aspect of research. The one most frequently stated is an ethical one of withholding services from persons who have requested them or who have been identified as requiring

them. I think that now there is sufficient responsible and legitimate questioning of both the efficiency of treatment and of the potential risks in providing it that we must re-evaluate our reluctance on this point. It is easier to do so in our present climate which favors short-term involve-ment. Because of this the delay in putting off treatment for clients or potential clients in control groups is much shorter and the potential risks lessened. But this is still something we ought not do lightly or forget that people can suffer if we deny them treatment whatever the reason. I suggest it is a risk we now have to take more often.

7. This recommendation and the following two are related to our professional responsibility to gather, utilize and make available data about our practice efforts.

In spite of the array of cynical humor, folklore and true stories that circulate in professional circles about the evils and misuses of recording, it remains true that responsible practice requires that we maintain accurate records. But this is difficult to do especially in the light of current practice styles. In this regard, it is both encouraging and discourag-ing in practice to observe: (a) how much our colleagues know about their clients in some significant life areas, and (b) how little they know about them in other equally significant areas, and (c) how unevenly this information gets reported, used, and collated. Thus, much effort is re-quired to develop and test new formats and methods of stan-dardized data gathering. An interesting approach to this would be to focus on convenient, yet comprehensive, pro-files for gathering data from large numbers of workers across a variety of settings and areas about their perception of individual clients, their objectives, their activities, and their outcomes. I am aware there are beginning thrusts in this direction and I mention it here to further underscore this as a required component of the essential tooling up process still required before we move into more rigorous research.

8. Not only must we begin to develop better systems of gathering data, we must make better use of the many tech-

nological resources available to us in gathering, storing, and analyzing large quantities of standardized data on many significant and presumed significant data. I am here suggesting data centers larger than single agencies or groups of agencies, yet smaller than national data banks. Such data collection centers would facilitate the examination of larger numbers of cases and phenomena in a more comprehensive manner than is usually possible in smaller centers.

9. Along with improved methods of accumulating data, there is needed a more efficient system of distribution of the myriad instruments that have been developed in the past few years to assess components of psychosocial functioning presumed to be related to treatment goals and outcomes. Obviously, they are not all of the same sophistication, utility, reliability and validity. Nevertheless, a most useful resource would be a system that would collect, report on, assess, and make available such instruments. Frequently agencies are eager to embark on some prudent small scale evaluative project and are seeking such instruments but lack easy access to them. How this resource can be best provided is not fully clear to me at this time. It might be through a new journal, a book, an organization of clinical researchers, a section of a journal or some other imaginative entrepreneurial activity. I suggest it could be a most useful resource.

10. My final point is to underscore some of Doctor Fischer's comments in his last chapter about the need for small, detailed, carefully constructed and controlled projects that examine discrete components of the various effects or non-effects of segments of practice in a form that permits replication and the opportunity for interconnected cumulative additional projects. Such projects can look at and correlate components of theory, new or old, components of client need, components of workers' perceptions, components of workers' activities, or any number of the almost

numberless variables that make our practice so rich, yet so illusive.

Conclusion

Research of the future that examines the effect and effectiveness of individual, familial and small group intervention will be marked by rigor, precision, and a focus on components of practice rather than entire practice methodologies. It should combine the discipline of the scholar with the ingenuity and imagination of the artist, the mark of any productive scientific endeavor.

In an earlier writing, Doctor Fischer suggested that casework had struck out. I suggest that in the light of the material here considered, this was an enthusiastically premature statement. If we can continue the analogy, I suggest the game has not yet started; we have only established which park it will be played in and which rules will be followed. Now at least the pitchers can begin to warm up!

CHAPTER 17 CASEWORK CAN BE EFFECTIVE

HAROLD D. WERNER

Chief Psychiatric Social Worker
Morris County Guidance Center
Morristown, New Jersey

JOEL FISCHER has made an original contribution of great value. If the foregoing text gives us nothing else but the framework he has devised for evaluating the designs and results of casework research studies, we are already in his debt. However, he has also provided us with a compact but thorough summary of basic research principles, which hopefully will help some of the new generation of social workers to lose their fear of research involvement. Still more, he has jolted us by bringing us face to face with the fact that not one of seventeen controlled studies can unequivocally demonstrate that social casework is effective. On the contrary, in some instances casework has appeared to be harmful to its clients.

When Fischer's conclusions about the seventeen studies are first read, I think large numbers of social workers will protest the severity of his judgment. Like myself, they will instantly recall countless cases that made obvious progress after casework attention. Before we go any further down this track, I think it is imperative for us to pause and reaffirm in our thinking the concept of the control. This act of reaffirmation will compel us to arrive at the only position that is possible: "I see definite improvement in my clients, but I must accept the necessity of comparison with a control group before the significance of the change can be determined."

Readers will wonder how they can reconcile Fischer's conclusions with their own certainty that many of their clients after casework service have become happier, less anxious, stronger, more successful, or more competent in problem-solving. I found my own answer to this dilemma after reviewing the characteristics of the client problems and the casework in the seventeen studies.

I discovered that in only one research project (Most, 1964) was there any possibility that all of the following three variables were present: (1) a client problem not massively influenced by the socio-economic environment or a chronic physical condition; (2) a nonanalytic casework orientation; and (3) periodic interviews not more than a week apart. The study by Most conceivably *might* possess all these variables by virtue of the fact that the clients were seeking marital counseling, the casework orientation was undetermined, and the number of contacts was unclear. Obviously, I am stretching things a good deal, but if we do not give this study the benefit of considerable doubt, then not one of the seventeen fits this model.

I chose this model out of my experience in a mental hygiene clinic, where the staff utilizes a nonanalytic approach that can be most simply described as a "reality" orientation, with the client selecting the goal whenever possible. Clients are seen once a week for short-term psychotherapy. Time and time again, we observe pronounced positive change in those individuals whose problems are within the capacity of one person to solve, given personal counseling and/or concrete services not requiring structural changes in society.

For example, a woman is depressed after a hysterectomy. Her pessimistic mood is reinforced by an introverted husband who avoids people, stays home all the time, and wants her to do the same. Another complication is a daughter with an alcoholic problem who is often violent and unmanageable. This woman shows marked improvement when we work with her to achieve her goal, which is to break out of her isolation. Securing the cooperation of her husband, we help the client to formulate and carry out a plan for learning how to drive, joining community activities, and studying for a new career. At termination, the client has helped her daughter to enter a residential treatment facility, where progress is reported.

Now I return to the disparity between Fischer's conclusions and my own observations that casework has been markedly effective with hundreds of clients. I think it can be explained by the fact that only one at most of the seventeen studies fits the model of the agency I described where I believe effective professional help is provided. Accordingly, I am prepared to offer this hypothesis:

> Clients whose difficulties are not massively influenced by the socio-economic environment or a chronic physical condition such as old age or alcoholism, and who are seen for closely spaced regular interviews not analytically oriented, will tend to score positively both on objective outcome measures and in comparison with controls.

Among the seventeen studies analyzed by Fischer, two dealt with neurotic and primary behavior problems of children. There were two studies of marital problems: the one by Most, and another which focused on concomitant problems of the spouses' alcoholism. The others were concerned with the readjustment of probationers, services for the aged, problems of families on public assistance, socially disadvantaged children in a pathological environment, and delinquent behavior. It would seem, therefore, that, with the possible exception of the first four studies as listed above, the researchers were dealing largely with multiproblem cases. These multiproblem cases were so intertwined with their surrounding circumstances that the functioning of the clients could not be changed without a simultaneous radical change in the very structure of their society.

Fischer has given us some mixed signals on this subject. He discusses the idea that "casework can't solve social problems" and seems to disagree, noting that several of the research projects did *try* to change the environment. However, it is important to indicate that they did not succeed. Fischer also states there is a view that casework is not supposed to solve social problems, but help the individual or family caught in them. In still another part of the book, he calls on caseworkers to become more involved in advocacy roles in an effort to effect basic changes.

We may have to recognize that casework cannot do everything that needs to be done. It may well be that casework cannot contribute much to making basic changes in society, and that this must be done through other means and under other auspices. My hypothesis, therefore, does not see casework as being effective with those problems whose solution is contingent upon structural changes in society. Likewise, professional casework is not apt to be significantly effective with chronic physical states such as old age or alcoholism. Clients in these and similar categories can probably get their material and emotional needs met better through non-M.S.W. sources ranging from Welfare Department workers, medical clinics, community centers and social clubs to Alcoholics Anonymous.

Fischer tells us that, in most of the studies, the orientation was clearly specified as "psychodynamic" of one form or another, i.e. Freudian or psychoanalytic. He believes that those studies whose orientation was unspecified suggest by the description of services and the dates they were done that they too have a psychodynamic orientation. As he puts it: ". . . virtually every model of social casework up until very recently was derived from some form of psychoanalytic theory." Not one of these traditional approaches provides clear statements of procedures or techniques to follow, so caseworkers have always done whatever seemed a good idea at the time, operating with their own individual styles.

Fischer goes on to point out that, because caseworkers have been enamored of a single model of practice since the early 1920's, there developed a long-lasting overdependence on a narrow approach whose dogmatism discouraged alternative views. Emphasis was on *understanding* clients but no techniques were provided for *changing* them. Fischer characterizes the union of casework with psychoanalysis as "disastrous" and calls for a new attitude of receptivity to all other available approaches and new ideas. He suggests we concentrate on technique-building, that is, developing specific methods to help our clients change. This commentator heartily agrees. My hypothesis calls for the utilization of nonanalytic approaches precisely because most of them specify definite techniques, which flow naturally out of the theory behind them.

The weakness of the classic psychoanalytic orientation in regard to providing practical help has also been noted in *Games Analysts Play* (New York: Putnam's, 1970) by Martin Shepard and Marjorie Lee, who describe many of its practitioners as antiaction therapists who forget or overlook the importance of activity. Regardless of what the clients bring to their sessions, the antiaction therapist always discusses their feelings. As Shepard and Lee express it: "Yet the tell-me-why therapist is not interested in the facts. He is concerned with proving that he is one step ahead of the patient. He can hide his ignorance of life-solutions by relying on a long analysis of *why*, rather than launching into *what* and what-to-do-about-it" (p. 62).

On the other hand, nonanalytic approaches have always been more action-oriented, the actual techniques being quite self-evident from the theory. By way of illustration, I refer to elements in the theoretical systems of Alfred Adler and Albert Ellis, both nonanalytic orientations which fall into the category of "cognitive" theory, also known as "reality" or "rational." A complete discussion of cognitive theory has been presented in *Social Work Treatment,* edited by Francis J. Turner (New York: The Free Press, 1974, pp. 239-275).

Adler saw behavior as shaped by an individual's goals in life. Each person decides what he considers success to be, and develops his goals accordingly. He then behaves in the way he thinks is most likely to bring him to his objectives, deactivating any instinctual drives that may interfere, e.g. the priest who adopts celibacy. The treatment technique which flows out of this theory is that we help the client change problem-producing behavior through reexamining and modifying the goals which shaped it. This concept has been utilized by many programs working with young people to prevent drug abuse. One of their principal techniques is to help the youth develop values and goals with which drug use is incompatible.

Ellis sees emotional distress as the result of saying sentences to ourselves which do not correspond to reality. Consequently, we feel hostile, frightened, inferior or guilty even though the objective facts do not justify such reactions. Again, the technique for helping is fairly self-evident. If the client is upset by distorted perceptions of himself, others and his environment, it is the task of the professional to challenge these inaccurate judgments and to encourage activities that will have a corrective influence. Ellis gives his clients "homework" assignments, such as taking a job for which one feels inadequate, or confronting a spouse with a grievance.

The third variable in my hypothesis has to do with sufficient frequency of casework contacts. Again, my own clinical experience suggests that, once the client's full participation has been obtained, regularly scheduled sessions not more than a week apart are a necessity. They provide a sense of continuity, maintain the psychological impact of the worker, keep the client actively engaged in the helping process, and increase his sense of security and certainty. Only about half of the seventeen studies met this level of contact frequency. The lesser frequency in the other projects may have played a part in their negative outcomes.

In other writings, Fischer has encouraged caseworkers to consider an eclectic approach. In his next book, I gather he will be telling us that, with such an approach, effective casework practice is possible. My own experience with the concept of eclecticism has made me very cautious, because I recall colleagues who described their orientation as eclectic. A closer look revealed they had no theoretical framework at all, and the term "eclectic" was a euphemism for playing everything by ear.

We need theory to guide our practice and should not try to function without it. Techniques cannot stand alone, and each should have a theoretical rationale to support it. Otherwise, techniques will become prepackaged mechanical devices to be identified by number: use number 5 for a rebellious teenaged girl, use number 6 for a phobia of elevators. Eclecticism in the choice of techniques that is not supported by a blend of compatible theoretical constructs gives us no professional basis for matching the technique to the client. Eclecticism without a theoretical frame-work is like the yellow brick road in the Land of Oz, with a false and empty idol at the end.

Fischer wonders about the risk of professional casework, if in some cases it is likely to harm the client. It seems to me that if the client sets the goal, as in the cognitive approaches, we mini-mize the risk of pushing him or her in directions subjectively de-termined by the worker which might have destructive results. I have in mind the cases of the elderly people in one study who were persuaded to make changes which might have shortened their lives.

In urging us to be open to new concepts, Fischer gives as exam-ples a greater use of direct influence, planning, and structure in the casework process; behavior modification; and training work-ers to develop the core characteristics of empathy, warmth and genuineness which have been found experimentally to be direct-ly related to effective helping. There can be little disagreement with any of these, but Fischer has made a serious omission, even though he states he may not have included all the new major thrusts.

I feel it is necessary to make the point that in none of his writ-ings does Fischer reveal awareness of the issue of consciousness. One of the major thrusts today, as we reexamine our overattach-ment to psychoanalysis, is a return to the idea of the primacy of consciousness. It is time for social work as a profession to think about the premise that the problems our clients bring to us are problems of consciousness. Educators like Fischer should be en-couraging debate on the contention of cognitive theorists that there is no "unconscious" that needs to be brought to conscious-ness, that what clients need to be conscious of is the real nature of themselves, their relationships, and the world around them.

By ignoring cognitive theory, Fischer reinforces the inaccurate notion that there are only two major treatment trends in exis-tence: psychoanalysis and behavior modification. This is unfortu-nate, because cognitive theory offers a unique conception of man. It regards people as having the ability to fashion their own lives by the force of their thinking, their creativity, and their will. In contrast, both psychoanalysis and behavior modification stress the animal nature of man, viewing his behavior as determined respectively by unconscious instinctual drives or by conditioned responses. It is ironic that social workers are not getting more exposure to the theoretical outlook which emphasizes the human qualities in man.

In conclusion, this commentator is not convinced of the general ineffectiveness of professional casework. What *was* ineffective was the specific casework studied in seventeen research projects. Casework with other types of clients, greater regularity and frequency of contact, and different theoretical orientations may produce better outcomes. It is no disgrace to grant that casework cannot help everybody.

PART III SUMMARY AND CONCLUSION

Not everything that is faced can be changed;
But nothing can be changed until it is faced.

—JAMES BALDWIN

"Remember that schools and professions are subject to the same deadening forces that afflict all other human institutions—an attachment to time honored ways, reverence for established procedures, a preoccupation with one's own vested interests, and an excessively narrow definition of what is relevant and important.
"The peaks lie ahead of you—but whether you scale them depends on your own vision and boldness."

—JOHN W. GARDNER
   Remarks
   Council on Social Work
   Education, 14th Annual
   Program Meeting
   January, 1966.

CHAPTER 18 THE END OF SOCIAL CASEWORK OR A BEGINNING?

I N PART I of this book, the existing evidence on the effectiveness of professional social casework was reviewed. The results—from a professional standpoint—were discouraging at best. Based on those results the concluding chapter of Part I contained a brief overview of a variety of suggestions for improving practice and research in social casework. The fundamental reasons for these suggested changes are two-fold: (1) There is a pressing need for the kinds of individualized services that caseworkers purport to offer, and the social work profession is in an excellent position—in terms of manpower and other resources—to offer them; and (2) given the complete lack of evidence of the success of any of the traditional methods used by the bulk of caseworkers, major changes, involving the use of demonstrably effective approaches to practice, are necessary. Indeed, without such evidence of effectiveness, the rationale for the continued existence of the branch of the profession now known as social casework may be untenable.

In Part II of this book, several noted educators, researchers, theoreticians and practitioners discussed the research presented in Part I, the evidence on the effectiveness of social casework derived therefrom, and the implications of these for the field. A number of important points were brought up by these authors, far too many, in fact, to summarize here. However, some of these points do merit discussion on the grounds that they were either made by several of the discussants, or that they have broad and major implications for the field. Thus, specific critiques or reevaluations of any of the seventeen studies such as the detailed reanalysis of all the studies by Polemis in Chapter 13, while important, will not be the focus here since ample information on these studies is available in Part I, in the discussants' presentations and in the original studies themselves.

The remainder of this chapter, then, will be focused on a discussion of the most salient of the issues raised in Part II. To avoid unnecessary duplication, issues that were already discussed in depth in Chapter 5 or in other places in Part I, for the most part, will not be addressed here. Thus, even though several discussants raised familiar questions regarding such issues as the definition and measurement of outcome in the original seventeen studies, the client groups and problem categories that were studied and so on, the arguments on these points are available in Chapter 5 and need not be repeated here. The issues that will be addressed, however, will be discussed in an effort to summarize the discussants' remarks, as well as with the goal of opening them up and clarifying them to the extent possible.

In the discussion that follows, each issue or set of issues will be considered separately.

Casework Is too Vaguely Defined to Study

This was one of the most common arguments presented in Part II. Several of the discussants (e.g. Cohen; Hudson; Polemis; Reid; Turner) touched on one of several variations of this issue. As the major basis for his response, Cohen states that because the casework treatment, or independent variable, in many of the studies was either unspecified or not clearly defined, possible changes in clients might have been negated or prevented. He argues that experimental studies evaluating the effectiveness of casework are impossible without being more specific about defining just what casework is. Cohen concludes that: "The failure of most researchers to define concisely the treatment variable makes it almost impossible to ascribe any outcome to the treatment, thereby invalidating any conclusions about a causal relationship between input and outcome." Hudson points out—and this should come as a considerable surprise to tens of thousands of practitioners—that it is impossible to provide casework to some clients and withhold it from others unless casework is defined in more operationally specific terms. He says that it is "silly" to try to answer the question of effectiveness when casework is defined so broadly, and even suggests that broad definitions of casework are somehow responsible for the overwhelming majority of the failures to show significant gains that could be attributed to treatment. He concludes that casework, ". . . has been so broadly defined that it cannot even be regarded as a variable from a scientific point of view." To try and study the effectiveness of casework, Hudson says, would be like trying to find out whether medicine or education are effective.

Polemis argues that defining casework broadly still leaves the question, in talking about effects, effects of what? She suggests that since obviously several different casework approaches were used, it is "sheer nonsense" to imagine that a single, unitary concept is being evaluated. Reid, too, thinks that it is unlikely that unspecified methods of casework would be able to achieve successful outcome, although he does add that, "Whatever the caseworkers were doing, it was apparently not powerful or enduring enough to register on the rather gross measures provided by the researcher." Turner argues that there is insufficient information about the social work input in these studies to conclude that a common variable (casework) is being considered.

Three variations of this general theme can be identified from the discussant's remarks: (1) Casework is not a single variable; hence, conclusions that are based on considering casework in such a manner are invalid; (2) vagueness in defining casework precludes casework or caseworkers from being effective; (3) lack of specificity in defining casework makes scientific assessments of the effectiveness of casework impossible. Unfortunately, the bulk of the discussant's comments on this matter reveal some serious misconceptions about the nature of scientific research, as well as what appears to be either distortion about, or overlooking of, some of the material presented in Part I.

The suggestions that, in the review of research in Part I, casework was considered as a single variable overlook the fact that in several places, particularly in Chapter 1, just the opposite was pointed out: Casework *is* not, and was not considered as, a unitary phenomenon. Some of the discussants seem to be setting up this issue as a straw man, easy to knock down in that, obviously, if casework is viewed as a single variable when indeed it is not, then any conclusions drawn about casework would be at least oversimplified, and, even more likely, totally inaccurate.

But, despite the fact that casework was specifically defined in Part I as "the services provided by professional caseworkers," hence, a multidimensional phenomenon, the discussants' argument might be justified unless—and this is a crucial "unless"—it can be shown that no matter what the model of casework informing practice in any of the seventeen studies, no matter what methods were being used, no matter whether one or twenty-nine interventive procedures were involved, there was consistent lack of clear evidence that any form of casework or any type of service performed by professional caseworkers produced effective results. This, in fact, was the case.

Again, the issue hinges, at least in part, around viewing casework as a variable package of services provided by professionals, differentially performed depending on the needs of the client and situation. It is true, of course, that, as pointed out in Chapter 5, in most of the studies, the services of the caseworkers in most of the studies were based on one or another of the psychodynamic approaches thus suggesting a greater degree of commonality among the services—certainly, at the theoretical level—than some of the discussants are willing to recognize.

Be that as it may, there is still no evidence in any of the studies where psychodynamic theory may *not* have provided the theoretical base for the services, that the services provided by the caseworkers (whatever their theoretical base) in those studies were any more effective.

The second part of this issue was the apparent claim that the *definition* of casework, or the fact that casework was not defined specifically enough, somehow was related to the ineffectiveness of the professionals providing the services. It scarcely bears mentioning that a rose, by any other name, is still a rose. Accepting the line of reasoning that changing the name of casework (or defining it differently or more specifically or less vaguely) would somehow facilitate more positive outcome would be like accepting the notion that an individual who inserts his hand in a roaring fire would not be harmed if he thinks the appropriate term for the fire is "peanut butter."

The third, and probably most basic, part of this issue is the charge that lack of specificity in defining casework precludes scientific investigation of the effectiveness of casework. After all, the argument runs, if you do not know every aspect of the input, how can the relationship between input and output be determined? The essence of this point appears to be that little, if any, knowledge can be gained by studying a phenomenon as broadly defined as "casework."

This myth about the nature of evaluative research must be dispelled. Under the umbrella of this "vagueness of definition" argument, a variety of methods with no evidence of effectiveness are permitted to dominate the practice of caseworkers on the grounds that since they cannot be properly evaluated, they cannot be properly dispensed with.

Inasmuch as Hudson brought up the analogy to medicine, an example from that field might be illustrative. Suppose a physician, using whatever professional secrets of medical treatment physicians use, decides to treat one half of his patients—with the broad range of medical problems they typically bring to this physician—with the best knowledge he has available, and to offer the other half of his patients either no treatment or placebos. Suppose also that after a given period of time of treatment, and with a long-term follow-up, the physician finds that the patients he treated with the best professional skills he possessed do no better than the ones who received sugar pills or no treatment. The conclusion: There would be little way to avoid the conclusion that whatever it was the physician was doing, it apparently was no more effective in helping the patients, whatever their problems were, than no treatment or sugar pills.

Suppose, further, that several physicians, operating out of a number of different clinics and hospitals around the country, decided to offer the best that their medical training had to offer to half their patients, whom they randomly selected from a pool of patients, and to the remaining half, they offered no treatment whatsoever, or treatment provided by practical nurses. Suppose, in addition, that this time the diagnoses of these patients—amounting in the aggregate to several thousand people—were known, and consisted, say, of children suffering from leukemia, rheumatic fever and chicken pox, and adults suffering from flu, pneumonia and emphysema. Of course, there would be large variations between individual patients in the severity of their illness, but in all cases, the general outlines of the illness and the diagnoses were known. Assume that, at the end of treatment and at an appropriate follow-up, it was found that the same percentages of patients in the treatment and control groups were either cured or still suffering from the effects of the illness, across all the diagnostic categories.

The conclusion: Although the exact methods of treatment were unknown, it would still be clear that whatever it was the physicians did, when comparing the two groups on an overall basis, the effects of that professional medical treatment were no more positive with the problems encountered than the effects of no treatment or the services of practical nurses. It would, perhaps, not be clear whether the lack of results would be due to the ineffectiveness of the physicians, the seriousness of the illness or the proficiency in some cases of the practical nurses. But it would be clear that, at least in the diagnostic categories studied, professional physicians appear overall to offer very little of value to their patients. And if these studies were the only data available about physicians, and the studies (and their results) were replicated many times, and if there were no data testifying to physicians' success with these or any other problems, what would be the recommended courses of action for people suffering from any of the above-mentioned illnesses?

Perhaps dismal results such as these are easier to accept in other professions. But the fact is that the situation described above is exactly the same situation that exists in social casework today. As much, or as little, is known about the methods of social caseworkers as was known about the methods of those physicians. But the results are equally clear: Whatever the methods used by those physicians or those caseworkers, as professionals, they achieved no more success in helping their patients or clients as a group than was achieved by practical nurses or nonprofessional social workers, or was achieved through no treatment at all.

So, in fact, a great deal is known about the effectiveness of social caseworkers *as professionals.* Now, in the hypothetical example about physicians presented above, a caseworker might still refer a client suffering from one of those illnesses to a physician. The physician, after all, is the socially acceptable resource for dealing with such problems, and one can always hope that, somehow, his or her case will be different. But the wise caseworker might also warn his client that his chances for recovery from his illness after seeing that physician (no matter what that physician's methods of treatment) were probably no better than receiving no medical help or seeing a practical nurse. Should not the same warning be provided for the clients of caseworkers?

The point, of course, is that broadness in the definition of casework (or of any professional services) is not at all a barrier to studying the effectiveness of those services. This is so even though it obviously would be more informative to know as much as possible about the ingredients of those services. Further, the broadness in the definition of casework used in this book—"the services of professional caseworkers"—still allows any specific form of those services, any type or model of casework, to be included in overall evaluations of caseworkers as professionals. It further allows any form of casework to be evaluated separately so that more specific conclusions can be drawn. But, to date, not a single type of casework, with any group of clients, has demonstrated successful outcome in controlled research. Thus, although it has been argued that it is absurd to debate the general question —"is casework effective?" (Orten & Weiss, 1974, p. 365)—it would seem that unless there is evidence that some form of casework is indeed effective, it might be even more absurd to ask the question—"what kind of casework?"—until some positive evidence of effectiveness indicates that such a question deserves an answer.

The Research Fails to Prove that Casework Is Ineffective

Several discussants (e.g. Cohen, Gochros, Hudson, Mullen, Polemis) believed that, despite the evidence presented in this book, the case against casework—that casework is ineffective—has not been proved. Cohen notes that it is "premature" to conclude that rigorous experimental research has evaluated casework and found ". . . it to be an ineffective method of treatment," although he acknowledges that, ". . . the opposite conclusion has not yet been proved either." Gochros states that the studies reviewed in Part I fail to prove, ". . . that most casework services do no good." Hudson says that the material presented in Part I, ". . . has not established many clear-cut cases to support the demise of 'mighty casework.' "

Mullen takes a slightly different tack in arguing that most of the research designs in question were not powerful enough to isolate and control the elements of social agency programs that are "casework" as distinct from other elements of social agency programs. He states that studies such as the seventeen reviewed in this book, ". . . provide little evidence concerning the question of social casework impact as distinct from the overall impact of programs." Mullen concludes that despite these seventeen studies, the question of the effectiveness of social casework ". . . has not been adequately researched and that as a consequence the information required to answer the question is not available."

Turner argues that the studies reviewed, ". . . do not prove that over the thirty to forty-year span studied casework has been ineffective." Polemis, in answer to her own question—Is the case closed?—succinctly summarizes this position: ". . . the case should be thrown out of court."

Most of these authors appear to be adhering to the "MacDonald principle" of casework outcome research which states: ". . . we do not have good scientific proof of effectiveness. On the other hand, we also lack good scientific proof of ineffectiveness" (MacDonald, 1966, p. 188). This dictum is undoubtedly true, technically at least. It is true because one of the basic principles of research is that the null hypothesis, e.g. that clients receiving professional casework services do not differ at the end of treatment from clients who did not receive services, can never be proved or even disproved. At best, the null hypothesis can only be accepted or rejected with more or less confidence in an individual study. Thus, even findings that show no difference between two samples, as pertained in most of the studies of casework effectiveness, do not "prove" that the populations from which the samples were selected do not differ. What mainly can be concluded is that there is no evidence that the populations differ, and that the notion that the two populations may be alike is a reasonable one. In other words, whether seventeen studies—or 170 studies—show no evidence that professional casework was effective, the same argument might be used—"but it hasn't been proved that casework is ineffective."

In fact, it never was asserted in Part I that casework is ineffective. What *was* asserted was that lack of evidence of the effectiveness of casework was the rule rather than the exception across the range of studies of casework effectiveness. However, this may be largely an issue of semantics.

Indeed, several of the discussants acknowledge that lack of evidence of effectiveness is the rule, as witness Turner's statement that the studies reviewed ". . . only support a conclusion that the practice activities of social workers in these studies have not been significantly effective."

The argument that nothing really is known about the effectiveness or ineffectiveness of casework might be characterized as the "nihilist approach to casework research": nothing is known, especially when the results of research are not to the liking of the observer. This issue actually presents an interesting problem in decision-making: just how many studies with negative results are enough? Just how much evidence is necessary to reach a conclusion? Without any substantial evidence of effectiveness after fifty years of research, it would appear that a conclusion regarding the necessity for major and radical changes in the nature of the casework enterprise would be unavoidable.

One way of clarifying this issue is to assume for the moment that the results of all the research reviewed in this book were the opposite of what was reported: instead of consistent negative findings, consistent positive findings, i.e. favoring the treated group, in all of the controlled research. What could be concluded given that pattern of results?

The first and most obvious conclusion would be that clients receiving professional casework services tend to improve across the range of studies. But this is a far different conclusion than one that states *why* those clients improved. Given the consistency of the findings in this hypothetical example, it would seem logical to conclude that the efforts of the caseworkers were responsible for the positive results. Or, if the caseworkers in all the studies were using an approach derived from a common theory, it might seem logical to conclude that adhering to such a theoretical orientation will lead to effective practice.

Unfortunately, such conclusions could be seriously misleading. There is too much evidence available documenting how changes in clients can come about independent of the practitioner's efforts. Thus, even consistent positive findings would not necessarily explain why clients improve. Similarly, even several studies with positive findings could not validate the use of the intervention theory underlying the intervention approach or even the specific techniques used by the practitioners in the studies. In both cases, further evidence based on extensive further research would be necessary to isolate out what part of the intervention was related to successful outcome. Was it the techniques (informed by a given theory), the personal style of the workers, the attention the workers paid to the clients? The list could be extended indefinitely.

The point is that the constraints on the conclusions that can be generated from studies (with experimental and control groups) with positive findings are somewhat different, and perhaps stricter, than those that can be drawn from studies with negative findings. Quite different levels of evidence are necessary to conclude, with positive findings, that the approach presumably under study is effective, i.e. caused, or was responsible for, the positive findings, as opposed to concluding with negative evidence that the approach is not effective. In the former case (while there would be reason to be optimistic about the impact of professional services), further research would be necessary to determine what part of the input produced the results. In the latter case, it would be clear not only that the approach used by the practitioners was not effective, but that the techniques, personality, attention, style, or any combination of these did not produce an overall significant, identifiable impact on the clients. In other words, there is more justification for condemning the methods used by practitioners when the results are consistently negative, than there is justification for praising them when the results are consistently positive.

Although this might seem to be an unfair discrepancy, the standards and rules of scientific evidence have been developed purposefully—as a safeguard against premature acceptance of unwarranted claims and to make the burden of proof difficult, but clear, objective and rewarding when established. Thus, finding significant differences between experimental and control groups must be a beginning rather than an ending point for research in seeking the aspect (s) of the input that made the difference. In research with null or negative findings, the conclusion is far clearer that no aspect of the input was sufficiently potent to produce a significant effect, and with consistent replication, would constitute sufficient evidence to warrant discontinuation of the use of the approaches implemented by the practitioners in the bulk of the studies.

Actually, the *research* findings pertaining to the lack of evidence of the effectiveness of casework are only a part—albeit a crucial part—of the entire picture. When the results of research on social casework—not one study unequivocally demonstrating success—are added to the results of research (or the absence of research) on the effectiveness of the major, predominantly, psychodynamic, models informing casework practice—lack of any research evidence validating those approaches as effective in helping clients (Marmor, 1968)—the need for major changes in the practice modalities of casework becomes even more apparent. And beyond the empirical or research evidence is the evidence that can be derived from casework "theory." Some of this was presented in Chapter 6 such as an almost total lack of identifiable techniques for caseworkers to implement in practice, overdevelopment of causal-diagnostic knowledge at the expense of intervention knowledge, vagueness in defining key concepts, and so on. Put this together with the research evidence and the conclusion becomes inescapable. Either casework (and caseworkers) changes, or casework disappears as a meaningful part of the social work profession.

The comments by Mullen, that the impact of "casework" has never really been assessed because it has never been separated from the impact of other elements of social agency programs, are somewhat puzzling. Obviously, if Mullen is correct, that nothing really *is* known about the effectiveness of casework, then caseworkers really need not be overly concerned with the dismal results reported here.

It would seem hardly necessary to point out, however, that in almost every one of the seventeen studies, casework *was* the program. Thus, the notion that there were other program components that might have interfered with, or confounded, the casework impact seems totally inaccurate. There are few, if any, instances where any other program component can be identified other than the direct services aspect (the "community program" described in Geismar & Krisberg, 1967, might be one exception).

But even if there *were* a variety of other program components available in each study, it hardly seems logical to assume that they so confounded results that it is impossible to conclude anything about the effectiveness of casework. In the first place, there is not a shred of evidence anywhere that any of these (largely unidentified) "program components" have ever been related, independently or in combination, to effective outcome. Second, it would be necessary to assume that if casework were indeed divorced from these other program components, it would be possible to obtain positive outcome from the casework alone. Of course, the research evidence points strongly to the opposite conclusion. Third, it would be necessary to assume that somehow, *subtracting* these other program components from the equation, casework *plus* program components equals negative outcome, will somehow *add* to the overall equation, casework *minus* program components equals positive outcome. Such an assertion is illogical on the face of it.

It appears that the most accurate conclusion that can be drawn at this point is that casework plus whatever other program components happened to be available in any given instance, has not yet demonstrated positive outcome. Placing the errors for this failure on program components—which cannot even be identified—other than casework is simply unjustified.

The Psychoanalytic Model Is Not Obsolete

Although other discussants alluded to this topic, Strean devoted essentially his entire chapter to an attempt to demonstrate that "psychoanalysis lives." He acknowledges that the ". . . psychodynamic model was used extensively by most of the caseworkers whose activities were studied . . ." but denies that ". . . it is the use of the psychodynamic model that makes the casework ineffective." Strean reasons that the "real" problem is that ". . . psychodynamic theory is poorly and fragmentally utilized, abused and misapplied by many if not most caseworkers in their practices."

He provides several examples of such abuse of theory, such as many instances that he has observed where, with poor and depressed clients, a full grasp of psychodynamics would have prompted the caseworker, to, instead of "gratifying and indulging" the client, ". . . work with the client's resistances against the expression of hostility toward all whom he distrusts and hates including his social worker and the profession of social work." This, according to Strean, will result in, ". . . an experience wherein the client can blast the caseworker who often represents in the transference everything or most things that the client thinks are evil."

Strean, whose emphasis of client hatred of social workers is perhaps best left to the psychoanalytically-oriented to interpret, argues in essence that critics of psychodynamic principles do not recognize that the "real" problem is this misapplication, misuse and abuse of psychodynamic principles, and that it is incorrect, therefore, to think that the theory is at fault.

It is difficult to avoid the implication in Strean's discussion that he is perhaps the only social worker who understands and properly uses psychodynamic principles, while the remainder of the profession and certainly the caseworkers in these studies are guilty of gross distortions of this body of knowledge in their practice. It is not clear if this really is Strean's position, or if this is actually a smokescreen (nee, "defense mechanism") for another problem—to wit, that a theory (and a theory designed to guide practice at that) that is misapplied, not understood and abused by almost everyone is not much of a theory at all. Of what value is a practice theory that cannot be properly used by anyone in practice?

Perhaps, as Strean says, psychoanalytic theory *is* misused by caseworkers and other helping professionals. Yet, it still remains a curiosity as to why, in the mid-1970's, advocates of psychoanalytic approaches still continue to insist that their approach has merit as a method of helping clients. To date, not a single piece of controlled evidence is available to clearly demonstrate the effectiveness of any form of psychodynamically-based approach in casework, counseling or psychotherapy.

It appears as though continued advocacy of the psychoanalytic model as a promising approach for casework—in face of the consistent negative evidence and lack of evidence—is a clear instance of what Kadushin (1959) long ago termed, endowing ". . . borrowed knowledge with a greater degree of certainty than is granted by the discipline which originally developed this knowledge" (p. 67). Even leading psychoanalysts have admitted that ". . . the high promises once held forth by psychoanalysis as a *technique of therapy* have failed to materialize (Marmor, 1968, p. 6). Glover has pronounced in *The Technique of Psycho-Analysis* that, "I have included therapeutic efficacy in the list of unwarranted assumptions [about psychoanalysis]" (Glover, 1955, p. 376). And Strupp has acknowledged: "In critically assessing the current status of psychoanalytic psychotherapy one cannot fail to record a certain disappointment with the achievements and promise of this method of therapy" (Strupp, 1968, p. 333).

Perhaps it may seem as though psychodynamic methods are being used as a scapegoat for the lack of effectiveness of casework. But the key issue must be—when an approach is advocated, *the burden of proof for establishing the efficacy of that approach must be with its advocates.* Thus, whether or not psychodynamic methods are to "blame" for the failure of casework, and whether or not those methods were used or were not used or were used improperly, it still remains a fact that there is no scientifically acceptable evidence—over a period of sixty years—warranting their inclusion in the interventive repetoire of caseworkers.

Casework Does Work

Several discussants, including Gochros, Strean, Werner and Turner, asserted that casework can be, and often is, effective. Gochros stated that ". . . there are desirable outcomes far different from . . . ideal cures or solutions. We can still reduce suffering, and help people get more power over their environment and even over themselves . . ." which eventually could ". . . generate a whole constellation of improvements in social functioning long after the caseworker and researcher have gone home." Strean points to numerous cases of improvement due to casework treatment that he has seen although he acknowledges that, ". . . the presentation of case examples is insufficient research evidence to prove a hypothesis." Turner takes an optimistic point of view when he suggests, "Our task should be to begin to identify situations more specifically in which we are helpful. . . ." He also assumes that ". . . within the vast quantity of good and bad practice that has gone on over the forty years there is a more highly effective cluster of interventive knowledge and skills than has been thus far demonstrated and tested." Werner is most definitive. He states that large numbers of caseworkers, ". . . recall countless cases that made obvious progress after casework attention," producing a certainty for these workers, ". . . that many of their clients after casework services have become happier, less anxious, stronger, more successful, or more competent in problem-solving." Werner asserts that he himself has observed ". . . that casework has been markedly effective with hundreds of clients."

It appears as though several discussants fail to recognize the distinction between *assertions* of effectiveness and *evidence* of effectiveness. Without proof of effectiveness, or even minimally acceptable evidence, any claims of effectiveness must be regarded as just that—unvalidated, subjective assertions. Gochros, of course, hedges his bet. He claims that while casework has been effective, the outcomes on which this effectiveness presumably has been demonstrated, ". . . are exceedingly difficult to measure. They are often diffuse and the 'benefits' not always predictable." Such logic is difficult to dispute, except perhaps for pointing out that outcomes that are too subtle or diffuse to measure, are probably also too subtle or diffuse to affect clients and hardly seem a substantial basis for continuing professional efforts. As noted in Chapter 5, it is somewhat mysterious as to how a profession can justify use of outcomes too faint to measure but too important to dispense with.

But there is still the problem of observed changes in clients. Indeed, it is likely that every caseworker (even the author!) has observed clients improve over the course of treatment. If casework has not demonstrated its effectiveness, how is this possible?

There can be no quarrel with the commonly observed fact that clients do indeed improve during and after casework intervention. But the key issue is, why do those improvements come about? Most of the discussants apparently assume that changes observed during casework treatment come about *because* of the casework treatment. Yet the controlled research on this topic specifically negates this possibility; when results for control groups are compared with results for treated, or experimental, groups, it is apparent that the same changes, across the range of outcome measures, can be observed in the clients who received no treatment.*

In Chapter 1, several criteria for evaluating research were reviewed, including the absolute necessity for the use of control groups so that this question—did the treatment make the difference?—can be answered. This is because the research has revealed

---

* This discussion is drawn from, and considerably expanded in, Fischer (1976).

that a variety of reasons can be responsible for changes in people, *independent* of any treatment experience. Some of these reasons, as noted in the framework for analysis of research in Chapter 1, are: (1) effects of "history"—any variable other than the treatment, including other treatment, changes in the environment, etc.; (2) effects of "maturation"—biological or psychological processes within the individual which would have occurred anyway simply as a function of the passing of time; (3) effects of "statistical regression"—the fact that people who enter treatment because they are at a particularly low point in their lives almost always show evidence of change whether they have had treatment or not; and (4) the "Hello-Goodbye" effect—the fact that people tend to exaggerate complaints on their way into treatment, and give socially desirable answers ("I'm very much improved," "I feel much better") on their way out. The point is that when caseworkers see changes occurring in their clients, they believe the changes occur because of the caseworkers' efforts. But, when a control group is added, these same changes occur in people who had no treatment at all.

Another reason for caseworkers believing that they are helpful in the face of evidence that they are not, is, in a way, related to the above—reports by clients, and actual observations by caseworkers, that, after talking with caseworkers, clients do *feel* better. There seems little question that people do tend to feel better after talking to someone else; the cathartic effects of "getting it off one's chest" have been amply demonstrated not only in clinical practice, but in the everyday living experience of most people. The question is, though, are such efforts significant enough to carry-over into the natural environment, and result in any more substantial changes in personal and social functioning, or even changes on psychological tests and inventories? Apparently, as the outcome research shows, the effects of "feeling better" during an interview are either temporary, or not substantial or strong enough to be reflected or measured in any other way, including the observations of clients by "significant others." And, finally and perhaps most importantly, as the research reviewed in Part I revealed, clients receiving professional casework services in fact do *not* report that they feel better in any more consistent or regular way than do people in control groups who have had no treatment whatsoever.

Deterioration of Clients Is Nothing New

The finding that in almost three fourths of the controlled studies of casework effectiveness there was evidence that some clients tended to deteriorate, is both striking and frightening. Strange it is, then, that most of the discussants either ignore this, mention it only in passing or, when they do address the issue, suggest either that they knew it all the time or that it is really not such a serious problem. Mullen addresses a portion of his chapter to this issue, and concludes that while ". . . it does appear that deterioration did occur among some of the clients in a large proportion of the [studies] . . . , these outcomes were not anticipated nor are they theoretically meaningful. Further the evaluation designs do not permit inferences that these consequences are attributable to the program or to specific program elements such as the casework."

Strean suggests that the reason for the deterioration may be the inappropriate use of psychoanalytic principles: ". . . gratifying people who have such hatred and self-hatred in them only induces them to throw up what the worker has delivered and can lead to deterioration and no change in functioning." Werner too, avers a way of avoiding deterioration: If clients are allowed to set their own goals, ". . . we minimize the risk of pushing him or her in directions subjectively determined by the worker which might have destructive results." Turner has the most startling revelation: "Any practitioner or teacher knows ['that casework could be harmful or has been harmful'] . . . and has long known it."

Hudson addresses a substantial portion of his chapter to "special problems in the assessment of deterioration." Much of his discussion, however, is a theoretical, or hypothetical, analysis of deterioration, largely removed from a discussion of the specific studies reviewed in this book. It is difficult to know exactly what Hudson thinks about the deterioration effects observed in the studies reviewed here because, when he does address them, he does so in a contradictory manner. For example, in his conclusion, he first states that, in certain studies, ". . . there does appear clear evidence of deterioration, and that cannot be ignored." He then says, "However, most of the studies . . . do not provide statistically significant results to support the claim that . . . deterioration is a function of casework." Later, Hudson notes that, ". . . when strong evidence of deterioration arises we have only the evidence of deterioration and do not know to what that should be attributed. It is meaningless to attribute it to casework." He then states, "On the other hand, we cannot pretend that we do not harm our clients, and we probably do so much more often than we care to admit."

It appears that most of these discussants accept the fact that deterioration of clients of professional caseworkers can or did occur, notwithstanding Hudson's appearing to take both sides of this issue. The differences are more apparent in two areas: (1) was it expectable (Strean, Werner, Turner and Hudson—"yes," Mullen and Hudson—"no"); and (2) was it the fault of the caseworkers or their theory (Strean, Turner, Werner and Hudson—"yes"; Mullen and Hudson—"no").

Strean's suggestion that improper use of psychoanalytic theory may be responsible for deterioration, once again seems to strengthen the case that psychoanalytic theory would be a good candidate for rapid interring. However, it should be pointed out that Strean offers no solid evidence that psychoanalytic theory really was misused, which opens the intriguing possibility that it may have been used properly and still caused the deterioration. Similarily, while Werner's suggestion that letting the client set the goals would avoid deterioration has a plausible ring, he cites no evidence that: (1) clients in the studies did not set their own goals; (2) setting one's own goals really does avoid deterioration; (3) setting one's own goals is really powerful enough to offset any other mischief the caseworkers may be up to, i.e. the rest of the treatment.

But adding these opinions that deterioration may be expectable, to Turner's assertion that this possibility has long been known, points to an ethical responsibility for all caseworkers to warn their clients—in advance of treatment—that *casework intervention may be hazardous.* This is as much a responsibility of caseworkers as it is of physicians who are using an experimental or potentially dangerous drug. Indeed, it seems that this knowledge about the hazards of casework is really one of the profession's best kept secrets, particularly from clients, who, when they do find out, do so only on their own, after completing their course of casework treatment.

Mullen asserts that since deterioration was not anticipated or hypothesized, it is theoretically meaningless, and, while perhaps deserving of further research attention, apparently is not deserving of over-concern on the part of caseworkers. This logic is hard to follow. The fact that deterioration occurred (and appeared to occur so frequently) makes it salient, and a valid fact, whether or not it was anticipated. It would seem to be precious little comfort to a client who has deteriorated after casework treatment to know that his condition is theoretically meaningless, and, because it was not hypothesized, not a matter of over-concern.

Similarly, both Mullen and Hudson reveal some naiveté about experimental design in arguing that cause and effect inferences cannot be drawn. Equally as curious are, first, Hudson's statement that deterioration may have been so frequent in these studies because the studies were selected on a "purely *post hoc* basis," and, secondly, his question—"What would be the results if we examined *all* published studies of casework intervention?" Surely he knows that this review *does* include all published studies of casework intervention using control groups, and that without control groups deterioration is impossible to determine in a scientifically acceptable way. And that is exactly the point. Use of experimental and control groups indeed does allow an inference about cause and effect. This is precisely the reason for control groups (to rule out alternative explanations). So, in every study, it is possible to conclude that some aspect of what the experimental group was exposed to that the control group was *not* exposed to produced the deterioration.

Now what were the experimental groups exposed to that the control groups were not? Professional casework treatment. The purpose of the control group was to rule out the effects of everything else *besides* the casework program. Now, it is true that the aspect of the casework program that actually *caused* the deterioration was not isolated in these studies. That is, the caseworkers' personal style, techniques or other dimensions may have been responsible.

In Chapter 6 evidence was cited showing that studies in related fields have isolated low levels of professionals' communication of the conditions of empathy, warmth and genuineness as related to deterioration (see Truax & Mitchell, 1971). Be that as it may, the casework intervention program as a whole stands indicted in the majority of these programs as the probable cause of deterioration.

It is interesting to note that Hudson appears to have dropped the bulk of his criticisms about the deterioration effect in casework clients which appeared in an earlier paper (Hudson, 1974). Instead, he relies on a purely hypothetical discussion (which concludes by noting at one point that his examples are, ". . . both fictitious and unrealistic."). It may be that Hudson has become increasingly persuaded by the evidence of the hazard of casework treatment. Thus, while his chapter is highly instructive regarding some of the intricacies of interpreting research findings, nothing in it specifically refutes, and rarely addresses, any of the findings on deterioration presented in Chapter 4.

Casework Was Not at Issue in These Studies; Social Work Was

In arguing that casework could not possibly be indicted by the findings in these seventeen studies, several discussants—intentionally or unintentionally—broadened the arena for the discussion. Berleman points out how social casework, particularly arising from psychoanalytic theory, ". . . did not significantly characterize the services of a number of these projects, particularly the 'delinquency studies.' " Several of these, he argues had a distinct "group/sociological" flavor. Cohen points out how, ". . . in three of the studies, the dominant intervention was group work, not casework. This is not serious except that Fischer never talks about the ineffectiveness of group work." Gochros states, "Many of the evaluated intervention efforts were not 'casework' activities, *per se,* but involved group approaches, advocacy and a variety of other social work activities. As long as the activities referred to loosely as 'casework' were so poorly defined, . . . much of the research cannot be considered an accurate test of the effectiveness of 'casework,' *per se.*" Polemis carefully reviews the services offered in all of the studies and concludes, ". . . there is a wide range of treatment modalities . . . ," and, ". . . there is among the various studies . . . a wide range of approaches. . . ." Turner states that there is insufficient information, ". . . about the social work input within and between the projects and their respective samples to conclude that a common variable is being considered."

Since Chapter 5 addressed the issues involved in making a judgment as to whether or not these studies involved casework, the types of casework being used and the use of a variety of methods by caseworkers including groups, environmental manipulation, etc., these points need not be duplicated here. But the discussants do raise an important issue; that is, if, in their opinion these studies all really did not involve casework, what *did* they involve?

The answer the discussants seem to favor is that these studies involved a far broader range of social work methods than "just" casework. They evaluated the impact of casework, all right, but also the impact of group work, advocacy, and what in broad terms, might be called clinical social work, interpersonal helping, social treatment, social work practice with microsystems and social work practice with individuals, families and groups. Indeed, the whole spectrum of social work services outside of community organization (although there were community programs in some of the studies, e.g. Geismar & Krisberg, 1967; Miller, 1962) was involved.

In fact, this review of research did include every controlled study of effectiveness of any type of social work that is currently available (Maas, 1966, 1971). There are, for example, no controlled studies of the effectiveness of any model of community organization, although available evidence about the results of community organization processes is primarily negative and extremely discouraging (e.g. Marris & Rein, 1974; Grosser, 1968; Schwartz, 1966, 1971; Morris, 1966; Rothman, 1971). Thus, to date, an overall evaluation of social work outcome must conclude that *there is not a single shred of controlled evidence that any form of social work is effective!*

Now, of course, it seems hardly appropriate to condemn those aspects of social work (such as community organization) that do not have any controlled research testifying to their effectiveness or lack of effectiveness. Similarly, the purpose of this book is not to make a whipping boy out of casework. Thus, since the controlled research does include social work with individuals, families and groups ranging from the direct use of counseling to environmental manipulation, the following conclusion, which some of the discussants, judging from their remarks, might prefer, seems justified: *across the range of clients, problems and types of social work services to individuals, families and groups studied in seventeen available controlled studies of effectiveness, fourteen studies show that professional social work services were not effective in producing any positive changes in clients beyond those that could be achieved by nonprofessionals or with no services whatsoever, while definitive conclusions could not be reached in the remaining three studies because of deficiencies in research design.*

Negative Results of Research Should Not Be Revealed

Perhaps the most disturbing argument in the discussants' chapters was that negative results such as obtained in these studies should not be revealed. Gochros questions whether ". . . the presentation and sensationalization of alleged evidence that casework does not 'work' really helps our field or does it justice." He also questions the effectiveness of such research, and doubts whether a book such as this serves, ". . . the cause of improving casework effectiveness," adding that it, ". . . serves neither the needs of the profession nor its consumers." He concludes: ". . . stop telling us that we are not doing any good." Polemis, a researcher herself, questions, ". . . the usefulness of the critical approach to research." She is especially concerned that research such as that reviewed in this book may be misused, but reluctantly concludes, ". . . if this is the effect of the truth, so be it." Surprisingly, Polemis also remarks that when the results of a study do not permit rejecting the null hypothesis, e.g. show no difference between treatment and control group, "there is no payoff for the reader. . . ." Finally, Turner concludes that the results of these studies, ". . . are scarcely cause for concern." Both Gochros and Polemis seem implicitly to second this motion by pointing out, "Physicians haven't overcome illness and death, lawyers and police haven't overcome crime, and politicians haven't overcome just about anything" (Gochros), and citing two studies showing that optometrists and ophthalmologists have trouble fitting glasses correctly (Polemis). The implication of both sets of remarks seems to be: "Why should social workers be particularly worried—nobody's perfect."

It hardly seems necessary to mention that a profession would not *know* that it is time to look for and develop new approaches, as Gochros so much desires, unless it has evidence that old methods have very little promise of success and must be radically revised or dropped altogether. Similarly, the point made by Polemis that studies that fail to reject the null hypothesis, i.e. show no differences between groups, have no payoff seems to ignore that this is exactly the kind of information necessary to make judgments about the direction of professional practice. Studies that show no significant effect of professional services, especially when replicated time and again as these findings were, are enormously informative, perhaps as much so as studies that do reject the null hypothesis. They indicate that it is time for a change. They suggest which methods do not work. They point to crucial areas of professional practice that need bolstering. They suggest which approaches to practice possibly warrant discarding on the grounds of lack of effectiveness. In short, they inform the profession when it is time to reject or radically revise old methods and approaches and search for new ones—feedback that is crucial to professionals interested in responsible and rational decision-making.

Regarding the assertion that these results are not cause for concern, especially in the light of the results of research in other professions, it must suffice to say that the fact that other professions have not attained 100 percent success is no reason for social workers to: (1) stop evaluating their services; (2) be complacent about either what they do in practice or the negative results of research; or (3) stop working continuously to develop optimally effective (even if it is not 100% effective) methods of intervention. Indeed, the fact that optometrists are imperfect in fitting glasses probably is little solace to social work clients who have invested significant portions of their time, energy and perhaps money to achieve little or no positive results or even negative results.

Perhaps the remarks of these discussants can serve as a warning signal for the profession. Unfortunately, the nature of the reactions to other reviews of research, as noted in Chapter 1, suggest that even if this is indeed a minority position, it bodes poorly for achieving positive changes in the field—changes that are made obvious as the result of the consistently negative findings regarding the practice methods currently used by most social workers. Indeed, the resentment toward publication of negative findings might best be illustrated by a recent article (Borenzweig, 1974) which concluded that any challenge to the effectiveness of the profession by its own members is, ". . . a phenomenon which . . . can be viewed as a form of our own self-hatred, our brutalization of our profession" (p. 629).

CONCLUSION: THE ONE-HORNED DILEMMA

Throughout the remarks of many of the discussants (e.g. Berleman, Cohen, Hudson, Polemis, Turner), there appears to be an implication which frequently becomes explicit that the material presented in Part I is, at best, "over-enthusiastic," and at worst, biased. The essence of this point should be that if the review indeed were biased, different conclusions could be reached through an unbiased analysis. That, at least, is what the essence of the charge of bias *should* be. But, in fact, none of the discussants' remarks have demonstrated the opposite of the conclusion that was reached in Part I—that there is no evidence that case-work is effective, and, moreover, that the evidence almost totally is that casework has not been effective. Thus, to substantiate the charge of bias, the discussants would have to demonstrate how the bias so clouded judgment that totally inaccurate conclusions were reached. This they have not done. Indeed, as Eysenck long ago pointed out, ". . . scientific statements, criticisms, etc., must be allowed to stand on their own feet regardless of the motivation of the critic. *Argumenta ad hominen* are not regarded as important or valid in science unless they are buttressed by factual demonstration of erroneous arguments or conclusions" (Eysenck, 1966, p. 95).

It should be clear that it is not the job of the reviewer to prove that casework is ineffective. Instead, the burden of proof must always be with the advocate of casework or any other approach to demonstrate the efficacy or validity of his approach. Again, it is important to note the distinction between *asserting* that an approach is effective and *demonstrating* that it is indeed effective. This discrepancy between claim and proof is the focus of this book. The facts are that there is as yet no evidence to support the claims of effectiveness of the casework establishment, or for that matter, any aspect or method of social work. It must be pointed out once more: those who assert that casework is effective have not produced a single controlled study providing even minimally acceptable scientific evidence of the effectiveness of any social work method.

Several of the discussants raised numerous criticisms about the research methodology used in the seventeen studies—design problems, measurement and criterion problems, statistical problems and so on. Many of these points were indeed valid; few of the studies were perfect. There is no question that evaluations such as described in this book are extremely difficult—time-, energy- and money-consuming—and that a variety of complications inevitably appear in such research. On the other hand, the methodologies in most of the studies were more than adequate to draw the conclusions made in Part I regarding the lack of evidence supporting the effectiveness of social casework. In addition, specific cautions regarding the conclusions that could be drawn for each study were delineated in Part I. Indeed, the great difficulty of such evaluative research, plus the dismal results produced thus far, are two of the primary reasons underlying the suggestions made in Chapter 6 for the use of new technologies of evaluation —objectified and systematic single case studies. Several of the discussants agreed with those suggestions. (Note Talsma's report in Chapter 15 that the bulk of cases in his family service agency are amenable to such evaluative methods.) Again, though, as clear as it is that it is difficult to conduct experimental research, it is equally clear that: (1) such research *is* possible, and eventually, is necessary; (2) several studies have been conducted showing negative or null results in social work; and (3) these findings do not support the implicit and explicit claims of the profession that they offer effective services.

Now again, the purpose of this book was not to use psycho-dynamic approaches as scapegoats for all the problems of case-work, even though one or another psychoanalytic model did un-derlie the treatment provided in most of the studies including many of those that used group methods (such as McCabe, 1967, Meyer, Borgatta & Jones, 1965). It is clear that no matter *what* the theoretical base of the workers in any of the studies, not a single study showed unequivocal positive effects. Thus, both the empirical and the conceptual evidence (some of which was re-viewed in Chapter 6) points to the conclusion that whatever were the methods that have been used by most caseworkers—or, social workers working with individuals, families and groups— they have not produced and are not likely to produce successful results in working with clients. Hence, the suggestions in Chapter 6 for major changes in practice using as a starting point for the redesign of the methods base used by most social workers, three already available approaches with considerable evidence of effec-tiveness. The point is that since these approaches *do* have their own evidence of effectiveness, they can be adopted for casework practice independent of the necessity for attacking psychoanalytic (or any other) theory. When one approach has evidence of effec-tiveness, and another does not, and both are concerned with the same phenomena (clients, problems and so on), there should be little question for professionals as to which should be adopted.

The discouraging results of research over a major portion of the history of the profession is a serious indictment of not only practice but the profession's educational establishment. Indeed, as evidence of this, at the current time, in the midst of the greatest knowledge explosion yet experienced in the history of the profession, and with an increasing number of new approaches with evidence of effectiveness becoming available, schools of social work are *decreasing* rather than increasing the time necessary to achieve a professional degree.

Perhaps social work educators know better than anyone else the value of their efforts, hence the change in many graduate schools to the "quickie" one-year and eighteen-month masters degree. Of course, the issue is not time alone; it is the *interaction* between content and time that is crucial. It is likely that increasing the time required for the professional degree to *four* years, or decreasing it to less than it is now, would not substantially affect the competence of most graduates, given the same traditional curricula that are currently being taught in most graduate schools of social work.

Indeed, added to the pressing problem of the lack of evidence of effectiveness of any form of social work *practice* is the equally appalling fact that, to date, not a single program of social work *education* has established through research its success in graduating effective social work practitioners. In other words, a demonstrated empirical base for social work education, both in terms of the educational inputs—what is taught—and the products—presumably competent practitioners—is totally absent. Thus, not only are the claims of effectiveness by practitioners apparently based largely on myths and wishful thinking, but the claims of social work educators to competence in *educating* effective practitioners appear also to be, if not mythical, totally unsubstantiated.

Now there is (or should be) an obvious interaction between what is taught in a profession and what is practiced by its members. It therefore seems clear that the profession must consider not only radical changes in its methods of practice, but major structural changes in its educational programming, including a serious look at the necessity for revising and increasing both the substance and time of graduate education. For example, given the current availability of several approaches with evidence of effectiveness, and the likely advent of new approaches from both within and without the profession, it is possible that a two-year graduate program may be insufficient. This becomes even more apparent given the idea that one place to begin such changes is in the selection and teaching of methods for practice that already have empirical evidence of effectiveness (as well as the development and testing of new methods), and systematically evaluating whether or not the teaching of those methods can be translated into objectively demonstrated benefits for clients (for expansion of these points, see Fischer, 1976).

What is the one-horned dilemma? Obviously, for a dilemma to exist, at least two alternatives must be available. And in a sense, they do. On one hand, the profession can continue as it is, with only minor changes, or no changes at all over the years, structurally, educationally or in practice methodology. On the other hand, the profession has the option of revitalizing itself by adopting new methods of practice and reexamining and changing the base of both its current practice and educational structures. If such changes are not adopted, it would indeed be difficult to justify the continued existence of the largest segment of the social work profession, and the future for the profession would appear cloudy at best. On the other hand, the potential for a new beginning points to the possibility of a far different future. When the vitality, indeed, the very life, of the profession hinges on making a choice between a dead end and a new direction, there should be little question as to which way to go; hence, the dilemma with really only one horn.

Now, unfortunately, it is not clear that social work will be able to respond to the challenge with the necessary vigor. There is, and always has been, strong opposition in the profession to making major changes in education and practice. Thus, optimism about the availability of a whole range of new and potentially effective modalities of practice and methods of practice research must be tempered with the more pessimistic observation that social work often is reluctant to implement such innovations.

It is probably unprecedented in this century for a set of concepts and methods to be so central to the functioning of the bulk of an entire profession, and yet be without a shred of scientific evidence validating their use, not to mention considerable evidence pointing to their lack of value. Casework—in fact, social work—must forcefully face the issue of effectiveness, and cannot countenance further concealment of the fact that its main methods have been found wanting. To the extent that these approaches may even be hazardous, in addition to simply not helpful, this may require, first, that they be applied on a far more limited basis in practice, and second, that clients be notified that, in lieu of positive evidence of effectiveness, the methods and procedures of the profession are of an experimental nature and potentially dangerous.

This book began with the idea that the core of the profession is a commitment to competence, and that competence refers specifically to being able to provide effective help for clients. But even this most basic idea of the profession—that a social worker cannot be competent unless he is also effective—is being questioned. A recent article in *Social Casework* typifies this destructive trend in asserting that: "The outcome of professional practice, when it can be measured at all, although of considerable interest in other connections is of little value in the assessment of competence . . ." and, "Since outcomes are obviously a questionable basis for determining and assessing social work competence a more hopeful alternative is required. . . . Its essential component is what goes into social work practice, not what comes out as a result. The essential component, in other words, is the inputs for social work practice rather than its outcomes" (Levy, 1974, pp. 377, 379).

Enough said.

REFERENCES—PART III

Borenzweig, H. "A Plea for Professional Unity," *Social Casework*, Vol. 55, 1974, pp. 628, 629.

Diloretto, A. O. *Comparative Psychotherapy: An Experimental Analysis.* Chicago: Aldine-Atherton, 1971.

Eysenck, H. J. *The Effects of Psychotherapy.* New York: International Science Press, 1966.

Fischer, J. *Effective Casework Practice: An Eclectic Approach.* New York: McGraw-Hill, 1976.

Ford, D. H. and Urban, H. B. *Systems of Psychotherapy.* New York: John Wiley, 1963.

Geismar, L. and Krisberg, J. *The Forgotten Neighborhood.* Metuchen, N.J.: The Scarecrow Press, 1967.

Glover, E. *The Technique of Psycho-Analysis.* New York: International Universities Press, 1955.

Grosser, C. F. *Helping Youth: A Study of Six Community Organization Programs.* Washington, D.C.: Office of Juvenile Delinquency and Youth Development (H.E.W.), 1968.

Hudson, W. W. "Casework as a Causative Agent in Client Deterioration: A Research Note on the Fischer Assessment," *Social Service Review*, Vol. 48, 1974, pp. 442-449.

Kadushin, A. "The Knowledge Base of Social Work," Kahn, A. (ed.), *Issues in American Social Work.* New York: Columbia University Press, 1959, pp. 39-79.

Levy, C. S. "Inputs Versus Outputs as Criteria of Competence," *Social Casework*, Vol. 55, 1974, pp. 375-380.

London, P. *The Modes and Morals of Psychotherapy.* New York: Holt, Rinehart and Winston, 1964.

Maas, H. S. *Research in the Social Services: A Five-Year Review.* New York: N.A.S.W., 1971.

Maas, H. S. *Five Fields of Social Service: Reviews of Research.* New York: N.A.S.W., 1966.

MacDonald, M. E. "Reunion at Vocational High," *Social Service Review*, Vol. 40, 1966, pp. 175-189.

Marmor, J. *Modern Psychoanalysis.* New York: Basic Books, 1968.

Maris, P. and Rein, M. *Dilemmas of Social Reform*, 2nd Edition. Chicago: Aldine-Atherton, 1974.

McCabe, A. *The Pursuit of Promise.* New York: Community Service Society, 1967.

Meyer, H., Borgatta, E. and Jones, W. *Girls at Vocational High.* New York: Russell Sage Foundation, 1965.

Miller, W. B. "The Impact of a Total Community Delinquency Control Project," *Social Problems*, 1962, pp. 168-191.

Morris, R. "Social Planning," Maas, H. S. (ed.), *Five Fields of Social Service: Reviews of Research*. New York: N.A.S.W., 1966, pp. 185-208.

Munroe, R. L. *Schools of Psychoanalytic Thought*. New York: Dryden, 1955.

Orten, J. D. and Weis, D. P. "Strategies and Techniques for Therapeutic Change," *Social Service Review*, Vol. 48, 1974, pp. 355-366.

Patterson, C. H. *Theories of Counseling and Psychotherapy*. New York: Harper and Row, 1966.

Roberts, R. W. and Nee, R. H. *Theories of Social Casework*. Chicago: University of Chicago Press, 1970.

Rothman, J. "Community Organization Practice," Maas, H. S. (ed.), *Research in the Social Services: A Five-Year Review*. New York: N.A.S.W., 1971, pp. 70-107.

Schwartz, W. "Neighborhood Centers and Group Work," Maas, H. S. (ed.), *Research in the Social Services: A Five-Year Review*. New York: N.A.S.W., 1971, pp. 130-191.

Schwartz, W. "Neighborhood Centers," Maas, H. S. (ed.), *Five Fields of Social Service: Reviews of Research*. New York: N.A.S.W., 1966, pp. 144-184.

Strupp, H. H. "Psychoanalytic Therapy of the Individual," Marmor, J. (ed.), *Modern Psychoanalysis*. New York: Basic Books, 1968, pp. 293-342.

Thompson, C. *Psychoanalysis: Evolution and Development*. New York: Thomas Nelson & Sons, 1950.

Truax, C. B. and Mitchell, K. M. "Research on Certain Therapist Interpersonal Skills in Relation to Process and Outcome," Bergin, A. E. and Garfield, S. L. (eds.), *Handbook of Psychotherapy and Behavior Change*. New York: John Wiley, 1971, pp. 299-344.

Turner, F. J. (ed.) *Social Work Treatment*. New York: Free Press, 1974.

Ullmann, L. P. and Krasner, L. *A Psychological Approach to Abnormal Behavior*. Englewood Cliffs, New Jersey: Prentice-Hall, 1969.